Business leaders and educators agree . . .

"The wisdom Whiddon offers in *The Mentor* aligns perfectly with our mission to support the children of our military service members around the globe. What a blessing he has provided for generations to come!"

—LEE SECHRIST
Cofounder, the Gratitude Initiative

"The timeless tools Jim Whiddon has provided our associates clearly set them apart by elevating both their business and social skills. *The Mentor* integrates these fundamentals into a fun and gratifying tale!"

—PATRICK J. LAUBACHER
CPA, Managing Shareholder, Judd Thomas, LLC

"Whiddon's stated goal is to pass on wisdom to the next generation. He is right on target with this mission! All of our college students and young professionals need this kind of practical instruction to develop the skills needed for their success."

—DR. JAMES HALLMARK
Vice Chancellor for Academic Affairs, Texas A&M University

"Whiddon has a unique ability to synthesize meaningful concepts into practical and actionable efforts that have an immediate positive impact. There is simply no way you are not enriched by the experience!"

—ADAM BIRENBAUM
CEO, Buckingham Strategic Wealth

"Whiddon powerfully reinforces the lessons that many in this generation have forgotten: the personal skills and qualities that provide tools for success in any working environment or social situation."

—SCOTT FRALEY, JD, MA
Director of Legal Writing, Baylor Law School

"Whiddon's work is thought-provoking yet accessible, masterful yet practical, and unearths the enduring wit and wisdom of the past to inspire the reader to live an examined, virtuous, and adept life. Our institute students all receive a copy of his book upon graduation."

—CHARLES J. EMMERICH, JD, LLM
Professor of Legal Studies; Founder, the Center for Law and Culture

"I am so glad J. N. Whiddon has collected his wisdom into this entirely engaging book. My class always loves his presentations, and now students all over the country will benefit from his insight and experiences."

—MCCLAIN WATSON, PhD
Director, Business Communication Programs,
the University of Texas at Dallas

"Whiddon provided concepts for our team that had an immediate and positive impact. His books were especially useful in bridging the culture gap to our young professionals as they started their careers."

—BRUCE GRAHAM
Chief Strategy Officer, Tyler Technologies

"Whiddon has an uncanny ability to stretch the imagination to reveal tried and true principles embraced by successful people. *The Mentor* displays his well-honed storytelling skills and is a must-read for anyone seeking an advantage in this highly competitive world!"

—DAVID C. ANDERSON
Former Chairman, Newark Resources, Inc.

"Whiddon is an authority on training and equipping people with simple strategies that empower them to become truly transformational leaders. *The Mentor* will captivate you and bring you back to the age-old paths and the good ways that have been forgotten by so many in our generation."

—BRIAN LEE
National President, Beta Upsilon Chi (BYX)

"Whiddon's insights are a foil to a world that is replete with ineffective communicators. He skillfully provides a compelling and clear framework to advance impact-oriented communication. His books have become required texts for my students. The storytelling chapter alone is worth the price of admission!"

—JEFF GROPP, PhD
Director, Management Fellows Program, DePauw University

"Whiddon takes readers down a road of discovering the ancient paths long forgotten. Our partnership with him has been transformational in the lives of our students."

—MICHAEL PINKSTON
Superintendent, Castle Hills Christian School

"Imagine wasting $150,000 on a bad college education when you could have learned what it takes to be successful by simply reading Whiddon's extremely practical and insightful books!"

—DR. FRANK TUREK
Founder, CrossExamined

"Whiddon's messages are rich with wisdom that can transcend across all walks of life. He will inspire and encourage you with simple yet life-changing truths!"

—STEPHEN MCGEE
CFP, "the Financial Quarterback"

"Whiddon provides much-needed focus on how to create and grow relationships in a tech-dominated world. *The Mentor* is a win for every reader!"

—DENNIS MCCUISTION
Executive Director, Institute for Excellence in Corporate Governance

"Whiddon provides the polish every professional needs. I wish I'd had this book thirty years ago! I'm so glad my children and grandchildren will."

—W. MARTIN YUNG
ARM, President, and CEO,
HUB International Insurance Services, Texas

"Our business leader's team in China was blown away by Whiddon's impact! Whiddon's mentoring is for all people far and wide."

—MIKE JORGENSON
Vice President, e3 Partners (I Am Second)

"Whiddon's enlightened story speaks wisdom about the essentials for a successful career—and life. If you're looking for that person your students will listen to, look no further. This book speaks to the matter in a wonderful journey you won't want to miss."

—KELLY MOORE
President, National Christian School Association

"*The Mentor* is a modern-day parable which draws readers into a captivating story of life lessons. Required reading for anyone interested in personal and professional growth!"

—SID WALKER, PhD
President, the Walker Group Executive Consultants

THE
MENTOR

THE
MENTOR

A Career-Readiness
Business Parable

J. N. WHIDDON

The Mentor
A Career-Readiness Business Parable

Brown Books Publishing Group
16250 Knoll Trail Drive, Suite 205
Dallas, Texas 75248
www.BrownBooks.com
(972) 381-0009

A New Era in Publishing®

Publisher's Cataloging-In-Publication Data

Names: Whiddon, James N., author.
Title: The mentor : a career-readiness business parable / J.N. Whiddon.
Description: Dallas, Texas : Brown Books Publishing Group, [2019]
Identifiers: ISBN 9781612543185
Subjects: LCSH: Business communication--Study and teaching (Higher)-
  -Fiction. | Vocational guidance--Study and teaching (Higher)--Fiction.
  | College seniors--Fiction. | Success in business--Study and teaching
  (Higher)--Fiction. | LCGFT: Didactic fiction.
Classification: LCC PS3623.H525 M46 HF5718 | DDC 813/.6 658.45--dc23

ISBN 978-1-61254-318-5 (PB)
ISBN 978-1-61254-345-1 (HC)
LCCN 2019932344

Printed in the United States
10 9 8 7 6 5 4 3 2 1

For more information or to contact the author, please go to www.JNWhiddon.com.

To the greatest mentor in my life,
Lawrence N. "Nate" Whiddon, and to all those
who mentor—past, present, and future.

CONTENTS

FOREWORD   xvii

INTRODUCTION   xxi

1. THE PROFESSOR   1

2. BUILDING INSTANT RAPPORT (Key #1)   13

3. THE GIRLS   29

4. TIME LEADERSHIP (Key #2)   35

5. THE OLD SCHOOL   49

6. WORDS THAT WOW! (Key #3)   55

7. THE RIVALRY   67

8. INFLUENCE AND PERSUASION (Key #4)   79

9. STORYTELLING (Key #5)   95

10. READY RECALL (Key #6)   115

11. THE MIDTERM   127

12. THE BREAK   131

13. You're Always Interviewing (Key #7)   145

14. The Future   155

15. Connectedness (Key #8)   165

16. The Game Plan   183

17. Dress for Success (Key #9)   193

18. The Game   207

19. Make Good Decisions (Key #10)   219

20. Ask Great Questions (Key #11)   235

21. Lifelong Learning (Key #12)   251

22. The Review   269

23. The Call   283

24. The Memorial   291

25. The Final   301

Afterword   311

Acknowledgments   315

About the Author   317

The 12 Keys to Professional Success   319

FOREWORD

Words have had a powerful impact on my life. They have transported me beyond social boundaries, taken me to my lowest moments, and captivated me in a romantic spell. But most importantly, words have led me to a purpose much greater than myself. A famous proverb says it well: Gracious words are like a honeycomb: sweetness to the soul and health to the body.

All books are simply a collection of words, but some more than others convey meaning and inspire change. *The Mentor* is just such a book. It is a story that will point you to the origin of success: the principles that extend beyond knowledge to a far-reaching realm of wisdom most don't reach until later in life.

When I first met Jim Whiddon, it was clear that he was a true mentor who spoke words of wisdom emanating from his unquenchable thirst for knowledge and a wide variety of life and professional experiences. This semifictional tale is heartwarming and at times heartbreaking. But it is interlaced with a reflective discernment that will take you back to the old-school years—the pivotal years of college during which you prepared for a lifetime of value. Jim has done a masterful job of exploring the truths of life with the wit of a storyteller and curiosity of an adventurer.

As a college professor, I have the great privilege of investing my days in the next generation as they seek knowledge in the classroom. Similar to Dr. John—the main character of this book—some of my greatest moments as an educator have come outside the classroom, in moments of mentorship and camaraderie with students.

Just as our agrarian forefathers of old did when planting, cultivating, and extracting the harvest from the land—often buried in weeds and brambles—this book will help you root through the mess and busyness of modern-day life to cultivate the best in yourself and in others. The pages that follow will lay a framework for timeless principles that aren't necessarily new but rather are rejuvenated through the narrative of a professor and his pupils. I could spend the remainder of my time telling you how so many of the keys in this book have impacted my life and that of my family—but I'll focus on one and allow you the privilege of exploring the others.

After my grandfather passed away, my father was going through some of his belongings and found a wooden box with a note inside he had sent to his father many years before. At the top of this handwritten note were the words "great letter from my son," and there were four or five subsequent dates spread across several years listed below that. My grandfather had reread that note from my father many times, each time noting the date at the top to remind himself of the power of the words within and the deep connection it provided with his son. And after personally surviving the most horrific event in American history, I received my own handwritten note in September of 2001 from that same "great son." The words it contained would forever change the trajectory of my life.

As I discovered, these very principles my father and grandfather held so dear are ably exhibited in this book—namely, the *connectedness* that comes through the simple act of hand writing notes and *telling stories* from one generation to the next. And as you will learn in a coming chapter, there is an art to letter writing and a "value that almost always exceeds the writer's efforts." If you were to learn only this one principle, you would be far better for it. However, this is but the tip of an iceberg of valuable insights you will soon encounter that will make a measurable difference in your life.

I invite you to find a comfortable chair or a porch swing and enter with me into the lecture hall with "my colleague" Dr. Johnathan Daniels. You are about to learn twelve keys that will unlock the power of your professional *and* your personal success. May the words contained herein inspire you toward authentic self-reflection and accountable action on your journey of lifelong learning—indeed, to a place of always being *wiser than your years.*

Nathan J. Harness, PhD

INTRODUCTION

Prepare the child for the path, not the path for the child.

—THOMAS P. JOHNSON

Do you remember that one special high school teacher? Or a professor you had in college? The one who taught you *how* to think—not *what* to think. The one who personified discernment and propriety and treasured the pursuit of truth no matter where it led. Perhaps you are picturing them in your mind right now. Some of us have had the good fortune to know more than one. What if those same beloved instructors could be here now for this generation . . . and for the next? Is it possible?

Even though our technology borders on miraculous, it seems at times that we are now adrift on an ocean of information without a drop of wisdom to drink. We are lost in the "Bermuda Rectangle" of electronic devices. Employers can find plenty of talented technicians to hire, yet finding candidates with exceptional communication and relationship abilities—or "soft skills"—is becoming increasingly difficult.

Imagine a professor that addressed all that. Imagine Professor Johnathan W. Daniels—"Dr. John" to his students. *The Mentor* is the story of the professor we desperately need today—a teacher of high moral character offering the practical instruction and personal support that is too often missing from formal education today.

Dr. John presents "12 Keys to Professional Success" in his capstone business communications course at "State U." The course was designed to equip his students with the tools they will need to go straight to the top—basic fundamentals that *never change*.

And as you follow along with Dr. John and his students, friends, and family, you will learn invaluable lessons *outside* the classroom as well. Whether it's study abroad, a team championship run, or an ill-timed ceremony, you will rejoice at their successes and mourn their losses as they experience the challenges of life under the sun. Whether you are a student or a grandparent or any age in between, as you read this story, you will be inspired to learn more, do more, and become more.

So now, it's time. Class starts today. Get your pen and notepad ready, because the most important course you will ever take is about to begin.

—J. N. Whiddon

ONE

THE PROFESSOR

*A teacher affects eternity; he can never tell
where his influence stops.*

—HENRY ADAMS

The air was unusually crisp on the State U campus. Even on a January morning, it was rare to see frost in South Texas. Professor Johnathan Daniels headed down Heroes Way to Academics Hall. The expansive neoclassical structure with its signature massive columns had been built in 1882. Daniels had been here as a student in 1982. And now, more than forty years later, he was teaching in the very same classroom.

Who am I to be here? How can I possibly meet the needs of these students?

The doubts came to Daniels at the same time every semester on this first-day walk . . .

Ninety-seven kids. Different dreams . . . different paths . . . different challenges. "A teacher affects eternity; he can never tell where his influence stops." I know, Dad. I know . . . Lord, please equip me . . . I need discernment . . . I'm no good by myself.

It was the first day of Johnathan Daniels's fifth spring semester teaching at State U, and his excitement had not faded in the least. He could not be more pleased about his decision to spend the fourth quarter of his life pouring into the next generation. After more than three decades managing his own firm, the last four years spent simultaneously obtaining his doctorate in business communications, he could hardly believe the university paid him to pursue not only his passion but also his *purpose*.

But he still got butterflies. It was game day. A new season. *Here we go*, he thought as he entered the building.

"Good morning, Maria!"

Dr. John spoke in a smooth baritone with no discernable regional accent. It was an unusual dialect characteristic that surprised many when they first met him, yet it was one common to those from the high plains of the Texas Panhandle, and it had served him well in his many media endeavors.

Maria Lopez smiled up at her longtime friend. Dr. John's tall frame had expanded some in the middle, but his full head of gray hair had a matching full beard. His eyesight required reading glasses—ever at the ready on a maroon lanyard draped around his neck during class—but the lack of crow's feet around his blue eyes made him look younger than his years. Starched shirts, creased slacks, and polished shoes were his standard uniform, but he never missed an opportunity to wear a sweater-vest or a cardigan if the projected high temperature dipped below seventy degrees. "Good morning, Professor."

"I can't thank you enough for getting here early to help set up. You are too kind," Dr. Daniels said. He knew what Maria's time was worth. Maria Lopez was an impressive person. She had emigrated from Guatemala seven years before and begun work at the university facilities department, but her capabilities had seen her quickly promoted to supervisor of maintenance at Academics Hall. Along the way, she had managed to begin working on her own degree in business communications. Dr. Daniels had become her academic advisor and had even officiated her wedding to her husband, David. Anyone who met her found her diminutive stature and gentle spirit endearing. Anyone who spoke with her for more than a few minutes was soon impressed by her exceptional intellect and determination.

"It's my pleasure!" Maria told him. "Do you want all the witnesses today?"

"Of course. Let's give them the full treatment!" Dr. John answered.

The first students of Business Communications 426 filed in around 8:45. They found his "full treatment" there waiting for them. The classroom had seating for 140 students, with a wide front staging area containing all the latest in audio-visual technology. But surrounding the entire front of the classroom were a dozen banners depicting famous historical figures: Lincoln, Socrates, Churchill, Mother Teresa, and Booker T. Washington, to name a few. At the top of each banner was written a virtue or characteristic, such as leadership, truth, or courage.

On the left side of the stage, there were life-size cardboard cutouts of action and cartoon figures. Easels holding charts and pictures seemed to be everywhere around the front and perimeter of the room. A giant yellow number-two pencil leaned on the lectern. A rubber chicken and a small red vault sat on a table in front, along with a football helmet, pennants, and a lava lamp. A scoreboard sat front and center with twelve minutes on the clock and a score of 82–0 illuminated. Above it all was a twelve-foot horizontal white banner with black lettering that said, "What do you mean by that?"

Most students entered and sat quietly, gaping at the spectacle. The question, *What is this?* seemed to be written on their faces.

At nine o'clock sharp, Dr. Daniels made his way down the stairs to the lectern. "Howdy and good morning, ladies and gentlemen!"

A few brave students returned a muted hello.

"I can't tell you how glad I am to be here with you today! Surrounding you are my witnesses from history. They will play an important role in your development this semester. Though they are dead, yet will they speak. But first things first: I have a simple question for you." Dr. John walked over to the character cutouts on the left side of the room and paused to make sure all eyes watched him.

Then, with the utmost seriousness, he asked, "Batman . . . or Superman?"

Many students looked confused.

"Who likes Superman better?" Dr. John asked again.

Suspecting a joke, only a few students raised their hands at first. Dr. John waited until about one third of the class followed suit. "OK, good . . . Now how about Batman?"

The majority raised their hands.

"Interesting. Someone tell me why they voted for Superman?" Daniels asked. "Yes, sir! In the back."

"Uh . . . he has superhuman powers," Chris Washington managed.

"Of course. Who else?"

"He's handsome, and I like that he doesn't hide behind a mask," Joy Williams volunteered.

Dr. Daniels chuckled. "Good. Thank you. Anyone else for Superman?" he asked.

"He just seems to be better adjusted . . . not as dark," offered James House.

Dr. Daniels considered this. "Well, that's a good point—although I think the old-school Batman wasn't like that. The newer movies have changed his personality. So what about Batman? Most of you like him better. Tell me why."

Katherine Reagan raised her hand and said, "I actually like his mask."

Students laughed. "All right. There you go," Dr. Daniels responded.

Taylor Martin chimed in from the second row. "He's a 'real person,' and he protects innocent people by fighting crime. And I think he uses his own money too."

"So, to clarify: his character is authentic, and he uses his resources to help others," Dr. Daniels said.

"Yes," Taylor confirmed.

"Got it. That's good. What else? What makes Batman so good at crime fighting?"

There was a pause. Finally, Aaron Woods, sitting front and center, gave the answer Dr. John was looking for: "His tools."

"Good! Say that again!"

"His tools. He has all the best tools," Aaron explained. "Even though he doesn't have superhuman powers like Superman—he's equipped to be the best at what he does."

"Exactly! Thank you, sir! Superman can't exist—sorry," Dr. Daniels added to the Superman fans in the class. "But Batman *could* exist. You see the yellow belt he has here? It contains twelve tools that make him every criminal's worst nightmare. From various projectiles to ropes to high-tech equipment. He's got them all. And his partner . . ." Dr. Daniels ducked behind a banner and pulled out another life-size cutout—Batwoman. ". . . She's the same way. This 'bat duo' is unstoppable. And it's because they have perfected the use of the best tools at their disposal," Daniels declared.

"Now, if I can bring you back from cartoon land for just a moment, that is what will happen this semester in Business Communications 426. I am committed to providing the training and tools that have been so often ignored in your generation. I want to make you a force for good in your chosen profession and community." He grinned. "Now, if you want to be a crime fighter, you'll need some additional training I'm not qualified to give. But the twelve keys to professional success you will learn this semester will help equip you for any career challenge that comes along—whether you encounter it over the next ninety days or the next ninety years."

Dr. John passed out the semester syllabus and went over the course description and a few other housekeeping items. As he spoke, he evaluated his class, planning for the year ahead. *They're listening. This is going to be a good group,* Daniels thought.

After answering a few questions, Daniels then announced, "Also, for anyone who might be interested—especially you World War II history buffs—during spring break I'm leading a study abroad trip that will start in London for three days, then head to northern France and Normandy. It will be an extraordinary opportunity and a life-changing trip! You can see me for details or check it out on the class portal.

"Please read **chapter 1** in your text for next time, and if anyone has any questions concerning the syllabus or what we'll be covering this semester, please catch me after class or send me an email. My office location and hours are at the bottom of page four."

Daniels paused. "Finally, I have one nonnegotiable class rule. I want everyone to sit in the place you sat today for every class. I appreciate your cooperation."

A few groans ensued, but in a class this size, Dr. John had found a seating chart to be indispensable in memorizing the names, faces, and personalities of all his students. Over the course of the class, they would find that the personal attention they received would be more than worth any inconvenience of having to sit in the same seat for every lecture.

"Have a great day, everyone, and please pass back the sign-in sheet, if you would. Thank you," he concluded.

Over the next several minutes, Professor Daniels visited with several of his new students as the classroom cleared. Then he perused the student list for thirty seconds and packed up his briefcase for the short walk across campus. As he exited the building, he heard, "Excuse me, Dr. Daniels?"

Dr. John glanced at the young man calling his name—Aaron Woods, another of his new students. He stopped and turned to give Aaron his full attention. "Yes?"

"Excuse me, sir. I just wanted to say I'm really looking forward to your class. It's my last semester. I can tell you have a real passion for your subject."

"Well, thank you . . . Woods, isn't it? . . . Aaron?"

"Yes sir . . . You know my name?" *There had to be a hundred students in class*, Aaron thought.

Dr. Daniels seemed to not hear the question. "So, it's your last lap, eh?"

"Yes, sir. I'm afraid it is. May I ask you a question?"

"You just did." Daniels smiled. "But first, let me ask you, Aaron—where are you from?"

"From Fort Worth."

"Ah yes. 'Cowtown,'" Daniels said.

"Yes, sir."

"The rodeo in January is always a phenomenal event. Quintessential Texas. Any family there?"

"Yes. My mom, and I have an older brother and two younger sisters," Aaron answered.

"That's a full house. You know, I have four children myself. Two of each. All close to your age. What are you studying?" Daniels asked.

"International finance with a biz-com minor," Aaron told him.

"Oh, did you know I was in the financial industry myself for more than thirty years? Sold my company five years ago. Never looked back. You have a position lined up after graduation?"

"No sir. But I'm working on it."

"I'm sure you are. Perhaps we'll have a chance to talk more about that soon. What do you do with your spare time, Aaron? Any hobbies?"

"Uh . . . I play guitar, harmonica, and pretty much love every sport." Aaron answered.

"We have a lot in common," Daniels remarked. "What sport is your favorite?"

"Well, I played basketball in high school—but a knee injury sidelined my career."

"No kidding! That was my sport too! You know, I coached basketball right here at State U when I was in grad school—before you were born." Daniels grinned, but he could tell Aaron was getting antsy. "Now, what was that question again?"

Aaron straightened. "You mentioned in your course overview today that you felt this generation has lost something and that you're hoping to provide some of the 'missing pieces' throughout the course. What do you mean by that?"

Professor Daniels thought to himself, *Mmm . . . eager young lad. Seems genuinely interested.* There was always one that stood out. Sometimes two. Rarely three.

In truth, Aaron Woods—tall and athletic, with a head of wavy and unruly sandy-blond hair—had been an A student throughout his academic career. His mother, a single parent, was raising four children on a teacher's salary. Aaron had gotten his first summer job cleaning bathrooms at his hometown high school when he was just fourteen. Anything extra he'd wanted—including something as simple as a new pair of jeans—he paid for. Like all in his generation, he was tech savvy, but as a sophomore in college, he had made the decision to cut back on social media. Keeping up with all the "likes" and the "friends" had become too much. Aaron was well liked—he was a good conversationalist and a walking encyclopedia of sports trivia—but he had always found his best friends among older adults as opposed to his less mature peers, though there were exceptions, such as his relationship with Amanda, his girlfriend of almost two years. It was an interesting young man who had come up to Dr. Daniels after class—one who possessed an unusual combination of confidence and humility born of wider experience than students his age usually saw.

"Excellent question! I'm so glad you asked," Daniels said. "Please have a seat." With the midmorning sun, the light frost had burned away from the roads and seats at State U. Daniels and Aaron took a seat on a bench along Heroes Way.

"Aaron, are you familiar with the author Aldous Huxley?" Daniels asked.

"Um . . . I think so. Didn't he write *Brave New World*?"

"Yes, that's correct. Huxley said, more than eight decades ago, 'Our appetite for distraction is nearly infinite.' And was he ever right! Americans look at their smartphone screens an average of about four hours per day. Ten years ago, we spent only eighteen minutes on our phones each day. It's not so much what this generation is missing as much as it is what they aren't seeing because their heads are always down. Constant distractions—what I call 'the tyranny of the rectangles'—are crowding out much of the wisdom you and your friends need to be successful. In fact, the secret of success boils down to that very thing, Aaron—*wisdom*."

Aaron frowned. "Can you be more specific?"

"Well, we live in a time where information has never been more readily available," Daniels explained, "so knowledge is perceived to be easy to obtain. Think how incredible it is. All of what has been learned in human history can be accessed on a machine the size of a deck of playing cards. Today, just google it, and in seconds, you'll have the answers you seek. But knowledge and wisdom are two different things."

Aaron was focused.

"Knowledge comes from information. How information becomes knowledge is an important thing to understand. But for now, just know that knowledge is *not* fixed. It has no limit.

"Then there's experience—and there are two kinds. One is related to the calendar. Your birthday is not up to you. However, the other relates to the *type*—or the *richness*—of the experiences you have. But wisdom . . . that's the goal," Daniels reiterated.

Aaron nodded.

Daniels continued, "Wisdom can't be forced, but it can be developed. Knowledge *multiplied* by experience *yields* wisdom. It's a simple equation. As an ancient proverb says, Knowledge in youth is wisdom in age."

Aaron pondered, "So you're saying that to be old and wise, you first have to be young and stupid."

Daniels laughed. "Well . . . I think I'd be a little kinder than that. Let's just say that wisdom is the most important thing to have, but it's also not something one can rush. But with every fiber of my being, over the next fifteen weeks, I will do all I can to teach you and your classmates how to obtain as much wisdom as you possibly can."

Aaron could tell Dr. John was passionate about this. "But wait—what about the 'tyrannosaurus rectangles' you mentioned?" he asked.

Dr. Daniels chuckled. "You mean 'tyranny of the rectangles.' There's plenty of time for that discussion. Just remember it's not the *use* of our machines that's the issue—it's the *overuse* and *abuse* of them that's creating the challenges."

"I agree with that!" Aaron exclaimed. "Thank you, Dr. Daniels. I really appreciate the extra time you took to visit with me."

Daniels stood, extending his hand. "Of course. It's my pleasure, Aaron. Your interest in my favorite subject is encouraging to me!"

After they took a few steps in opposite directions, Daniels turned and said, "Oh, and Aaron?"

"Yes, sir?"

"My friends call me 'Dr. John.'" He smiled.

"Thank you again, Dr. John."

As they turned and parted ways, Aaron couldn't wait until nine o'clock Monday morning.

TWO

BUILDING INSTANT RAPPORT

*Be faithful in small things because
it is in them that your strength lies.*

—MOTHER TERESA

"Good morning, ladies and gentlemen!" Dr. John exclaimed as he made his way down to the front of the classroom.

Students had mostly adjusted back into campus life after Syllabus Week. But they were still excited about the big men's basketball win Saturday night. It had been four years since State U had prevailed against Tech U—their archrival just ninety miles to the west. The Eagles were a perfect 20–0 for the first time in twenty-two years, and while there was no bigger fan than Dr. John, it was time for class.

The students kept talking about the game.

SCREECH!

A gasp went up around the room.

SCREECH!

Aaron winced. *What is that?!*

Dr. John chuckled as he held up a rubber chicken he loved to use to silence the room.

He grinned. "Works every time."

Several students laughed with him at the classic sight gag.

Dr. John's elaborate classroom setup from the week before had shrunk to a single banner depicting Mother Teresa with the word *Compassion* emblazoned across its top. To her left was a small round table with a lava lamp from circa 1970 bubbling its black substance in slow motion up and down.

At the lectern, as expected, Dr. John looked out over a wall of computer backs. He sighed. "First things first, I want to mention that the best way to take down my lecture notes is with pen and paper—and not by keyboard."

A few grumbles sounded around the room.

Dr. John shook his head. "By some estimates, you are as much as *five* times more likely to remember what I say if you write it down—as opposed to typing it. Just a word to the wise. Your choice."

Dr. John paused a moment for those who might like to take his advice. About a dozen did. He continued, "It's no accident that Business Communications 426 is the capstone course the university has chosen to set aside until your last year. That's because it's almost time to launch. It's time to think of yourselves as the professionals you will soon officially become. You've had excellent technical training during your time here, but I intend for you to one day look back on this course as the most important training you received in your four years . . . or five . . ." There was scattered laughter. "Or six . . ." More laughter with some pointing. "And I know you will soon be representing yourself, your family, and your university in a way that will make us proud.

"I also mentioned during our syllabus review that I will provide twelve *keys* to ensure your professional success. And keys open doors. And the doors we will open will provide rooms full of opportunities you can't even imagine right now. Shall we get to work?" he asked.

Dr. John stepped out from behind the lectern. "Humorist Will Rogers once said, 'You never get a second chance to make a first impression.' The first 'key to professional success' is **building instant rapport** *with anyone, anywhere, anytime.* I call it 'the LAVA conversation.' LAVA is an acronym that I will explain more in a moment."

He continued, "Let's begin by imagining you are at a networking event or holiday party six months from now. What is the first question you think people will ask you?"

Calli Clark, on the first row next to Aaron, answered, "'What do you do?'"

"That's it, Ms. Clark," Dr. John told her. "Thank you. All agree?"

Heads nodded yes.

"I want you all to remember this . . . *Never* ask that question!"

Some puzzled faces looked up from computers and the occasional notebook. "Life is not just about *what we do,*" Dr. John explained. "In fact, it's *who we are* that makes the difference—and from this, *what we do* often emerges. Asking someone 'What do you do?' as soon as you meet can easily bias or stigmatize your view of them—or their view of you—socially or economically. This can happen within just a few seconds. You don't want people 'counting your pockets,' right?"

Several students rolled their eyes at Dr. John's attempt at being hip. Smiling a little, Dr. John continued. "What if the person you are visiting with is between jobs, underemployed, or still seeking their first career opportunity? You never want to create an atmosphere of envy or inferiority—especially during a first introduction. We all have misfortunes and challenges from time to time, don't we? When you meet someone new, the encounter should be about *connecting* on a personal level. You must build rapport with a genuine attitude of empathy and goodwill. Today we'll learn just how easily this can be done with *everyone* you will ever meet. Now, how many of you ever entered a project in a science fair?" Dr. John asked.

Half of the class admitted they had done so.

"Good. Now, how many of you went with the old stand-by of the baking soda and vinegar volcano?" Twenty to twenty-five hands went up to the amusement of all.

"Excellent! In order to *warm up* a conversation—and get it *flowing*—we're going to use LAVA. That is, the acronym 'L-A-V-A.'" Dr. John pointed to the lava lamp. "It will become your blueprint for introductory conversations—otherwise known as small talk. And small talk is the doorway through which almost every person you ever meet will enter your life.

"The LAVA conversation is going to make you an expert in the art of small talk. It will allow you to consider yourself a *host*—not a guest—in any initial introduction. This means being active, not passive, no matter how introverted you may feel. As a leader of the dialogue, you can fill awkward pauses, introduce others, and make everyone feel welcome and comfortable.

"Most feel that the key to being a conversation leader involves having the 'gift of gab,'" Dr. John observed. "But ironically, in almost any dialogue, the person who talks the *least* directs the conversation. *Listening* is the most critical rapport-building skill. Many of your mothers probably told you that you have two ears and one mouth for a reason. LAVA is a surefire way to guarantee that you will talk *less* than your companions by simply *asking questions*. This will allow you to connect with people on a personal level without getting too personal.

"Now, as we go through the questions represented by LAVA, I want you to note that each one is designed to provide a form of minibio of the whole person. Remember, it's *who you are,* right? Let's talk about the initial step."

Dr. John had noticed that Natalie Nguyen, who sat on the front row next to Aaron, was very attentive. He rubbed his hands together briefly and stepped toward the center of the classroom. He smiled and made eye contact with Natalie and slowly extended his hand. "Hello, I don't believe we've met. I'm Johnathan.'"

Catching on immediately, she replied, "I'm Natalie."

"It's a pleasure to meet you, Natalie." As they shook hands, he looked up at the class and stated, "*This* is a critical moment."

Natalie smiled as Dr. John nodded a thank-you, gently released her hand, and stepped away.

He then asked the class, "Have you ever forgotten a name within three seconds of meeting someone? Me too. It's embarrassing, isn't it? In your text in **chapter 1**, there is a section—'Nine Ways to Never Forget a Name or Face.' We don't have time to cover them all in class, but here are three that are particularly important:

"Number one: **listen and focus.** Often, we are just nervous and afraid we'll forget someone's name. So, what happens?"

Several students chorused in unison, "We forget their names."

"That's right. We freeze up. But remember—you're the *leader* in this conversation. Have an empathetic attitude. That means paying close attention.

"Secondly, if you didn't hear the name or forgot it immediately—**ask again. Don't wait.** You won't be held responsible if you do it right away. Most people are understanding and will appreciate the effort to get it right.

"And thirdly, **repeat the name back immediately.** Besides being courteous, everyone likes the sound of their own name. Repetition also starts the process of embossing their name in your memory. Your goal is to repeat their name at least *five* times in the course of the initial conversation."

Dr. John looked across the classroom and noticed only about half of the class typing. *Not bad for the first lecture*, he thought.

He continued, "After this initial greeting, you would then say, 'So nice to meet you, Natalie. Are you from this area?'"

Aaron turned his head slightly as though something sounded familiar.

Natalie grinned, pleased to be the example. "I live in Chicago—born and raised."

Dr. John interrupted the conversation with Natalie and interjected, "We become—to a great extent—like those around us . . . the culture . . . the mores . . . the values of our upbringing. The communities in which we live and work shape us, don't they? Returning to our volcano analogy, this first question gets the conversation flowing back to the beginnings of *who we are* by focusing on our geographic roots—our *locations*—which is the *L* in LAVA.

"Think of how much information can be derived from this simple first query. If you've traveled, read, or keep up with current events at all, you can almost always follow up with a question such as . . ."

Dr. John looked back at Natalie. "Oh, from Chicago, eh? White Sox or Cubs?"

Natalie bounced in excitement. "Definitely Cubs!"

"Oh, you must be happy after 2016," Dr. John said.

"Yes, I am! My grandmother cheered for eighty years and never thought she would see it in her lifetime."

Dr. John looked back at the class and asked, "What just happened?"

Robert on row two answered. "You know she's a baseball fan."

"That's right, Mr. Harris. And I'm only just beginning to build rapport. I could easily go from baseball to another 'windy city' where I grew up in west Texas—or the several conferences and vacations I've had in her hometown. I could ask if she went to school there, or maybe about her favorite restaurant in Chicago." Dr. John glanced back at Natalie and smiled.

"These add-on questions would further create rapport and a personal connection. Geographic origins and their unique characteristics typically create a comfortable atmosphere of nostalgia. Nostalgia can be bittersweet—but it's a mostly positive emotion packed with relationship power. It's a kind of gateway to the past that makes the present meaningful. Just think about all of the TV commercials that use nostalgia to connect you to their products."

Aaron could only smile as he thought about his LAVA conversation with Dr. John last week. "*Ah . . . 'Cowtown' . . . the rodeo in January is always a phenomenal event. Quintessential Texas.*"

"By the time I leave the *L* in LAVA, my new friend Natalie and I will have connected in three or four lighthearted ways that will begin to weave a friendship that might last only for the duration of the event we're attending—or for a lifetime. Either way, we are just getting started."

Dr. John straightened. "Now to the second question—or the *A* in the LAVA acronym—which stands for *associations*. Natalie, do you have family still in Chicago?"

Natalie raised an eyebrow. "Yes. My husband and I have two boys—ages two and six. And my parents and two sisters and their families all still live there."

Dr. John chuckled. Natalie was inventing an imaginary family to play along as an example. That she'd done it so quickly was impressive. "Ah, I have two boys that are also four years apart. I know you have your hands full!"

Dr. John turned his attention to the class again. "Notice the connections piling up? Two boys . . . parents and siblings all still live in the same town. These are clues that might be an indicator of a close-knit family.

"Alternatively, I could have asked Natalie about other associations—whether she knew anyone at the meeting. That would be safer than asking about family. But since she already offered the fact that she was 'born and raised' in Chicago and that her grandmother was a Cubs fan—likely living in Chicago—the opening to ask gently about family was available."

"That's a full house," Aaron remembered. *"You know, I have four children myself. Two of each. All close to your age."*

Dr. John stepped to the other side of the stage. "Now that we have discussed comfortable topics such as hometowns, favorite teams, friends and family, or alma maters, it's time to broach the topic of *vocations*—or the *V* in LAVA. Watch how I approach this area.

"Natalie, I'm curious . . . How do you spend most of your time?"

"Well, working, for sure. I'm a logistics analyst for the ABC company," Natalie fabricated.

"Oh, interesting. How long have you been doing that?" Dr. John asked her.

"Just a couple of years—but I'm really enjoying it."

Natalie was having so much fun imagining her future self. It made Dr. John smile. He looked at the class. "Note that by asking, 'How do you spend most of your time?' I leave the door open for her to tell me something other than a vocation. Perhaps she is taking time off to be with her boys for a season. Again, I would never ask, 'What do you do?' because I want to avoid the 'you are what you do' mind-set that dominates our culture. It should always be about the whole individual you're getting to know.

"Now, suppose I had a good idea that Natalie is engaged in a full-time occupation. Maybe she had given me a clue in a previous answer. I then could have also asked, 'What line of work are you in?'" he explained. "When my new friend tells me about her *vocation*, I can also ask, 'Have you always been in this line of work?' or 'How has the economy affected your industry?' If I sense a good rapport and want to have an even more connecting conversation, I can ask a question such as, 'What did you want to be growing up?' Do you see how that question will bring up some nostalgia?

"The last question, or the second *A* in LAVA, is *avocations*—a fancy word for hobbies and interests." Dr. John turned back to Natalie. "Natalie, I'm assuming you don't just work, so how do you spend your free time—any hobbies?"

"Yes, I snow ski a ton, and I love to travel," Natalie answered.

"Oh, nice! I don't ski like I used to, but I travel a lot too. What's the most memorable trip you've ever taken?" Dr. John asked.

"Oh, definitely Italy! I've never seen a place there that didn't look like a postcard!" she exclaimed.

"Yes, I've been blessed to go there myself. You're right. Italy is extraordinary," Dr. John agreed. To the class, he added, "As you can imagine, a topic such as travel could go on for several more minutes . . . or hours. In the interest of time, I'll conclude the LAVA conversation with Natalie by saying, 'Well, it looks like the program is about to get started. It was so nice to get to know you. I hope we can cross paths again.'"

"Yes, Johnathan, I enjoyed it as well."

"Take care, Natalie—and enjoy the evening."

Dr. John walked back behind the lectern. "Notice I said it was 'nice to get to know you' instead of 'nice to meet you.' I also said her name *five* times within four to five minutes of small talk. I would try to find her to say, 'So long, Natalie,' once more toward the end of the evening if possible. I want to deeply ingrain her name in my memory.

"So, tell me," Dr. John challenged his class. "What do I know about Natalie because of the LAVA conversation that I would not have known if I had taken the standard 'What do you do?' approach?" Dr. John asked. "Yes, Ms. Williams?"

Joy answered, "You know where she was raised, that she loves the Cubs, and that she is married with two young boys and probably has close family ties."

"Good . . . What else?"

Aaron spoke up next. "You now know her profession, specific position, her years of experience, and the name of the company she works for. You also know she loves winter sports and enjoys traveling—particularly to Italy."

"That's right, Aaron. You have a nice minibio, don't you? I would suggest that anytime you have a LAVA conversation, you document in some way what you've learned about your new friend within twenty-four hours so that you maintain a high probability of retaining it in case you see them again in the future." Dr. John instructed his class. "I use a simple note app on my phone for convenience, and then once I'm back at my office, I'll write on the back of their business card or on a three-by-five card to put in a recipe box—just because I'm a stickler for writing things down. Just make sure you have a way of recalling this valuable information about *who they are* when you want to refresh your memory. Yes, Calli? You have a question?"

Calli Clark was pensive. "I know we shouldn't ask, 'What do you do?'—but aren't people going to ask us that question? How should we answer?"

"Good question, Calli!" Dr. John said approvingly. "When people ask me, 'What do you do?'—I just quickly say, 'Whatever it takes!'"

Students laughed.

"Seriously, I may use that quip if the situation feels comfortable. Otherwise, I try to answer first with a question: 'You know all the great students we have at State U? I have the privilege of teaching a senior-level communications course there. I also do some consulting and training for companies on how to become exceptional communicators and leaders.'

"Think of a short question you could ask at the beginning of your answer to engage them—and then simply tell them the gist of the work you do. But then get right back on track with LAVA. Does that help?"

Calli nodded. "Thank you," she said.

"OK, now it's your turn," Dr. John announced. "I want you to turn to a classmate and have a LAVA conversation right now. I don't care how well you think you might know them—you're about to learn something new."

The class followed instructions, and within twenty seconds, the scene became what it always was—a delight. Laughter, high fives, and an occasional "No way!" were common. Nothing energized Dr. John's class at the beginning of each semester like LAVA.

After seven or eight minutes, Dr. John checked the clock and then reached behind his table and brought out an old-school megaphone. "May I have your attention please . . . attention please," he echoed. "This is a microphone from back in my day," Dr. John joked, holding up the antique. "Thank you all for your participation today—especially you, Natalie. Let's give her a hand."

Polite applause followed.

"I wish we had time to hear all of the things you just learned about each other. Here is what we are going to do instead. As I told you on the first day of class, throughout the semester I will be issuing several challenges. You will only have a midterm exam and a final—so these challenges will make up one-third of your grade. They are designed to allow you to 'test drive' some of the keys to success in real time. And you're going to uncover some interesting opportunities along the way—I promise.

"The first challenge is this: conduct three LAVA conversations—just like we did here in class today. Write down your observations as soon as you can afterward, and then access the class portal and submit them. They must be date-stamped prior to class two weeks from today to avoid a 50 percent penalty. Note that you will not be asked to provide names online. So, feel free to tell them about the LAVA assignment if you wish. We'll take a few minutes during class to hear what you learned about a new acquaintance—or even an old friend."

Dr. John waited for complete silence and then said, "Here is the most important thing I want you to take with you concerning this first key: **everyone is important and should be treated as such.** At the end of any LAVA conversation, *what* you talked about may be forgotten, but the way you made them *feel* will always be remembered."

Dr. John stepped out to stand near the banner. "I'm sure you noticed the single witness from history I have with me today. Mother Teresa understood what it meant to make the poor and downtrodden feel special. She was born in Macedonia in 1910. She lost her father at age nine and grew up to become a missionary in the slums of India. She eventually helped start more than six hundred missions, schools, and shelters in more than 120 countries. She is quoted as saying, 'If I look at the masses, I will never act. If I look at the one, I will.' We can all learn something about compassion from her. And compassion should start with the first conversation," Dr. John concluded.

"Please also look over **chapter 2**, concerning time leadership, for next time. See you then, and don't be late!"

Aaron stood up to go talk to Dr. John, but several other students had already queued up. The professor took his time with each student—never failing to ask them that first LAVA 'location' question. Aaron waited so he could be last.

When it was his turn, Dr. John greeted him with pleasure. "Howdy, Aaron. How are your classes shaping up so far?"

"Pretty well, thank you. Dr. John, I was just thinking . . . You did a LAVA on me, didn't you? When we first met? I had a question for you, but you just kept asking *me* questions."

Dr. John smiled. "I suppose I did 'do a LAVA.' I've never used that term . . . I like it."

"But how did you know my name already?" Aaron asked. "It's not like you had time to put all our names with our faces before the first class."

"Great question, Aaron." Dr. John turned toward the classroom, gesturing for Aaron to look out at the desks as he saw them. "Aaron, you did something very important on the first day of class. You sat on the first row, in the middle. It's the best seat in the house, yet most students avoid it like the plague—or the front row in church." He chuckled.

"Yes. My mom is a teacher and always encouraged me to do that," Aaron offered.

"She taught you well, Aaron, because by sitting there, you communicated some meaningful things to me as the professor. You showed interest in the subject, you showed a willingness to participate, and you showed respect for authority. These are all critical elements of success that many people just don't think about."

Dr. John gathered his things, and he and Aaron headed up the stairs to the exit. "Now, how did I remember your name, you ask?"

"Yes, sir," Aaron answered.

"After every first class, I immediately grab the roster and check the three names of those sitting front and center, because at least one of you always has a question for me." They continued to walk together outside. "'Aaron Woods' was the name in the middle. Memorizing you, Calli Clark, and Natalie Nguyen wasn't a huge task—even for an old guy like me. Fortunately, no one from row three approached me today. Know what I mean?"

Aaron nodded and grinned.

Dr. John explained, "But for other people, if you want to remember their names, mnemonics can help. If you and I had met in a different circumstance, for instance, I might picture you in my mind as the Aaron who was the spokesman for Moses in the Old Testament. Picturing you in the 'woods' instead of the wilderness would also make your last name easy to remember."

"Interesting." Aaron liked the creativity. *Me working with Moses*, he mused.

"I know that may sound silly," Dr. John admitted. "But the important thing is that I would find a way to remember your name—to honor you in that small way for when we meet again. Within a few weeks, I'll have every student's name committed to memory with this method. And remember, it's all in **chapter 1** of your textbook—so you have no excuse not to use these methods as well." Inside his office building, Dr. John smiled at Aaron. "Well, this is my stop. Let me know if there's any other questions I can answer. See you next time!"

Dr. John disappeared down the hall. "Thank you, Dr. John!" Aaron called after him. *I can't believe how fast he got to know me*, he thought. *So simple . . . yet so powerful!*

THREE

THE GIRLS

*Friendship is born at that moment when one person says
to the other, "What! You too? I thought I was the only one."*

—C. S. LEWIS

Ten minutes after Dr. John's class ended, Aaron blew through
the revolving door into the main library with his scarf in his
face and hair disheveled. He wanted to find a quiet corner
to set up and get some studying done so he could go see
Amanda later. The first round of exams would be here soon
enough, and he felt behind already. Chances were slim, but he
thought he might just be able to score a private study room.
He rounded the corner on the third floor. *Yes!*

He entered an empty study carrel with six comfortable
chairs and a table. *This will be perfect . . .*

A voice spoke up from behind him. "Hi, I don't believe
we've met. My name is Lisa, and this is Nicole." Aaron turned
around to see a hand firmly extended.

"Uh . . . oh, hi . . . I'm Aaron. Aaron Woods."

"A pleasure to meet you, Aaron Woods." Lisa's smile was
broad and genuine.

"Me too," Nicole followed.

"So where are you from, Aaron?" Lisa asked.

"From Fort Worth. How about you?"

"We've lived here for about five years now, but originally we're from Dallas," Lisa answered. "So I guess we were neighbors for a while. You go to the rodeo much? We love Cowtown."

"Uh . . . yes. I like it." Aaron's head tilted. *Chatty girls.* He wasn't quite sure what to make of them. "Are y'all related in some way?"

"Yes, sisters," Lisa told him. "Do you have family in Fort Worth?"

"Yes, I have a brother and two sisters. How about you?"

"We have two older brothers that went to school here too," Lisa said. "So what are you studying, Aaron?"

"International finance with a business communications minor."

"That's a pretty hard track. *¿Hablas español?*" Nicole asked.

"*Un poco.*" Aaron gestured with his thumb and forefinger. "But I'm learning, and I love to travel, and the whole international banking system is intriguing to me. I'm guessing you know some Spanish?"

"*Si, señor,*" Nicole said. "We learned it from our mom."

These girls are nice, Aaron decided. "What are y'all majoring in?"

"I'm in business management," Lisa said.

"And I'm a sophomore in psychology," piped up Nicole. "I want to be a family counselor."

"What do you like to do when you're not studying, Aaron? Any hobbies?" Lisa asked, moving into the study room. Aaron made room for both girls, and they all sat down.

"Yes, I play guitar and harmonica. I also like to sing. I'm a fan of pretty much any sport. What about you?"

"Nice! Music, definitely. And our dad has made us sports fans over the years," Lisa said.

There was an awkward pause. "It's getting a bit warm in here," Nicole said, removing her jacket.

"Hey, nice shirt! Where did you get that?" Aaron asked.

On the front was an elongated, distressed black diamond logo with the words "The Old School" in the middle. Underneath, it read, "#noschoollikeit."

"Thanks! It's probably my most comfortable shirt," Nicole answered.

"It's awesome! Where can I get one?" Aaron asked.

"I have another one in State U colors!" Nicole said. "It's maroon with a white logo."

Aaron tilted his head. "No way!"

"Haven't you heard of the Old School movement?" Nicole asked.

"No. What's that?"

"Well, it's a student organization. Ta-da!" Nicole waved her hand in front of the logo on her shirt like a game show hostess. "Old School is the new cool!"

Lisa reached out to playfully shove her sister. "Our mission is to bring back timeless wisdom, like old-school communication techniques—things like that," she explained. "I mean, social media can be fun and convenient, right? But it's really becoming a burden. Wouldn't you agree?"

"Yes, I do agree." Aaron responded. "So, you've obviously had Dr. Daniels's class. You sound just like him."

"No, I haven't had his class—and unfortunately, my remaining schedule is not set up where I can take it. But we have a copy of the textbook he uses in his class, so we're very familiar with all the concepts you're talking about," Lisa told Aaron.

So that's why these girls just did a LAVA on me, Aaron thought to himself. *They read the textbook. Crazy . . . and a little strange.* "So you're telling me there is actually a campus organization that you can join called 'The Old School'?"

"Yes," Lisa answered. "We have about a hundred members. I'm the current president, and Nicole is public relations chair."

No surprise there, Aaron thought.

Lisa continued, "There are thirty-four campuses that have chapters now. It's growing fast. Dr. Daniels speaks at our meetings a couple of times each semester. We also have some other great lecturers—including the author of your text."

"No kidding. Really?" Aaron responded.

Lisa nodded. "Yes, and our service projects involve going into local high schools where students may have limited economic or social opportunities. We teach them old-school principles so that they might have an advantage as well. Right now, we're teaching them sales and marketing skills as we sell these shirts to companies and organizations throughout the community. Working with those kids is the most rewarding experience I've had at State U. We get into some deep conversations about life."

"That's amazing. I had no idea," Aaron replied. "There's so much to do on this campus. It's hard to keep up."

"Well, maybe you can come with us sometime . . . and get a shirt," Nicole said, gesturing theatrically at hers again. Aaron noticed she was messing around with what looked like a glue gun.

"What are you doing there? Arts and crafts time?" Aaron asked.

Nicole giggled. "I'm trying to get notes out to all of the companies that supported the program last year before we call them again." She squeezed hot liquid onto the back of an envelope.

"So, is that a wax stamp . . . like from the Middle Ages?"

"*Like* yes." Nicole smirked.

"Man, now *that's* old scho . . ." Aaron caught himself. The three of them laughed.

"So I just realized, I know quite a bit about y'all, but I don't even know your last name," Aaron said.

"It's Kosta." Nicole extended her hand with a big smile, as though she and Aaron were meeting for the first time.

As Aaron shook her hand, he said, "Kosta. Pleasure to meet you, Nicole Kosta. So, what's the origin of that name?"

"It's actually Greek," she informed him.

"It's our mom's name—but she's from Cuba originally," Lisa added.

They use their mom's last name . . . Won't go there, Aaron decided. "Cuba? Really? Man, I bet she has some incredible stories."

"Oh, she definitely does," Lisa agreed.

"Have you ever been to Cuba?" Aaron asked.

"No, but we hope to all go some day. My mom is a little hesitant. Some bad memories there," Lisa told him.

"You should go over spring break," Aaron encouraged them.

Nicole shook her head. "We're going skiing with the Old School."

"Oh, does your mom ski?"

"She and my dad both did for years. But since he sold his company, they've taken a break."

So there is a dad, Aaron thought. "What does your da—"

"Uh-oh, time flies," Lisa interrupted. "Actually, we need to run meet somebody."

"Take care, Aaron! *¡Hasta la vista!*" Nicole called as they rushed out.

"Uh . . . OK . . . see you later," Aaron mumbled, shrugging and opening his laptop to get to work.

FOUR

Time Leadership

Do you love life? Then do not squander time,
for that's the stuff life is made of.

—Benjamin Franklin

"Good morning, ladies and gentlemen! I have a story to tell you."

Dr. John waited a few seconds as the class settled in.

"In 1912 . . ."

He stopped as Aaron rushed in and slid into his seat on the front row—disheveled and out of breath. "The first rule of *time management* is 'if you're not early, you're late.' Right, Mr. Woods?" Dr. John cajoled.

Aaron knew he had a good reason for being late. He wanted to explain to Dr. John, but his mother had always taught him: "*No whining, no complaining, and no excuses.*"

"Yes, sir. I apologize."

"No worries, Aaron. As I was saying, in 1912, the president of the Bethlehem Steel Company was Charles M. Schwab. His company was struggling with inefficiency, and Schwab didn't know how to improve it. He called Ivy Lee, a well-known efficiency expert. Lee agreed to help the company, with his fee being 'whatever Schwab felt the results were worth' after three months of implementing his new idea.

"Six weeks passed, and Lee returned with this advice. Each member of the company's management team was to compile a list at the end of each day that consisted of the six most important tasks to complete the following day. They were then to organize the list by ranking the tasks in order of priority. The next day, the managers were to work through the list from top to bottom, focusing on a single task at a time. At the end of the day, anything left on the list would get added to the top of tomorrow's list. As the story goes, the company was so much more efficient after three months that Schwab sent a check to Ivy Lee for $25,000—equivalent to more than $500,000 today," Dr. John concluded.

He spread his hands over the lectern. "This story might seem trivial because of its simplicity. 'Make a list, and check off the tasks as you complete them.' It's hardly rocket science. But a century ago—it was a breakthrough idea. Surprisingly, few people follow this simple advice even today. Those who do know the secret of its power.

"I want to make a slight adjustment in your thinking concerning time management," Dr. John told the class. "I want you to use a different term from now on: **time leadership**. American philosopher William James said, 'The art of being wise is the art of knowing what to *overlook*.' Imagine that—wisdom and time management are tied together. Handling time wisely through prioritization is a hallmark of an effective leader. And one of the most important aspects of time leadership is to distinguish the important from the *un*important. Doing what needs to be done *when* it needs to be done. That means you're *telling* your time where to go instead of *asking* where your time went. To put it succinctly, as a leader, you must **set priorities**, **do less**, and **become more**."

"Here are some of my favorite quotes concerning our most important commodity," Dr. John told them, pointing to some writing on the board and reading each quotation aloud.

"Until we can manage time, we can manage nothing else."
—Peter Drucker

"The bad news is, time flies. The good
news is—you're the pilot."
—Michael Altshuler

"Take care of the minutes, for the hours
will take care of themselves."
—Lord Chesterfield

Dr. John paused for a moment and looked out over the classroom. He was pleased to see more students were writing things down this session. He saw that Maria Lopez had snuck into the back row. She waved, and Dr. John nodded and smiled. "Perhaps my favorite quote is from today's witness from history—Benjamin Franklin." Dr. John motioned toward the banner bearing Franklin's likeness. The word *Innovation* was blazoned boldly across the top. "Early to bed and early to rise . . . Can you finish it for me?"

". . . makes a man healthy, wealthy, and wise." As usual, only a handful of students joined in unison in this classic American saying he had learned in the third grade. "By the way, which president was Benjamin Franklin? Third, fourth, fifth?" Dr. John asked.

The class was silent. Finally, Aaron raised his hand. "I don't think he was president," he said politely.

"That's not true! He's on the one-hundred-dollar bill, right? Which one was he?" Dr. John asked again.

No answer.

"OK. Make a note," Dr. John instructed. "Benjamin Franklin was the sixth president—"

Has Dr. John lost it? Aaron thought.

"—of Pennsylvania, when it was a commonwealth between 1777 and 1790." He grinned at the class. "That might be a good bonus question on the midterm, by the way."

After a short pause, he continued. "Did you know that 40 percent of the freshman class that started here at State with you just over three years ago is no longer here? That's right—on average, only three out of five students earn a degree within six years. Congratulations for even being here! Who would like to take a guess as to the biggest reason your classmates are no longer with you?" Dr. John scanned the classroom. "Ms. Reagan?"

"Maybe they partied too much?" Kate offered. Laughter rippled in agreement all around.

"I'm sure that's the case for many," Dr. John allowed. "But by far the biggest reason is their inability to handle the scheduling freedom that college affords. In high school, the day was structured for you. Your teachers and parents directed you to the next activity, and you never gave it much thought. But college brought with it this problem of freedom. You were able to eventually get your schedules under control. But I'm sure you would admit it wasn't easy. Let me assure you, the transition from college life to professional life will be just as challenging when it comes to stewarding your time . . . maybe even more so."

Dr. John lifted up the textbook. "There are several time-leadership techniques mentioned in your text. They could all be on the test, by the way. But today, I want to review a few in particular that I believe will help ensure your smooth transition into the working world. Are you ready?" Dr. John asked.

Heads nodded.

"Let's get to work!

"The most important time-leadership technique builds on the concept that Ivy Lee showed Charles Schwab: **review tomorrow's schedule and task list every evening on paper**."

"Great leaders plan ahead—and they do it in *writing*. Now, please understand that I'm not knocking the tech-driven tools that surround us. I love them too. Music, all of my books on my tablet—it's truly amazing. But what we're talking about here is time efficiency. And just as Mr. Schwab learned more than one hundred years ago, sometimes the simplest ideas can be the most effective. As I've alluded, there are two aspects to this technique: (1) timing of the activity—the night before—and 2) going analog—on paper.

"Despite warnings to the contrary in your freshman orientation classes, I know many of you have 'pulled all-nighters' or woken up early to cram for an exam. These were both bad ideas because what you gained in additional study time you lost in fatigue, and thus in memory. It will be no different in your professional life. Your performance will be adversely affected if you don't establish a reasonable routine for rest.

"There will also be times when you don't wish to think about tomorrow's work because it might 'stress you out' and you're afraid it will keep you from falling asleep," Dr. John observed. "But the opposite is true. Taking a few minutes to review tasks and organize your schedule before bedtime puts your mind at ease. Knowing is better than not knowing because there are no lingering questions in your mind. And get this—your mind can actually be working on issues *while you are sleeping.*"

"How can that be?" Joy asked. "I sleep like a rock!"

Dr. John chuckled, "Yes. I understand. But there is science behind it. Research suggests that rapid eye movement— otherwise known as REM sleep—enhances creative problem solving, thus fostering associative networks in the brain. Your brain is very active when you sleep, and it becomes more active if you've just learned something new."

Joy followed up. "And the tasks we reviewed and wrote down before we went to sleep count as 'something new'?" she asked, putting "something new" in air quotes.

"That's exactly right!" Dr. John exclaimed. "And the advantages don't stop there. Think about it. Have you ever had a great idea—or an answer to a nagging question—pop into your head first thing in the morning? Maybe getting ready for class, or on a jog? That's anecdotal evidence that supports this concept."

Aaron raised his hand and asked, "Dr. John, why does it have to be on paper? That seems a waste of time when everything is saved on our devices and we have them with us all the time."

"Well, it doesn't *have* to be on paper," Dr. John answered, "but remember how I mentioned last week that it's better to take notes with pen and paper rather than with a keyboard because you are up to *five* times more likely to remember it? When you write something down, as far as your brain is concerned, it's as if you are actually *doing* the very thing you're writing about. It's a type of minirehearsal, if you will. It's in the same vein as athletes who visualize their performance before a game.

"Going analog also increases your focus," added Dr. John. "Interestingly, surveys show that a majority of your generation prefers to read hard copy books instead of e-books because it limits or avoids distractions. In the same way, keeping your activities and schedule on paper limits distractions.

"Finally," Dr. John finished, "the additional effort of writing promotes mindfulness, which can help you gather your thoughts and reflect for a few minutes each day. This practice can also promote creativity. And, as a bonus, your schedule and task book can serve as a convenient place to journal and keep a chronological record of your activities. Which takes me back to ole Ben Franklin—he also coined the memorable phrase 'time is money.' And while he was more famous as an inventor, statesman, and framer of our constitution, he loved to identify himself as simply a *printer*. As a print-shop owner, he created one of the early daily journals—a sample of which is found in **chapter 2** of your text. I love the evening question he has at the bottom: 'What good have I done this day?' You should take three to five minutes to ask yourselves that same question at the end of each day. This is a motivating activity because it reminds you of the positive progress you made instead of the things that you left incomplete. Closing the door on each day's work in this manner will help energize you for what lies ahead the next day."

Dr. John looked out at the class. "Twenty-four hours a day is what we all have in common. Just as Mr. Franklin did, we must make every day our masterpiece.

"Now, I'm no founding father, but many years ago, I developed an analog tool for our team that I call simply *The Day Book*. I eventually got a copyright and published it." Dr. John held up a copy. "In every new edition, I put the same poem in the front to remind users how important all of our days are—especially 'normal days.' This verse is by Mary Jean Irion."

Normal day, let me be aware
of the treasure that you are.
Let me learn from you, love you,
bless you before we depart.
Let me not pass you by in quest
of some rare and perfect tomorrow.
Let me hold you while I may,
for it may not be always so.

"As part of your rite of passage into the working world, I look forward to presenting you with your own *Day Book* at the end of our time together. The summer edition is at the printer now," Dr. John told the class.

He heard a chorus of "nice" and "awesome" from around the room.

"Moving on," Dr. John said. "The other time-leadership technique I want to discuss today is **scheduling in time blocks**.

"When I was about your age, I was into the latest technology. The jogging craze was at its peak, and I bought a Walkman—a historic device on which one listens to music by way of AA batteries and a cassette tape." Dr. John paused to a few snickers. He continued, "I also had a running watch that had a countdown clock in addition to a stopwatch. This countdown clock became a tool that provided me a way of getting things done more efficiently. My friends teased me, but by setting an hour to read history, an hour to work on chemistry, and then an hour for English, I was able to focus and finish my work sooner."

Dr. John held up his left arm and pointed at his watch. "You all have these watches now—or smartphones and tablets—that give you beautiful graphics. I schedule a time block for every class. See? We have eleven minutes and twenty-seven seconds to go in the class time block."

Dr. John lowered his arm. "There's an old saying: a goal without a deadline is just a dream. And while this is typically applied to long-range planning goals, the time-block method applies this principle of working to a deadline with short-term goals as well. Remember, 'Take care of the minutes and the hours will take care of themselves.'"

Dr. John saw a student had raised her hand. "Yes, Rachel, you have a question?"

"Yes. I can see the advantage of this in school, but I'm about to graduate. How would this help us at work?" she asked.

"Thank you. Great question. Let's say you arrive at the office at 8 a.m. and have a lunch meeting at 12:30. That four and a half hours can be broken down into three time blocks of ninety minutes each. Since you've prioritized your list of tasks the night before, you can easily evaluate which ones fit into the first ninety-minute segment. If the tasks slated for the first time block are completed early, then reblock the remaining two time periods in the four-and-a-half-hour window. If you finish the first time block twenty minutes early, blocks two and three get ten more minutes each."

Dr. John saw another hand go up. "Yes, Ms. Wilson?"

Aisha asked, "I've heard that you should do certain types of tasks in the morning and other types in the afternoon. Is there anything to that?"

"Actually, there is something to it. And it's very interesting what the research has uncovered." Dr. John answered. "For the majority of people, analytical tasks or important decisions are better scheduled in the morning, while brainstorming or creative tasks are best left for after 1 p.m. or so. Now, if you are part of the 20 percent of the population who are 'night owls,' the opposite is true. But regardless, you are more likely to make a positive impression in the morning. You should take note of that for interviews, by the way.

"Now, here is the critical part of the time-block method: you must wait until the end of each time block to check texts and emails. The average American checks their phone or email *eighty* times per day. Furthermore, studies have shown that it can take up to *eight* minutes to return to the same level of concentration that was achieved before an interruption. At that rate, it doesn't take many interruptions to blow an hour of productivity."

Dr. John spread his hands. "We all get anxious when we hear our phone buzz or ring. In fact, it's proven that your blood pressure goes up, your pulse quickens, and your problem-solving abilities decline. That's why silencing phones and placing them out of reach during each time block is important."

Dr. John paused and smiled as some students looked up from their laps. A few slowly slid their phones away with less subtlety than they were hoping for. "One more bonus tidbit— who knows what 'ASAP' stands for?" Dr. John asked.

"As soon as possible," Natalie answered.

"That's correct!" Dr. John exclaimed. "As *slow* as possible." After a short pause, a few students snickered.

"ASAP has been so overused that it no longer contains the sense of urgency intended. I'm wondering if you've ever heard of Parkinson's Law?" No one responded. "I'll take that as a 'maybe,'" Dr. John quipped.

"Parkinson's Law says, 'Work expands so as to fill the time available for its completion.'" Dr. John paused to let that sink in. "If this is true, imagine the inefficiency when no deadline is given! From now on, I want you to use a different acronym for a time-sensitive task: GMAD—which means 'give me a *deadline*.'

"A deadline is especially valuable as it approaches, because people naturally get more energized to close the small gap that remains," Dr. John explained. "Think of finishing a race. When you see the finish line, you have a burst to finish strong. Establishing GMAD is a small concept that can be a big way to save time and eliminate frustration."

The class was getting close to ending. Students began to whisper to their neighbor and shuffle their backpacks. Dr. John tapped his watch and said, "Wait, I have thirty seconds left!"

Everyone froze.

"Next time, we're going to take a look at the power of *words* and which ones matter the most. Please read **chapter 3** before Monday." Dr. John looked at his watch as a timer beeped. "See you next time. Have a great day!"

Several students lined up to ask questions after class. Most of the queries were about *The Day Book*, which Dr. John was planning to give them at the end of the semester.

Aaron waited until Dr. John was packed for his daily jaunt to his office. Dr. John looked up when he approached.

"Aaron, you don't seem like the type that likes to be late. Is everything OK?"

"Uh . . . yes, sir. I mean, I think so. I just wanted to apologize."

Dr. John frowned. "Of course. No worries . . . but you don't sound too convincing. What's wrong?" he asked.

"I was checking on my girlfriend," Aaron explained. "She was not doing that well this morning. She was lightheaded and nauseated last night. She just was not herself. She plays volleyball and is a great athlete, but she said practice was extra hard yesterday and that she almost fainted a couple of times during it. I just texted her, though, and she said she's feeling better."

"I'm sorry to hear about her fainting spell. That can be scary. Glad she's feeling better," Dr. John empathized.

"Thanks. I just wanted to let you know why I was late. It's no excuse. I know it was rude."

"Again, don't worry about it. Thank you for explaining. We all have things happen that we can't control," Dr. John reassured Aaron as the two of them headed toward his office once again. "Tell me about your girlfriend. What's her name?"

Aaron lit up, and in his face Dr. John saw all the signs of a young man in love. "Her name is Amanda."

He smiled. "Did you meet here at State U?"

"Yes, sir. We became chemistry lab partners. She saved me in that class. Science is not my field of expertise."

Dr. John nodded, "Believe me, I'm in that nonscientific boat too. How long have you been dating?"

"Almost two years. We're best friends—and our values are pretty aligned, which is not all that easy to find nowadays.

And her family is great! My mom always told me, 'Remember, Aaron—you marry the family, not just the girl.'"

Dr. John grinned and raised his eyebrows. "Marriage? You thinking about popping the question?"

Aaron nodded. "I'm thinking about proposing this semester. I'll be graduating in May, and she will get out in December if she takes summer classes, so I'm thinking maybe now is the time to get something on the calendar. You know, GMAD!"

Aaron's answer provided more details than Dr. John had expected. "It may well be the time, Aaron, it may well be. Two years is plenty of time to know if she's the one. Keep me posted!"

Aaron stopped at the door of Dr. John's building. "I will," he promised. "Thanks, Dr. John. I'm really enjoying your class."

"Thank you, Aaron. I'm glad." But as Dr. John watched Aaron walk away, he felt a strange uneasiness come over him.

FIVE

The Old School

Stand by the roads and look,
and ask for the ancient paths,
where the good way is: and walk in it,
and find rest for you souls.

—Jeremiah, the prophet

"*. . . and to the Republic, for which it stands, one nation, under*
God, indivisible—with liberty and justice for all."

"Thank you, Robert," Lisa Kosta said. *Bam!* She thumped her gavel on the podium to bring the meeting of the State U chapter of the Old School to order, and a hush followed. "Welcome! First things first: I'm so excited to see everyone!"

Lisa Kosta had an infectious smile that filled every room she entered. Her pearly whites, combined with her naturally blonde hair and blue eyes, were always attention getters. An achiever both in and out of the classroom, she never seemed to sit still. As president of the Old School student organization, she had helped double the membership to more than two hundred students in the fall drive. "Tonight, we're going to go over the plan for the spring fundraiser," she announced. "It looks like we have forty-two kids signed up—which is the most ever. Nicole, how many potential business partners are on the list currently?" Lisa asked.

Nicole, Lisa's younger sister by two years, was often mistaken for her twin—even with her amber hair and brown eyes. The more extroverted of the two sisters, she was perfect for her job as marketing and public relations chair for the spring campaign. She had the gift of gab and a magnetic personality. She combined these traits with a particular toughness—likely born out of having two older stepbrothers and being the youngest in a blended family. She could hold her own in any debate. "We have about thirty right now," Nicole answered. "But I'm confident we can get that number way up once we start calling on our list of alums in the area."

"Excellent," Lisa replied. "Now let me go over the logistics of the program for those who have not been involved yet." Nicole handed her sister a T-shirt. Lisa held it up. "This is our classic Old School shirt."

"We know!" Peter Jacobs shouted from the back.

"Thanks, Peter," Nicole replied wryly.

Undeterred, Lisa continued, "We have three options from which companies can choose. This classic black-on-gray, a white-on-maroon—State U colors—and then we can also do their company colors. I think we're up to forty-four different color combinations. And on all of the shirts, we can put their company logo on the back collar." She turned the shirt around to show.

Lisa tossed the shirt back to Nicole. "There are five things we want to stress in our presentation," Lisa said, "Starting with the benefits for the *customer*. Remember, everyone is listening to the same radio station: WIIFM—What's in It for Me?

"So first, comfort. These are the softest T-shirts ever, and they will become favorites. Second, it's a good perk for employees that includes company branding. Third, these shirts make great gifts to customers. Fourth, the shirts represent *who these companies are*. Being Old School indicates that the wearer knows the importance of the *fundamentals* and has the wisdom that goes with understanding the things in life that *don't change*. Finally, and most importantly for our mission, their financial support will help transform the lives of kids in our community. Kids who have faced many more challenges at a young age than they should have."

Lisa continued, "For our next couple of meetings, our faculty advisor, Dr. Daniels, will be here to go over some sales techniques. We will not only use these ourselves but also teach them to our kids to help them develop a marketable skill. If you can sell, you can do just about anything—and we think this kind of training and experience will be extraordinarily valuable to our kids. In particular, Dr. Daniels will give us a refresher on building instant rapport, using words that WOW!, influence phrases, and customer follow up. If you haven't had a chance to be in his business communications class—you're in for a real treat."

Randy Parrish raised his hand.

Lisa recognized him. "Yes, Randy, you have a question?"

"Yeah, how much are we buying and selling the shirts for? And do we have a goal?"

"Good questions." Lisa said. "We can get the shirts made up for $8 each. We want to sell them for $20. If we can get our list of prospective companies to one hundred and then sell an average of twenty-five shirts to half of them, then our gross profit will be $15,000."

Lisa's business acumen was obvious as she continued, "If we can meet these numbers, after some additional nominal expenses, we will have enough to send fifty-six kids to Camp

Eagle this summer. Last year we sent twenty-seven. But if we're going to meet this goal, the key is making sure you are here for the training and making a commitment to pour into the kids you're assigned. It's an opportunity to show responsibility and to bring some stability to the lives of our protégés. In that regard, I would like to ask one of our freshmen members, Nahla Robinson, to come up and say a few words."

Nahla made her way up to the podium. She carried a small piece of paper. "Thank you, Lisa. Hi, everyone." The microphone squealed, and Nahla waited for the sound to adjust, took a deep breath, and said, "Four years ago, I was a freshman in high school. I never met my dad, and my mom worked all the time. My two brothers had left home, and I had not heard from them in a long time. I was ready to quit school. I was drinking, and I had tried weed as well. The friends I had were not good. I literally didn't know what to do."

Nahla paused. "On one of the few days I decided to go to school, my history teacher, Mrs. Bailey, asked me to go with her to a meeting right after school. I went, and when I entered the classroom where the meeting was, a banner with a picture of an African American man was at the front of the room. His piercing eyes grabbed my attention. I couldn't look away from him. Three students from State U talked about the Old School and said that this man—Booker T. Washington—was an American hero who had achieved incredible things in his life to benefit the lives of the people in Alabama, primarily African Americans."

She continued, "The students talked about learning communication skills that would help us for the rest of our lives. I listened, and for some reason, I decided to give it a chance. I learned how to relate to people in ways I know I never could have before. My grades turned around almost immediately, and over the next three years I climbed to the top 10 percent of my class, which allowed me to get into State U. I attended Camp Eagle as a high schooler. It was an extraordinary experience I will never forget.

"I had never heard of the Old School," Nahla finished. "I didn't want anything to do with any school four years ago, much less an *old* one." Several students gave her a courteous laugh. "But the Old School changed my life. And now—" She stopped. "And now I know there is *no school like it!* I want to do the same for someone else. Thank you."

Members applauded as Nahla returned to her seat. Lisa stepped back up to the podium. "Thank you, Nahla. You've reminded us what the Old School is all about. I'd like to ask Tim to come up and lead us in the oath. Don't forget that next time, Dr. Daniels will be here for training—it would be a good session to invite a friend to!"

Tim Weathersby stepped to the podium, adjusted the mic, and said, "Please recite the oath with me."

The members of the organization joined him in their pledge:

> I will be authentic and consistent in my actions.
> I will be responsible, accountable, and reliable.
> I will be determined, and I make no excuses.
> I seek to be wise beyond my years.
> I am OLD SCHOOL.

"Please don't forget to check in at the portal at TheOldSchool.cool for any updates," Lisa reminded the students. She banged the gavel on the podium. "This meeting is now adjourned."

As the meeting broke up, Lisa and Nicole watched Nahla as her many friends surrounded and embraced her. The beaming expression on her face told the whole story.

SIX

Words That WOW!

Short words are best . . .
and old words are best of all.

—Winston Churchill

"Good morning, ladies and gentlemen!"

As usual, Dr. John paused to allow students to get pen and paper ready. He noticed that Aaron was one of the first to arrive. "I'm pleased to report that we had 100 percent participation in our first challenge—the LAVA conversation. I've seen many of your responses but wanted to know . . . Who might care to share something unusual or interesting from your dialogues?"

Two dozen hands went up. Dr. John smiled and said, "Ms. Martinez?"

"Yes. I met a new friend named Tui who's from American Samoa," Rebecca reported.

"Oh, let me guess: he plays football here," Dr. John responded.

"Yes, he does. How did you know?"

"Just an educated guess. I know they love football there!" Dr. John winked. "And I keep up with our team pretty closely. Good 'location,' Rebecca. Nice work. Who has an interesting 'association' to report?"

Joel Simpson raised his hand, "I met a girl whose mom is the president of Tech U!"

Dr. John's eyes widened. "Is she a student here?"

"Yep."

"Her name, please?"

"Her name is Maggie Roberts, and her mom is Patricia," Joel answered.

Dr. John laughed. "I love it. The president of our biggest rival, the ugly orange, sent her daughter to State U. Well, like I often say that every parent wants their children to do better than they did. Who can top that one?" Dr. John asked. "Mr. Washington?"

"I met a guy at a party this weekend who said his hobby is wingsuiting," Chris answered.

"Hmm . . . Tell me more." Dr. John prodded.

"It's those guys who jump off cliffs in body suits that open up—" Chris did his best to demonstrate, holding his arms up. "He said they go 150 to 200 miles an hour."

"Oh, I've seen those guys on extreme TV shows," Dr. John recalled. "Wow, I would love to do that! I think you're seeing what kind of interesting and fun things you can learn about people by just asking these simple questions. Thank you for the feedback. I look forward to hearing more of these, but it's time to move on to the next key."

After a brief pause, Dr. John continued. "Wise King Solomon of ancient days said, 'The tongue has the power of life and death.' And our witness from history today—Winston Churchill—said words are the only things that last forever." Dr. John turned and motioned in the direction of the banner, which had Winston Churchill's famous photograph sitting with a cigar and the word *Courage* embossed across the top. "Boy, did he believe it! In his combined works, he published more than seventy volumes and nearly ten million words. To put that in perspective, Shakespeare wrote only about one million words.

"Words matter," Dr. John emphasized. "Words are at the center of the human experience—the *currency* of communication—and, as such, they have an untold impact on the people around us. There may be nothing more important in life than *words*. That being the case, our third key to professional success will center on what I call **words that WOW**!"

Dr. John spread his hands on the top of his podium. "Today, I'm going to show you how words and phrases can present you as a person of depth and substance. This positive impression is based on a concept known as *the magic of attribution*. The meaning and connotation of your words are imputed or attributed to you *personally*. This happens naturally. It is a powerful and—in the wrong hands—even a dangerous phenomenon."

Aaron could not recall Dr. John opening a class with such emphatic claims. *This should be interesting*, he thought to himself.

"Before I give you some examples of those powerful words and phrases," Dr. John told them, "we need to 'scrub' some words from your vocabulary that are destined to *limit* your opportunities. Tell me, anyone, what words might be overused today?"

Silence prevailed as students looked around the room.

Dr. John broke the pause. "Let me give you a hint. When people are nervous, what are some 'pause words' or 'crutch words' they use in order to buy more time to think of what they want to say next?"

Megan spoke first. "'You know'?"

"Yes, Ms. Smith. Good one. What's another?"

Mary responded, "'So'?"

"Yes. That's one I struggle with myself," Dr. John admitted. "Thank you, Ms. Wright."

There was a long pause.

"No one has said the most obvious one yet," Dr. John said.

Finally, Ryan Dotson yelled from the back row, "'Like'!"

Many in the class laughed—but a few grumbled, discomfited by the truth Ryan had brought up. "Yes, Mr. Dotson, thank you!" Dr. John replied in a mocking half yell. "*Like* may be the worst verbal tick of this generation. And you know what? Simply by bringing it out in this conversation, we can eliminate half or more of the uses of such lazy words.

"Here's another that I mention with some hesitation. It's such a great word. But when everything is 'awesome,' what is *really* awesome?" Dr. John asked.

"Nothing," Aaron answered.

Dr. John agreed. "That's right. The Grand Canyon, a spectacular thunderstorm on a distant horizon, the birth of a child. These are truly awesome. But when words are overused, their meaning is diminished. Awesome is a prime example. I'm not saying you should no longer use it. But use it less often. I'll give you some *awesome* alternatives to awesome in just a few minutes."

He continued, "Other words we need to scrub are so subtle we might not think of them. They're called *drama words*. Some examples are *very*, *really*, *absolutely*, and *totally*. You don't have to say, 'I'm very excited.' 'I'm excited' will do. This issue is another one I have to watch myself. Excessive adverbs and adjectives add unnecessary drama. See how soon you can eliminate these common verbal ticks from your vocabulary. If you can do so, I estimate that your perceived IQ will rise by twenty points. No kidding. That's how important the right words are.

"Now, the IQ part is not scientific, I know. Everyone is proficient in the technical aspects of their jobs—even at the entry level—and working hard is a given if you want to advance. But once you're in the midst of your careers, your command of words will play a major role in determining how high you will go. All things being equal, exceptional soft skills will show you to be wise beyond your years and thus create opportunities beyond what you can even imagine now."

Dr. John opened the textbook on the podium. "In **chapter 3** of your text, there are thirty words and phrases that WOW! For class today, I've chosen a sampling to discuss in some detail. Let's get started.

"*First things first* is a phrase I use often. By using these three words, you communicate as someone who follows the rules, does not rush their work, is a logical, sequential thinker, and knows how to set priorities. *First of all* is a good alternative phrase to use.

"The next word is one of the most impactful words in the English language: *imagine.* It is so powerful because it has a different meaning for each person who hears it. Imagine blends your mind with your heart, your aspirations, and your hopes. In all of creation, only humans can see things as they *ought* to be—and that's what this word is all about."

Dr. John went on, "Next is a group of five words called *-ability* words. They are *responsibility, predictability, accountability, reliability, and stability.* These are known as quality attributes. All five words describe characteristics admired by everyone. They signify individuals who will do what they say they will do—on time—and who will exceed expectations. These words are about personal integrity.

"Yes, Ms. Martinez, you have a question?" Dr. John asked, looking at a student in the corner of the fourth row. Aaron shook his head. *I can't believe Dr. John knows every student's name already.*

"Yes, sir," Rebecca confirmed. "You said that by using these words and phrases they would be attributed to us. But these -ability words sound like descriptions we might like to be used *of* us. How would we use them to receive the attribution you're talking about? I don't get it."

"Excellent question." Dr. John smiled. "Let's *imagine* you're in an interview, and the interviewer asks, 'What do you see as the most important characteristics of a good employee?' You answer, 'That's a good question. *First of all*, I believe everyone should take personal *responsibility* and be *accountable* for their actions. This seems to be happening less and less these days. I also want to work with someone who is *predictable*, someone who can be *relied* upon when the going gets tough.'"

Rebecca Martinez smiled and looked down to capture the moment in her notes.

"What just happened in that short answer *Ms. Martinez* gave? Did she kill it?" Dr. John asked.

Several students agreed.

"Notice that in her three-sentence answer to what makes a good employee, she provided a description of an *exceptional* employee by using four of the five -ability words," Dr. John stressed. "She was actually providing a de facto description of herself at the same time. At least, that's how it would likely be perceived. Using these terms in this manner is precisely how the positive aspect of their meaning is imputed or attributed to you, the speaker. And whether consciously or unconsciously, more often than not, the listener will instinctively give you credit for abilities you may or may not have.

"Let me give you a few more examples of attribution. By using the term *people centered*, for instance, you are likely considered to be a friendly person who cares genuinely for others. Or, if you say you are 'concerned about the *consequences*' of a certain action, you must be a responsible person who thinks things through."

Dr. John sensed he was getting some converts to the concept of attribution. He pressed on. "Here is one of my favorites: *in my opinion*. When you say *in my opinion*, you are in effect saying, 'For what I am about to say, I take full responsibility.' That shows confidence. In addition, you can say just about anything you want as long as you say 'in my opinion' before or after. It's also a good way to test the waters with an idea without making a firm declaration. If others glom onto the idea because it has merit, then you can take it further—if and when it's appropriate," he explained. "If you prefer a stronger phrase, then *according to my assessment* indicates you did some research or collaborated to form your position on the matter. In the military, for example, this phrase may be more credible.

"The next one on the list is the phrase *no excuses*."

Aaron thought of his mom.

"When you say you have *no excuses*," Dr. John told them, "you are saying to the listener that *you will succeed, period*. It is especially effective when you know that you do actually have an excuse—even a reason—yet choose to move on and keep striving for excellence.

"Here's another of my favorites: *let's get to work*."

"We've heard that one!" a voice from the back rang out.

"Like I said—it's one of my favorites," Dr. John agreed. "It indicates a positive attitude and an eagerness to engage the next task. Anyone with this attitude is an asset to their team, and it's a phrase that can spur others to action. I can assure you that it's impressive when you receive instructions from a supervisor and respond by saying, 'Let's get to work!' It brings the term 'a real go-getter' to their mind very quickly."

Dr. John paused to let note takers catch up. "Here's a bonus word that can be fun: *unbelievable*."

Some confused faces looked up.

"When asked the question, 'How are you doing?' try answering with just one word—an enthusiastic *unbelievable!*" Dr. John said.

Several sleepyheads perked up, and others laughed at Dr. John's wide-sweeping, circular arm movements.

"Here are three reasons to say *unbelievable*. First, it's an 'interrupter.' People expect you to say a standard and boring, 'Fine, how are you?' Instead, you get their attention with one word. Second, even though the word *unbelievable* does not necessarily connote all things are going well for you, when said with a positive, upbeat tone, you are seen automatically as an optimist. Everyone loves positive people—especially in leadership. Third, saying *unbelievable* usually elicits at least a chuckle from most people. That makes *you* feel better too—no matter how things are going. Use it! It's unbelievable!

"Now, I'm going to give you two last words to fulfill my earlier promise. When you're tempted to say *awesome*, instead try either *exceptional* or *extraordinary*. Like *awesome*, both of these words connote 'above and beyond.' They also carry far more weight than other pedestrian words such as *cool* or *nice*. Sprinkling in these two strong words will turn heads—I promise," Dr. John said.

Dr. John smiled. "I wish we had time to talk about all of the WOW! words and phrases today—but you get the idea. If you take time to practice speaking this way, these words will become second nature to you. And believe me, there has never been a better time to speak well. Strong communication skills in our society are on the decline. You can witness this every day at school or in the workplace. But guess what that means? This presents an extraordinary opportunity if you're willing to work hard to improve and differentiate yourselves. You can all be exceptional conversationalists, public speakers, and writers. You can achieve practically anything with effective communication skills."

Several students had caught onto the vision. They were arrested by the opportunities they could imagine using Dr. John's technique.

"I'm passionate about this topic because I have four kids about your age—or a few years older," Dr. John told them. "One of the biggest compliments someone can pay me as a parent is when they say, 'Your son or daughter is wise beyond their years.' And nothing gives clues to wisdom like the words you use. Using the right words shows you to be not only wiser but also more intelligent, well read, and highly qualified in your chosen field."

Dr. John straightened and gave the class a sterner look. "Now, with all of this said, I want to warn you that this word attribution business can be a double-edged sword. How is this so? Anyone?" he asked.

Several hands shot up. "Yes, Ms. Anderson?"

"You mean if we use foul language or inappropriate words?" she asked.

"Yes. That's an obvious way to make a bad impression. But I'm talking about those who might use words that WOW! for nefarious reasons or unfair advantage. Because of word attribution's power, the words you use become a leading indicator of your character and trustworthiness. If you're earnest in your character, right actions will generally follow. But if your words lack authenticity because they are contradicted by your actions, then the influence you are hoping to have will be justifiably diminished," Dr. John explained. "Because there is such power in the words you use, there is an accompanying *responsibility*. You must speak not only with sincerity but also with integrity. Understanding that words and actions must match can provide a safeguard against those who might want to try and fool you simply by learning and using these powerful words. Now, listen closely to what I am about to tell you. This may be the most important and exciting aspect of the lesson today . . ."

Dr. John paused to make sure he had every student's attention. "As you increase your usage of these positive words and phrases, *they will have an effect on you*. They can make you a better person. When you make using WOW! words a habit, you'll see constructive changes occur in your life as a result," he promised them. "The words we choose shape the world around us—the way we perceive our environments and the way we act in turn. For example, when you use the word *determined*, you will act with more resolve. When you say, 'I believe it is important to be *consistent*,' you will become ever more consistent yourself. The power of words is truly unlimited.

"Be sure and review all thirty words and phrases in your text," Dr. John reminded the class. "Any or all of them could be covered on the exam. Let me finish with this story:

> Years ago, a construction supervisor was ready to retire. He told his employer of his plans to leave the house-building business and live a leisurely life with his wife. He was getting older, and he wanted to see his grandchildren more. He would miss the paycheck but felt like it was time to slow down.
>
> The builder was saddened to see him go and asked if he would build one more house for the company as a personal favor.
>
> The supervisor agreed; however, he was in a hurry to retire, so he never put his heart into this last project. He resorted to shoddy workmanship and inferior materials because they were readily available without ordering.
>
> When he finished his work and it was time to inspect the house, his employer never set foot inside. He smiled and handed the key to his longtime employee. "This is yours," he said. "It's my gift to you!" The retiree would now live in the home he had built.

"Eventually, we will all live in what we build. Every day, we are constructing a life, and the primary materials we use are our words. With our words, we hammer a nail, place a board, or erect a wall. All of us must recognize the power of the words we use—for better or for worse—because we're going to live in what we build with them.

"A limited vocabulary limits your life. Whether on an essay exam, a first date, a job interview, a sales presentation, or as a keynote address at a national convention, words make all the difference," Dr. John concluded.

"Now, before I let you go, I want to issue the second challenge of the semester. You will need to refer to the list of thirty words and phrases in **chapter 3** of your textbook. Choose five words or phrases—one for each day between now and next Monday. I want you to then use a different word on your chosen list *ten times* per day and then write down any observations you have. Please submit your work via the portal as usual. I look forward to hearing about what opportunities arise from this effort. Have a great weekend! Please read **chapter 4** for next time."

SEVEN

THE RIVALRY

Always surround yourself with individuals
who will help to enable your courage
when it is lacking from within.

—MIKE KRZYZEWSKI

Dr. John ambled to the kitchen around 6:45 a.m. As he poured his first cup of coffee, he smiled at the sign that hung over the antiqued credenza: "A yawn is a silent scream for coffee." His kids had given it to him last Christmas. He was short on vices, but caffeine was protected, and Sunday mornings were sacrosanct. A warm cup of joe, reading, and quiet time before Mrs. Daniels woke up and joined him for an hour prior to church services—Sundays were his favorite time of the week.

But his phone rang at about 8:15 a.m. Feeling a slight sense of annoyance, Dr. John answered, "Hello?"

"Johnny!" a voice bellowed on the other end.

"Coach Joe?" Dr. John asked, smiling now.

"You got him! And you know what they say?"

Dr. John chorused with his old friend and coaching mentor. "'If you can't shoot the 'J,' you can't play!'"

Joseph Dempsey Sullivan was a legend at State U. Coach Joe had been the men's head basketball coach for forty-five years. Opposing fans loved heckling Coach Joe by calling him "the Bald Eagle." He had embraced the moniker as a badge of honor, always responding, "At least I'm not a turkey."

Sullivan had been hired as a coach in a very different way than big-college coaches had been hired in recent decades. After winning back-to-back state championships in the small Texas town of Caldwell, Sullivan had been offered the State U head basketball coaching position for one year. He was told that in order to keep his job for year two, he had to win the South Central Conference. It was an unusual stipulation for such a football-crazed university—but he did it. In fact, he had done it eight more times since then and made two trips to the regional final—"the Elite Eight"—of the college basketball national tournament. Still, he had always been overshadowed by the successful State U football program and Tech U's illustrious basketball program, which had won three national championships under the direction of coach Clark "the Silver Fox" Thorn. But this season, with a 27–0 record the likes of which only about a dozen teams in college history had ever posted, Coach Joe's chance at basketball immortality was nigh.

Dr. John's connection with Coach Joe was a special one. It had started long ago when he was a graduate assistant under Sullivan in his fifth season as head coach. Sullivan had given him a break at age twenty-two that Dr. John regarded as one of the pivotal opportunities of his life.

"Coach—27 and 0! Are you kidding me?!" Dr. John exclaimed.

"Yeah, well, we've gotten a break or two along the way. Hey, where have you been? How's your class going?" Coach Joe asked.

Dr. John answered, "Hey, I've been following every game! Just trying to stay out of your way! Class is *unbelievable!* I still don't get why they're paying me for this."

"I'm sure they're asking the same thing," Coach Joe teased.

Both men laughed. "Hey, Johnny, I apologize for interrupting your Sunday morning, but here is why I'm calling." Dr. John noted a serious tone in Coach's voice. "You know we are the national game of the week against Tech U."

"Of course! I'll be there! The top two teams in the country—absolutely," Dr. John said.

"Yes, great, but I'm wondering if you would come to the locker room and say a few words before the game. Most of the guys already know you from taking your freshman seminar course, and they still talk about you."

Dr. John sat stunned for a moment, then replied, "Well, Coach, of course. Anything you need, if you think I can help."

"Excellent. We're set, then. I'll have the SID leave a floor credential for you and a guest at the main ticket office by 11 a.m. on game day. It's a seven o'clock start. And let's talk again soon. We're overdue." Coach Joe hung up.

Wow. How great is this! I need to call John Jr., Dr. John thought. Athletics were the pulse of any college campus. As a student, he had once written a term paper on the subject in which he had stated, "Sports are the 'front porch' of the university, where the public visits and where students of all colors, backgrounds, and beliefs meld together to support a common cause. The spirit that is created by simply supporting *your team* is uniquely American in that it has a cross-cultural unifying effect like few—if any—other areas of our society can."

And for Dr. John, there was no sport like college basketball. He had been making posters of tournament brackets as a student at State U long before ESPN was on the air.

The day of the Tech U game, Dr. John arrived at Metcalf Arena having had little to no sleep the night before. John Jr. met him at the will call window. Dr. John's oldest son was the spitting image of his mother with a perfect set of teeth and a disarming smile. He had his dad's gait but his own personality, but when anyone had a few minutes' conversation with him, there was no mistaking that the traditional values that Dr. John espoused had stuck with his son.

Both father and son were hyped for the game. "You ready for this?!" Dr. John exclaimed, exchanging a high five with his oldest.

"Yes! This is gonna be *unbelievable!*" John Jr. responded.

They had never heard a buzz like the one on campus this day. More than four hundred more spectators than would normally be allowed had crowded into the venue, but no one was going to call the fire marshal to tattle this night. As they entered the court level, John Jr. screamed, "It's so loud!"

Dr. John was walking right beside his son, but the only way to be heard was to scream right back: "I know, and we haven't even started! The 'sixth man' will be here in force tonight!"

The television announcers on their pregame set were just as excited as the crowd. Dr. John heard them on the speakers. "Welcome, ladies and gentlemen, to tonight's showdown between the two biggest rivals in Texas—undefeated, number-one-ranked State U versus archrival Tech U with a 26–1 record, their only loss coming at home to, you guessed it, State U!"

Dr. John and John Jr. stood behind the bench, watching warm-ups and taking in the crowd. "Dr. John! Dr. John!" someone screamed from the fourth row behind the bench.

It was Aaron, bobbing up and down, face painted, in the student section. A girl beside him was laughing and waving. Dr. John waved back and smiled as he and Aaron exchanged thumbs-ups. *I bet that is Amanda next to him.*

Coach Joe caught sight of Dr. John. He signaled for Dr. John to follow him and the team. "Let's go!" They went up the tunnel and into the dressing room. Emotions were sky high. Dr. John had no available saliva, and the lump in his throat made him feel as if he had swallowed a basketball during warm-ups.

I can't believe I'm this nervous. He'd spoken at hundreds of events, but there was something special about addressing his home team right before their big game.

"Settle down, gentlemen, settle down." Coach Joe gathered the team around and stood like a statue until he had complete silence. "Did everyone wash their hands?" Coach Joe asked.

Dr. John smiled. *He never changes. Same savant-like attention to detail. "Removes natural oil from your hands and cuts down on turnovers by 10 percent," Coach always said.*

Coach Joe continued. "I've asked my good friend Dr. Johnathan Daniels to say a few words before we go out this evening and play basketball."

A few players nodded and said howdy to Dr. John. He waved and acknowledged them before continuing. "Thank you, Coach, it's an honor to be here with you on this exciting night. Gentlemen, we can all hear the crowd. They love you. Some of them love you only because you are 27 and 0."

A few players laughed nervously as the dull roar of "*BEAT THE HECK OUT OF TECH!*" sounded again and again through the thick arena walls. Dr. John pointed at Coach Joe. "But *this* man," he emphasized, "loves you no matter what, and four decades ago, when I had the privilege of helping with this program as a graduate assistant coach, he told me something on my first day I will never forget.

"He said, 'Johnny, General Douglas MacArthur was a boyhood hero of mine. And he once said,

> Competition teaches the strong to know when they are weak and the brave to face themselves when they are afraid. To be proud and unbowed in defeat and yet humble and gentle in victory. And to master ourselves before we attempt to master others. And to learn to laugh and yet to never forget how to weep. And to give the predominance to courage over timidity.

"I have that quote framed and sitting on my mantle to this day," Dr. John finished, voice breaking as he choked up for a moment. He looked over at John Jr., who nodded respectfully to his father. "Tonight, as always, you will be defined not by the outcome—but by your *courage*. I wish you all the best in this endeavor. Now let's go BEAT THE HECK OUT OF TECH!"

The game started at a torrid pace. Coach Joe was not at all pleased, since State U liked to control the ball with a more methodical tempo. By halftime, the home crowd was subdued by an eleven-point Tech lead.

But after the intermission, the Eagles cut the lead to two points within five minutes. But Tech maintained control, with leads hovering between four and ten points throughout most of the second half. Each time State made a run, Tech staved it off. Revenge was clearly on the mind of the "Ugly Orange," as State U fans liked to call them.

Then, a run! State hit three consecutive three-pointers within thirty seconds! A shot, a steal, a shot, a steal, and a shot—and boom! Just like that, the Fighting Eagles found themselves ahead by one with possession of the ball, out of bounds after a traveling violation on Sterling Sharper, Tech's all-American point guard.

With twenty-eight seconds remaining, Coach Joe called time out.

The Eagles huddled closer than usual on the bench because of the deafening crowd noise. "Listen, fellas, look at me," Coach Joe told his team. "All we need to do here is protect the ball. The shot clock is off. If they foul us, make the free throws. They will be playing man to man to overplay our passing lanes, trying for a steal, so look for a back door cut or give and go. If it's not there, keep the ball out and run the clock. We have our best ball handlers and free-throw shooters in the game. We've got this! 'Courage' on three—"

The players all stood and placed their hands together in the middle of the huddle. "*Courage*!" they said in unison as they broke to return to play.

The plan was spot on. Tech overplayed on defense as expected, and State ran the perfect back door to their star small forward, Eli Driver. As he gathered himself to go up for a dunk, the ball was deflected out of his hands to State teammate Cade Carson. The best ball handler and free-throw shooter on State U's team then inexplicably turned to attempt a sixteen-footer. It was blocked by Sharper.

Tech's best player headed unimpeded the other way. A streaking Eli Driver raced downcourt and was able to reach Sharper in time to foul him and prevent the easy go-ahead basket.

Tech now had two free-throws to take the lead. Sharper stepped to the line . . . three dribbles . . . shot . . . he made the first. Tie game. Three dribbles . . . shot. It bounced off the rim. No good.

State rebounded and quickly passed downcourt. Driver took a shot from the short corner for the win—in and out—overtime!

State took advantage of the first possession of the extra period and went up by two points. Back and forth it went as the two top-ranked teams in the nation traded basket for basket in prime time.

With twenty seconds remaining, the Eagles held a two-point advantage with possession of the ball under their own basket. Coach Joe signaled 'bombs away' from the bench. It was an out-of-bounds play they had saved all year.

State forward Brae Browning slapped the ball. Driver broke free for an uncontested layup . . . He missed! Coach Joe put his head down, clasping his knees in disbelief. Tech rebounded, and Driver was called for reaching in. It was an ill-advised foul based on an emotional reaction—and it was his fifth of the game. State's best player was disqualified.

On the other end, Tech made their first free throw. They missed the second, but Tech rebounded and took another shot to take the lead by a single point!

State hurriedly inbounded the ball and passed it down the court to work for one last shot . . . Over to freshman Kit Potter . . . He turned and dribbled the ball off his foot out of bounds.

"Time out!" Coach Joe screamed to the referee. There were twelve seconds on the clock.

Coach Joe said nothing in the huddle for the first ten seconds as he drew up a play on his lap-sized white board. The crowd was nervous and subdued.

"We have one time out left. *I will call it if we need it.* The good news is they have to go the length of the court here. Let's go with '41 double-jump spy' on the inbounds. We are going to steal this ball. If they get by you to the frontcourt, try for the reach-around. It's OK if you foul them. Got it?" All heads nodded.

"'Courage' on three."

As the ball was thrown in, State's Potter, guarding the Tech man with the ball, allowed him to get by him. As he slid by, Potter tapped the ball from behind . . . right into the waiting arms of State teammate Matt Hall. Hall went straight toward the basket, then faded left for a fall-away ten-footer. No good. The rebound came down quickly and bounced off a Tech player's foot. It would be State's ball under their own basket, with a chance to win it here . . . Wait . . . Tech ball?!

Coach Joe was hopping mad, literally. Assistant coaches calmed him down.

The crowd jeered as the slow-motion replay showed the ball bouncing off a Tech player's foot. For some inexplicable reason, the referees chose not to review the play and handed the ball to the Tech player to resume play.

Tech inbounded the ball, and Sterling Sharper was fouled with 4.4 seconds remaining. Sharper had made 86 percent of his free throws this season. The State student section counted his dribbles. He missed! State grabbed the rebound!

"Time out!" Coach Joe yelled.

Dr. John grinned as John Jr. buried his head on his shoulder. "I can't watch!" Johnny knew what play was coming next.

Coach Joe was calm again. He looked into the eyes of his seated players and said, "We've got 2.9 seconds. That's plenty of time. Let's run our long double screen away. We inbound to Matt coming off the half-court screen. Stevie, remember, as soon as the ref hands you the ball, you've got to give a convincing long-pass fake to get Matt's man leaning back one step. Matt, it's a catch, turn, and overhead pass . . . Don't get in a hurry. We have time, but it's got to be perfect. Patrick, come hard off that back screen to the corner. Matt is going to hit you with a pass in perfect triple-threat position, ready to shoot. You got it?"

"Yes, sir!"

"'Courage' on three!"

It was one of those slow-motion moments from the movies *Remember the Titans*, *Rocky*, and of course, *Hoosiers*.

State got the ball from the ref. Steven made his long-pass fake followed by a perfect pass to Matt. Matt turned and hit the wide-open Patrick, who caught the ball and shot.

BUZZZZZZZ.

The ball bounced off the back rim. NO GOOD.

State players collapsed to the parquet floor as if it had been choreographed. Tech players leaped, screamed, and pointed to the stunned crowd as they waved their orange towels above their heads and ran to their dressing room.

With the win, Tech U and State U had identical 27–1 records. College basketball in Texas had never seen a year like this one. The number-one and number-two ranked teams in the country had traded places this evening. But the postseason tournament was about to begin.

The longest and most intense rivalry in state history would almost certainly be revisited soon.

EIGHT

INFLUENCE AND PERSUASION

*There is no power on earth that can nullify the
influence of a high, simple, and useful life.*

—BOOKER T. WASHINGTON

"Good morning, ladies and gentlemen!" Dr. John's organic enthusiasm was in stark contrast to the miserable weather outside—and inside—his classroom. "I trust you all are having an extraordinary week in spite of the unfortunate results for our Eagles the other night?"

The class groaned. Dr. John had been expecting a melancholy class after losing the big game against Tech. The truth was he was still licking his own wounds. *I get one chance to give the big pregame locker-room speech . . . and we lose. I hope Coach Joe will forgive me.*

But he put on a brave face for his students. "It's OK. Having just one loss at this point is still amazing, and I think there are big things ahead for our Fighting Eagles. Before we get into our topic today, I'm excited to hear about how challenge number two went for you. Who would like to share? Yes, Ms. Anderson?"

"I don't know if anyone else thinks this, but it felt pretty awkward using the same word so much in one day," Rachel opined. "But then I realized I was using the same word with ten different people. It actually became natural by the end of the day."

"Interesting. Was there a particular word that you felt impacted any of your conversations?"

"Yes. Definitely," she replied. "I noticed that every time I said 'simple truth' or 'common sense,' people just shook their head and agreed with me. I even tried to bring up semicontroversial topics—and they still wouldn't argue that much."

"Hmm . . . interesting. Who else would like to share?" Dr. John asked.

Robert Harris raised his hand. "I used 'because.'"

A confused silence stretched over the class. "OK . . . Would you care to elaborate?" Dr. John asked Robert.

"Well, I was in a ridiculous line at the creamery, and I just went to the front and asked, 'Can I cut in *because* I'm really hot and need an ice cream?'"

Students laughed. "And they just let you push in?" Dr. John asked.

"Yeah. It worked like a charm. They didn't even hesitate. I did kind of feel bad, though. I bought the cones for the next three people in line, but it was worth it," Robert said.

"Well, it sounds like this challenge opened up quite an opportunity for you, Robert, and at least you were courteous enough to treat your new friends to an ice cream. But I would be careful . . ." Dr. John said. He winced inwardly. There was always one who employed the words he taught them somewhat recklessly. "One more want to share? Megan?"

"I decided I would challenge myself to see if I could avoid using the words 'awesome' and 'like' in a LAVA conversation," she answered.

"How did that go?" Dr. John asked.

"It was extraordinary!"

"Nice. You get extra points. So you were able to do it, then?" Dr. John asked.

"I think so. I may have slipped in one or two 'likes'—but it was a good exercise. Like you said—just bringing attention to the issue is going to help me a lot," Megan said.

"Thank you all for sharing. These are typical experiences —even Robert's. That's the power of words. I look forward to reading all of your remarks. One last follow-up item as far as words go: make sure you have both a *dictionary* and a *thesaurus* app loaded on your phones and tablets. Use these often, and your WOW! words will increase even more."

Dr. John took a moment before moving on. Then he began the day's lesson. "One of my favorite sayings is 'Perfect vision is to see the faults in yourself and the good in others.' With that in mind, today's subject matter comes with a warning. You've learned the value of words and phrases that allow you to speak powerfully. By adding the fourth key to professional success—**influence techniques**—you can build a formidable rhetorical arsenal.

"Therefore, I want you to make a commitment before we go any further. I want you to promise that you will use these techniques for good and decent purposes—which will include for your own defense and protection. Does everyone agree?"

Heads bobbed around the room.

"I would like to see a show of hands, please," Dr. John pressed. After a few seconds, every hand went up. "Good. Thank you. *Let's get to work!*

"The first technique is one you're already familiar with: **building instant rapport and likability.** The LAVA conversation framework is in this category. We've discussed how you can build a connection with others with the foundational information you uncover in that short first conversation—hometowns, alma maters, family, occupation, hobbies, etc.—but other things, such as physical attractiveness, compliments, and even dressing the same, can help create likability through what is known as the *halo effect*. This occurs when positive characteristics dominate the initial impressions you give," Dr. John explained.

"So, would a bad impression be called the 'pitchfork effect'?" Nick Berry interrupted. There was scattered laughter.

"I've never considered that, Mr. Berry, but that may be a bit harsh," Dr. John returned. "Let's just say you will have a *devil* of a time making a good impression without understanding these concepts."

Aaron grinned. *Nice.*

Dr. John continued, "Let me tell you about an experiment that was conducted wherein, before a negotiation, the parties engaged in getting to know a few things about one another's background. In other words, they engaged in small talk. Researchers paired up students enrolled at two elite US business schools. Half were simply given the instructions to negotiate; the other half were provided with a photograph and some brief biographical information about the negotiating partner—what amounted to a mini LAVA conversation.

"In the groups where no small talk took place, 30 percent failed to agree to a deal. In the pairs that had some background information, 94 percent came to an agreement. The negotiated prices were also 20 percent higher in these more familiar groups."

Every head was down, taking notes. Students always perked up in this lecture—only one reason of many why it was one of Dr. John's favorites. "Influence technique number two is known as **reciprocity**," he said. "It is based on the widespread understanding that a favor deserves repayment—typically 'in kind.' We don't like people who take without giving back. The rule of reciprocation creates in us an unpleasant feeling of indebtedness. This can make us agree to something when logic otherwise suggests we should say no. This happens even when relatively small favors, like ballgame tickets or dinner at a nice restaurant, are designed to elicit bigger favors or large purchases in return. In most cases, it is not abused, and our culture generally deems this all to be acceptable behavior."

Dr. John tapped the podium. "Being *aware* of reciprocity is your best defense against it. There's nothing wrong with accepting a favor graciously. But if you feel you're being taken advantage of, then you should not feel obligated. Leonardo da Vinci gave this sage advice centuries ago: 'It is easier to resist at the beginning than at the end.'

"The third technique of influence is known as **authority**. This one may be the *most abused*—and so I want to spend a little more time on it," Dr. John said.

"When someone is presenting their side of an issue or argument, you often hear them say, 'We have it on good authority.' The word *authority* evokes thoughts of sound judgment and knowledge or expertise. But you must always ask, 'Why is this authority so good?' Don't just take their word for it.

"Here are some more subtle ways *authority* is used to influence. Academic degrees carry the weight of authority. A PhD carries more weight than a high school diploma. Likewise, *position titles* in business, government, or any organizational structure make it clear who has more authority."

He continued, "*Attire*, such as military uniforms, signifies various levels of authority. In the corporate world, professionals 'dress for success' partly in an effort to gain credibility—or authority—within their hierarchy or with customers. Research has shown that physicians who wear a tie or a white lab coat are likely to be trusted more than those who dress more casually. Even at sporting events, supporters wear their team colors to try to intimidate the opponent and motivate their own team."

Dr. John took a moment to look hard at the class. "So, where are you vulnerable to authority? Someone who is well-dressed, well-credentialed, and well-spoken has a powerful combination. Yet you must not equate confidence with competence. Always ask, 'Is this person really an expert?' and 'Why should I believe their opinions?'

"When you evaluate those who are presumed to be experts or authority figures, there are three critical considerations that will help you judge whether you can rely on that authority or not.

"First of all, in addition to considering a person's credentials, make sure you evaluate their reasons for their opinions. There is a common error known as 'the fallacy of the expert witness.' In a trial, credentials alone are not enough to certify an expert witness's testimony; they must convince a jury that the judgments behind that testimony are adequate. Even eyewitnesses get it wrong—and fairly often. Mistaken eyewitness identifications are the main cause of three out of four wrongful convictions that are later overturned by DNA evidence."

Megan Smith interjected at this point, concerned. "If expert witnesses and eyewitnesses get it wrong so often, how can we have any confidence in our justice system?"

"Good question, Ms. Smith," Dr. John replied. "I don't want you to get the wrong impression here. Juries get it right the overwhelming majority of the time. And our system of justice is still the best on the planet. But juries sometimes are wrongly swayed when the appeal to authority is overemphasized. That's why important decisions must ultimately rest on the *evidence*. We'll have a guest speaker later in the semester who will be the perfect person to answer questions like this.

"The second consideration to make when you are evaluating a person's authority is whether it is based on the authority of the group—whether they are attempting to convince you of something everyone thinks. The idea that the majority is always right is a prevalent and dangerous one.

"Third—"

But Natalie's hand had shot up.

"What do you mean, the majority is always right is dangerous? Isn't that just democracy?" she asked.

Dr. John acknowledged the point. "Good question! Yes. You could use the term *majority rule* and *democracy* interchangeably. But would it interest you to learn that the United States is not a democracy? In fact, the word *democracy* does not appear in either the Constitution or the Declaration of Independence."

All students stopped taking notes and looked up.

"Wait . . ." Natalie interrupted. "You're saying we are not a democracy?"

"Yes. That is what I am saying." Dr. John saw some puzzled looks and decided to pursue the topic. "The United States is a *constitutional republic*. The word *republic* comes from the Latin *res*, or 'thing,' and *publica, or* 'public.' The *law* is the 'public thing.' *Democracy* means 'people rule.' It sounds good, but unchecked majority rule is a danger because the majority could become unrestrained. If more than half of the people are so persuaded, they could take your house, your business, or even your children. This has happened consistently in democracies throughout history. That's why the founders were adamantly against this form of government and why they even referred to 'democracy' as 'mobocracy.' Alexander Hamilton stated, 'We are a republican government. Real liberty is never found in the extremes of democracy.'

"Our American ancestors knew the history of the failed democratic city-states in Greece. Even Rome—which established a republic—eventually transitioned to a democracy as the government grew bigger through high taxes, regulation, and welfare. Eventually, this led to financial ruin, and mobs demanding 'bread and circuses' became commonplace. The citizens then traded freedom for security. This supermajority rule, which had little or no opposition, paved the way for tyranny under the Caesars."

Natalie just stared in apparent disbelief. "I can see some confusion out there," Dr. John observed.

Many heads nodded.

"It's no wonder. Politicians on both sides of the aisle now routinely—and, in my opinion, incorrectly—use the term 'spreading democracy' when they talk about expanding American values worldwide. It's interesting to note that in the early twentieth century, the Socialist Party first began using the term democracy to describe our form of government.

"Just remember that without law, there can be no freedom. A republic is where the government is limited by law—leaving its citizens alone to pursue life, liberty, and happiness. It's a genius form of government. Making us a nation of laws is designed to eliminate *rule by fiat*—the very reason the pilgrims fled Europe in the first place. The Constitution sets up a government that protects the minority against the 'tyranny of the majority,'" Dr. John concluded. "I hope you will forgive the long answer, Natalie. I know what people mean when they say democracy. But I think it's important that you be aware of the nuances. The good news is that none of that will be on the exam," Dr. John teased. Natalie seemed satisfied for the moment. "But as our government guards against the tyranny of the majority, so should you."

Dr. John continued, "Now, back to my third point concerning the use of *authority*. If there are any marketing majors in here, you know all about the effectiveness of repetition. That's what advertising is all about, right? Getting the most views. The third thing to think about when you evaluate a person's authority is this: familiarity is not easily distinguished from truth."

Dr. John spoke slowly, letting his words sink in. "Authoritarian governments know this. Often, when tyrants don't have the credentials themselves or can't assemble experts to back their position, they will influence through repetition—and sometimes volume (as in raising their voices). Nazi Germany's minister of propaganda, Joseph Goebbels, worked for a guy that liked to raise his voice. Goebbels made this notorious statement: 'Tell a lie enough times, and it becomes the truth.'"

Joel Simpson raised his hand, "So, Dr. John, do you think the Holocaust could happen today? It seems like Hitler was able to pull that off because he controlled everything, like the German media. But today we have so much more access to information, with social media and everything."

"That's an insightful question," Dr. John answered. "Let me see if I can help you find an answer. There is a small but powerful book I want to assign over the weekend." Many students grumbled and glared at Joel Simpson, and Dr. John smiled to himself. He had always planned the assignment—a warning against the more dangerous applications of influence. "It's called *How Do You Kill 11 Million People?* I'm confident it will provide the answer to how Hitler was able to pull off his atrocities in the midst of many good and religious German citizens. By the way, fewer than one in five Germans were members of the Nazi Party. This little book will provide big insight into how the evil use of the *authority* influence technique can get a foothold in the hearts and minds of the populace—and how this eventually can lead to the use of brute force and murder . . . even in this technological age."

Dr. John looked at his watch. "Uh oh. We had better speed it up here if I'm going to get through all of these.

"Influence technique number four is known as **consensus**. If you are looking to gain consensus, you are trying to get everyone on the same page or, to use a WOW! word from **chapter 3**, to get them *fully aligned*. *Consensus* uses the principle of *social proof* by asking, 'What do others think about this? What are other people doing?' While you should always be wary of being tyrannized by the majority, the 'wisdom of crowds' can be helpful in many cases. But what else can happen when everyone is looking to others for the correct answer and nobody really knows?" Dr. John asked.

There was a pause. "Everybody's wrong?" Aaron offered finally.

"Good answer, Aaron. Write this down: *pluralistic ignorance*. It can get us all into trouble. Maybe you've heard the concept this way—the blind leading the blind? John Adams said, 'The people that wish to be ignorant and free wish to have what can never be.'"

Dr. John paused.

"The fifth influence technique is known as **commitment and consistency**. *Commitment* is also on the WOW! words list. It connotes concepts such as *offering assurance* and being *dependable, forthright*, and *sincere*. Commitment also involves *consistency*, another word on the WOW! list that implies doing what you say you will do."

Dr. John continued, "Influencing people via commitment and consistency involves helping people commit to making a choice, which they then will consistently find a need to validate. A commitment can take several forms or modes. For example, a *verbal* commitment to one person can be effective—especially if given to someone you love or respect. You can see a version of this in fitness programs with accountability partners.

"Alternatively, influencing someone to make a verbal commitment publicly—such as to your team at work—is even more powerful because the likelihood of following through increases when there are more people to keep you accountable. In addition, a *written* commitment often carries more weight. That's what contracts are all about. Even a written goal that no one but you sees can help you achieve at higher levels.

"Here is the bottom line with *commitment and consistency*: you can use external pressure such as threats or bribes (as with children) to effect certain actions, but to truly get a commitment that is meaningful and lasting, you must appeal to an inner sense of personal responsibility and authenticity."

Dr. John paused a moment to allow everyone to catch up with their notes. "The sixth and final influence technique is **exclusivity and scarcity**. It is one of my favorites because it's about supply and demand.

"What compels you to answer your cell phone when a call comes in—even when you are in a face-to-face conversation with someone whose relationship you value?" he asked.

"FOMO!" George cried out from row five.

Dr. John nodded. "That's it, Mr. Denison. Fear of missing out. Another word for it is *scarcity*. The chance that the caller may be unavailable later can cause you to rudely interrupt the person who is right in front of you. The technical term for FOMO is 'loss aversion.'

"Make a note of this: the fear of loss motivates people much more than the thrill of gain. Some studies have shown up to *seven* times more! I saw this often in the investment business as financial markets went up and down. Knowing about loss aversion comes in handy when you're marketing a product or service—and it explains why professions such as insurance, accounting, medicine, and law pay so well. Their first job is to help people who are in *trouble*—or at least who want to protect belongings, avoid a tax problem, get well, or be in compliance with the law.

"Exclusivity and scarcity are cousins," Dr. John explained. "When something is unique, difficult to obtain, or available for a limited time, its value increases. This is true with cars, houses, plane tickets—or even phone calls. In America, our attitude is generally 'the more choices, the better'—even though too many options can cause 'paralysis by analysis.' But when fewer options are offered—or a thing we want becomes scarce—our desire for it can increase to the point that we become anxious and make rushed choices that create regret.

"In order to avoid the panic that tempts you when faced with situations of scarcity or with the pride that accompanies exclusivity, you must slow down and collect your thoughts, relying on wisdom to rule the day. 'Haste makes waste' is not just something your grandmother told you. It's true. Good decisions are not usually made quickly—especially important long-term decisions."

The lesson was wrapping up, so Dr. John stepped to the whiteboard and said, "Here is an easy acronym to use to help you remember the six influence techniques. We are all in a *race*, but we'll spell it like this: R-R-A-C-C-E."

He wrote the acronym on the board:

> **R**apport
> **R**eciprocity
> **A**uthority
> **C**onsensus
> **C**ommitment & Consistency
> **E**xclusivity & Scarcity

He waited for students to copy the acronym before continuing. "Please review the fifteen influence phrases at the end of **chapter 4** for the exam. If you are going into any kind of sales, these are golden.

"Challenge number three is a short assignment on the portal in which you are to identify the type of influence techniques that are being employed in a public speaking situation. I can verify that each of the techniques is used at least once. This challenge is due one week from today by class time."

Dr. John looked at his watch again. "I want to conclude by telling you a story about today's witness from history." He walked to the banner bearing an old photograph of an African American gentleman. At the top of the banner was the word *Humility*.

"Booker T. Washington was a true American hero. He is probably best known for leading the Tuskegee Institute in Alabama for over thirty years. His widespread positive influence was felt throughout the post–Civil War south. But the story I like best about him is one that finds him wielding great influence as an impromptu waiter."

Dr. John stepped back to the front middle of the classroom. "Washington was forced to work in a salt furnace from ages nine to fifteen. He would start the agonizing work of shoveling salt at 4 a.m. and devote nearly every waking hour to the activity. From this humble state, he eventually was able to attend school and achieve great prominence. As a leading educator, an internationally renowned author, and an advisor to governments, he was arguably the most famous black man in the world. One night he stayed at a hotel in Des Moines, Iowa. As he walked through the restaurant, a female guest mistook him for a porter and asked him for a glass of water. Without hesitation, he went to the front desk and secured the water. Booker had every right to take offense. But he took none. Humility was not only a matter of principle with him"—Dr. John pointed to the top of the banner—"it was an everyday natural occurrence. He achieved great influence not through money, position, and power but as a result of his humble spirit during one of the most difficult times in our nation's history. That's why I consider him an exceptional American role model."

Dr. John smiled. "That's it for today, everyone! Have a great day!"

Students scrambled to gather their belongings and head out. Aaron filled in a few of the cryptic abbreviations in his notes while he waited for the rush to clear. After a few minutes, he headed toward the exit.

On the way, he overheard Dr. John talking to Maria. "I like that section very much. I think you're going to change lives all over this hemisphere, Maria. It is very exciting! Keep me posted!" He handed a binder back to her.

"I will. *¡Adios, Doctor Juan!*" Maria smiled.

Aaron made way for her to exit the classroom first. *Change the hemisphere? I wonder how she's going to do that?*

But before he could follow her, Dr. John got his attention. "Hey, Aaron, got a sec?"

"Uh . . . oh . . . sure. What's up, Dr. John?"

"I was going to ask you the same. Is Amanda feeling better?"

Aaron frowned, trying not to show how worried he was about his girlfriend. "She is a little bit. The nausea and fainting spells are less severe and less frequent. But her coach wants her to sit out of practice for a while until she feels normal again."

Dr. John looked like he understood. "Ah, gotcha. I know what it's like to be worrying about the health of those close to you. Keep me posted," Dr. John encouraged.

"Sure will, Dr. John. Thank you for asking."

"Of course."

NINE

STORYTELLING

*The difference between the right word
and the almost right word is the difference
between lightning and the lightning bug.*

—MARK TWAIN

Dr. John entered the classroom for the next lesson at ten seconds before nine o'clock. "Good morning, ladies and gentlemen! I have a story I'd like to tell you."

His class stared at him as he made his way up to the front. For reasons unknown, the professor today carried a giant yellow number-two pencil. "Before we get to my story, I have a statistic for you to ponder: Did you know that 90 percent of all statistics are made up on the spot?"

Dr. John waited for that to sink in. A few students laughed.

"Today's witness from history—Mark Twain—famously said, 'There are lies, damn lies, and statistics.'" Dr. John pointed with his pencil toward the banner with Twain's portrait, showing his characteristic unruly white hair. The word *Storytelling* was printed across the top. "But seriously, research shows that people have a 5 percent chance of remembering a fact—and a 63 percent chance of remembering a story. Here's a simple example."

Dr. John propped his pencil up against the podium and went to the whiteboard. He wrote:

FACT: The cat sat on the mat.
STORY: The cat sat on the dog's mat.

He looked at the class and then slowly underlined <u>dog's</u>. "You see the difference?"

Dr. John continued, "Mark Twain—whose birth name was Samuel Clemens—was perhaps America's greatest master storyteller. He wrote twenty-eight books and numerous short stories with a distinctive narrative style of irreverent, often satirical humor. In 1861, he headed to Nevada and California to try and hit it big in silver and gold, but by that time, the rush was winding down. However, his keen ear for stories and incredible memory brought him a different kind of riches. He took careful notes from the myriad stories told by veteran prospectors around the nightly campfires and became one of the best-known storytellers in the West. His professional success as an author is a testament to the importance of being observant if you want to be a great storyteller.

"Now . . . about my story for you."

Aaron sat up with his classmates to pay closer attention.

"Once upon a time, there was a farmer in the central region of China.

"He didn't have a lot of money, or a tractor, so he used an old horse to plow his field.

"One afternoon, while working in the field, the horse dropped dead. Everyone in the village said, 'Oh, what a horrible thing to happen!'

"The farmer said simply, 'We'll see.'

"He was so at peace and so calm that some in the village got together and, admiring his attitude, gave him a new horse as a gift.

"Everyone's reaction now was, 'What a lucky man.'

"And the farmer said, 'We'll see.'

"A few days later, the new horse jumped a fence and ran away. Everyone in the village shook their heads and said, 'What a poor fellow!'

"The farmer smiled and said, 'We'll see.'

"Eventually, the horse found his way home, and everyone again exclaimed, 'What a fortunate man.'

"The farmer said, 'We'll see.'

"Later in the year, the farmer's son went out riding on the horse and fell and broke his leg. Everyone in the village said, 'What a shame for the poor boy.'

"The farmer said, 'We'll see.'

"Two days later, the army came into the village to draft new recruits. When they saw that the farmer's son had a broken leg, they decided not to conscript him.

"Everyone said, 'What a fortunate young man.'

"The farmer smiled again and said, 'We'll see.'"

Dr. John paused, giving the class time to absorb the story. "What life lessons are contained in this short story?"

"Things change," Brandon answered.

"Well *under*stated, Mr. Siegel. What else?"

"Don't count your horses before you ride them," blurted Jacob.

"Oh, nice derivation of the hatched chicken story. I see what you did there, Mr. Connors." Dr. John chuckled.

"Anyone else? Yes, Mr. Freiburg?"

"Isn't this fable really about perseverance?"

"Go on . . ." Dr. John encouraged.

"It's like Kipling's poem, 'If.' I think it says something like, 'If you can treat success and failure the same, then you will be successful.' The farmer faced each situation the same way."

"I'm impressed with that answer!" Dr. John replied. "In fact, the famous poem by Rudyard Kipling says, 'If you can meet with Triumph and Disaster/And treat those two impostors just the same . . .' So, you are correct, David. The farmer faced adversity with calm resolve and, notice . . . even with a smile. Nice job. Let me offer a few more lessons this story teaches—which could be on the midterm by the way."

Dr. John stepped back behind the podium. "Lesson 1: Most people in this world react (or overreact) to every event as though it's the last event that will ever occur. They're tossed to and fro by the news of the day. I saw this all the time in the financial business. People deduced—or extrapolated—that good stock markets would always be good and bad markets would stay bad. It's known as the extrapolation fallacy.

"Lesson 2: Many times, what looks like a setback might actually be a gift in disguise.

"Lesson 3: *All* events and circumstances can provide valuable lessons if we have discernment.

"Lesson 4: This gentleman farmer personifies a person we all should aspire to emulate. One who has lived and seen. One who understands. One who has wisdom ever at his side.

"To the point of today's lesson," Dr. John told the class, "if you were to ask me, 'What one skill could have the greatest impact on your career?'—I would tell you, unequivocally, *storytelling*. It's your secret weapon for professional success. The best news is that this is a learnable skill. You can become a master at it. You've heard that a picture is worth a thousand words? Well, a story is worth a thousand pictures.

"Each of the lessons I just mentioned concerning the wise farmer has filled volumes throughout the centuries. Yet the sheer economy of words and the context in a short story like this one benefit the listener each time it's repeated. It's important—especially in our information age, where we are inundated with innumerable facts—to place these facts in a story format to deliver an emotional impact. Also, stories are easier to remember, so the message can spread further—and in less time. There is no walk of life that escapes the influence of stories. Who can give me an example? Anyone?" Dr. John asked.

James answered, "There are a ton of shows now that give you the story behind a game or an athlete. Sometimes I like watching those more than the games."

"Good point, Mr. House. I agree—and the thing is, once a game is over, unless your team won the championship, we rarely go back and watch the whole thing again. But I'll watch stories or movies *about* games or particular players more than once because the human element is so much more interesting. But did you ever consider that *every* athletic contest you watch is a prime example of a story?" Dr. John asked.

"Every one of them is different," he continued, "and no one knows how the plot will play out or how it is going to end—not even the players. We all watch the game unfold together. This storytelling element is why sports are so popular and compelling. We love the challenge, the struggle, and the resolution that games—and stories—bring!

"Here's another example. Have any of you ever been to a major art museum?"

Many hands went up, and Dr. John heard a few moans around the room. "Yes, I know. They can be boring as one painting blends into another," Dr. John empathized. "But what happens when you know the story behind the painting? Here's an example."

Dr. John leaned over his laptop, quickly connected it to the classroom's projector, and picked up his pencil to point at the projection. "You may recognize this famous painting," he said. "It's called *Washington Crossing the Delaware*. It's located in the Metropolitan Museum of Art in New York, and it is huge—twelve and a half feet tall by twenty-one feet wide.

"You may recall the story that inspired the painting— General Washington on his way to a Christmas surprise attack in New Jersey at the Battle of Trenton. But I'll bet you didn't know this painting was painted in 1848 by a German American, Emanuel Leutze, to encourage Europe's liberal reformers through the example of the American Revolution.

"I'll bet you didn't know the painting was destroyed in a British bombing raid during World War II. In art circles, it's a joke that this was Britain's final retaliation for the American Revolution. Leutze had fortunately made multiple copies.

"Did you know the people in the boat represent a cross section of the American colonies? Not all are actual people. The man standing next to Washington and holding the flag is Lieutenant James Monroe, who became the fifth president of the United States."

Dr. John indicated the flag in the painting. "That flag there was the original flag of the United States. The design didn't exist at the time of Washington's crossing." His pencil flicked to another part of the painting. "Despite the rising sun, Washington crossed the Delaware in the dark of night.

"Take a look at Washington," Dr. John encouraged the class. "He looks very heroic standing up in the rowboat like that. But if he had done that during the actual crossing, he might have taken a nasty topple into the Delaware on Christmas Day.

"Now, do you need to know these particular facts about this painting?" Dr. John asked.

"Only if it's on the test!" Ryan blurted out.

Dr. John chuckled. "That's true, Mr. Dotson. Or perhaps if you are studying art history. But the point is that when you see this painting, your experience is now laced with new details—an enriched story that involves the backstory of its creator. The painting—while already important because of the historical event it depicts—becomes even more interesting. Next time you go to an art museum, pay the small fee for the audio, and see the richer experience it becomes.

"One other place I believe stories are important—but from which they are now largely missing—is the hearth."

"Dr. John, did you say 'the heart'?" asked Chris, confused.

Dr. John chuckled. "Close, Mr. Washington. I said 'hearth'—as in a fireplace. But our *hearts* are missing a lot of stories because the *hearth* is not being utilized for storytelling much anymore. Throughout history, stories have been told in living rooms and dinner tables. Cross-country family vacations were also a common storytelling venue once the automobile came along. Most of us have stories we can remember that our parents and grandparents told in one or more of these settings. Today, it seems the electronic rectangles have limited these valuable teaching moments. Maybe together we can start to bring them back."

Aaron nodded in agreement.

Dr. John seemed to be somewhere else for a few seconds. "Enough reminiscing. Please make a note that 'The Ten Effects of Storytelling' in **chapter 5** will also be on your midterm exam. But right now, I'm going to stop telling you about storytelling and let you witness it at its highest level."

A man began walking down the aisle toward the front, and there was a ripple of interest through the class as they realized there was a guest speaker today. "Dr. Christian B. Harnesty is a distinguished professor of economics at our own Maison Business School," Dr. John told the class. "He received his undergraduate degree in Arkansas and did his graduate work in Georgia. He is married to a wonderful lady, and they are blessed with three children. He enjoys hiking, biking, and basketball. And he is not only one of the finest storytellers I have ever heard—he is also one of the finest men that I have ever known. Please help me welcome today's guest speaker—Dr. Harnesty."

Aaron smiled at Dr. Harnesty. He had enjoyed taking other classes with the professor. He was as intelligent as he was humble. Tall, with sandy blond hair and a tenor voice, he didn't look his age. He'd always reminded Aaron vaguely of a fair-haired Abe Lincoln.

Harnesty stepped slowly to the front of the class and paused. Then he began. "September 11, 2001, was only the second day of my professional career. I was on top of the world—both figuratively and literally. At 8:45 that morning, as I exited the restroom on the sixty-first floor of the South Tower of the World Trade Center, I remember pausing to look out over the Manhattan skyline. . ." Harnesty turned and gazed out the window. ". . . surveying my kingdom, and thinking to myself, *If my friends could only see me now. I'm going to be a billionaire one day.* It was my dream job: a boy from small-town Arkansas had made it big. Good bye *Leave It to Beaver.* Hello *Great Gatsby.*"

He turned suddenly back to face the students. "At 8:47, I turned from the window to return to my desk. At that very instant, my life changed forever."

The students were on the edge of their seats, Aaron in particular. *I've never heard this story before.* Dr. Harnesty turned and said, "Thank you, Dr. John, for that more than generous introduction. It is such a privilege and a pleasure to be with you and your exceptional students. I'm not a State U alum—but I got here as soon as I could!"

Harnesty turned back to the class. "The story I will share today is, regrettably, true. I tell it because my hope and prayer is that, in some way, it can have a positive impact on your lives, as it has on mine."

He nodded decisively. "The events of 9/11 reinforced—with unequivocal fury—two universal truths I had been taught since I was born: first, ten out of ten of us will die. It is the final statistic. But second, we will all live forever . . . somewhere. The only question left to answer is, When will that happen?"

Harnesty paced in front of the class, commanding the room. "Like most young people right out of college, I ignored the reality of these truths and that question because they all seemed so far off. But that reality was brought vividly and meaningfully to my attention through the experience I gained on that infamous day.

"As I tell my story, I want you to keep in mind one word in particular. That word is *heroism.* I know Dr. John will tell you about the hero's journey and the story circle that is the pattern for almost any great story. But the story I am about to tell has myriad heroes. Heroes defined by bravery and courage—standing in the face of fear. Heroes defined by self-lessness. Heroes defined by humility—the kind of humility that Abraham Lincoln spoke of when he quoted his favorite Bible verse in Micah 6:8: 'To do justice, to love kindness, and to walk humbly.' I believe we are all called to heroism, but it does not suddenly appear in an instant simply because it is needed. It is fostered in the days . . . the weeks . . . the years . . . in living a life of excellence and in understanding the value of others."

Harnesty continued, "I will never forget the plane ride to New York and the nice lady who told me all about the city. I was so excited! I was an avid reader, and I discovered the world through books. I never dreamed I would one day be working in a place like Manhattan. Morgan Stanley—a world-renowned financial firm—was making my impossible dream a reality.

"As you can imagine, coming from a town of only ten thousand residents, I was completely awestruck by the skyscrapers of New York City. I soon noticed the incredible diversity that existed there. It was a waypoint where so many people from every culture on the planet came together in one place. It was fascinating.

"My first day on the job went as expected. Orientation, exercise facility tour, and a free lunch. On Tuesday, September 11, briefcase in hand, I stepped on the elevator of a 110-story building and pushed button number sixty-one. I got there early, because if you're not early, you're late, right?" Harnesty teased.

Many students smiled and nodded.

"At about 8:40, I took a break and made my way across the open architecture of my floor, which housed the cubicles of about 250 coworkers. That's when I stepped into the restroom, then out to the window for that immense feeling of pride and accomplishment.

"Then I turned around—and my entire world turned upside down. I walked back into the room, and *everything* had changed. The atmosphere of the room, the demeanor of my associates—I saw shocked faces, blank stares. As I looked past the sea of silhouettes and then out through the long, narrow windowpanes that spanned the width of the floor, I noticed burning papers floating in the sky. Something was wrong. People were pressed against the windows. I heard a strange crashing, jingling sound that seemed very out of place. I couldn't tell what it was until I was able to jockey for a position to look down to see. Huge sheets of glass were falling. Fires were burning everywhere. Within just a few minutes, I went from a state of complete pride to a place of intense fear like I had never felt before.

"As I tried to get a feel for what was happening, I looked up and down the other tower for clues. I could not see what was going on above our floor because of the close proximity of the two buildings. I would learn later that people watching on television had just heard reports that a plane had crashed into the North Tower at about the ninety-fifth floor."

Dr. John had never seen his students so still. They were riveted.

Harnesty continued, "About that time, we heard our floor manager say over the intercom, 'Please return to your desks.' I complied—as did everyone else. I collected my papers and put them into my briefcase. After a few minutes of silence, I felt an overwhelming urge to get out. Over and over in my head, I heard my own voice screaming, 'Get out! Get out! Get out!'

"But I had just started with this company. It was the opportunity of a lifetime. They had a rule in place that said if you left the floor without permission, you would get a strike against you. Too many strikes, and you were gone. It's almost unimaginable now, but the fear of damaging my career was actually competing with my instinct to run for my life.

"After a few minutes, the intense feeling of danger won out, and I decided to leave. Just as I stood to begin my exit, the intercom blared that we should vacate the floor via the stairs. I found myself on the far side of the room—away from both of the stairwell exit doors. As I inched my way over, I considered the difficulty of evacuating 250 people from our floor alone—much less evacuating the thousands of people who would be streaming down from floors above and those already flooding in from the lower floors.

"When I finally entered the stairwell, I was still unaware of what was actually happening outside. About ten floors down, someone hushed everyone and said, 'I'm on a cell phone with my wife, and she said a small plane has hit the tower next door. All is OK.' I remember feeling relieved. Some headed back to their floors. Yet, I felt a tug, a pull. *Keep going. Keep going.* I continued my descent, and then, at 9:03 a.m., when we had reached the forty-fourth floor—BOOM! A shockwave like an earthquake, combined with the feeling of being in the top of a tree that is hit by an eighteen-wheeler going eighty miles per hour. The shaft we were in listed back and forth several feet. Drywall popped and crumbled. The lights went out. I couldn't stand up. I heard ladies screaming, 'We're all going to die!' None of us knew what had happened.

"Some thought it was a bomb in the basement like in 1993. Many started back up the stairs at that moment. In reality, the second plane had been flown into the eightieth floor of our building, a jetliner full of fuel traveling at almost six hundred miles per hour. It was surreal. I went to my knees, and I screamed to myself, *This is not fair! No goodbyes! I'm twenty-two years old!* Then . . . a strange calm came over me. I felt a pull to, *Just keep going. This will NOT be my final moment.*

Dr. Harnesty surveyed the class. "I remember thinking about my mom and the glass elevator in the tallest building in my hometown. It had only four stories. I remember my mom took me to the elevator and we went up and down . . ." He stopped, as though he had lost his breath. He looked down. Then he took a sip of water as he composed himself.

". . . I clung to her leg." He stopped again. "I'm sorry, Dr. John. I don't know why I'm having trouble telling this today. I guess it's kind of cathartic for me." He made a strangled noise, halfway between a laugh and a sob.

"It's OK, Christian," Dr. John said in a reassuring voice. "You're with friends here. Take your time."

After another few moments, Harnesty continued. "I clung to her leg, and she said, 'It's going to be OK.' She was building heroism in me. Little did she know the impact that small lesson would have in my life when I needed it most.

"Well, the building stabilized, and the lights came on. Fifty-six minutes later, the tower would collapse. There was very little time to get out. But no one pushed. No one yelled. I was in a stairwell full of heroes. Some of them gave their lives that day. I saw several heart attack victims. Others stayed to perform CPR. There were piles of high heels at every doorway we passed. Survival was the only thought and the only goal.

One young lady in front of me completely froze after the initial impact, and I had to carry her the next two floors before she could garner the strength to carry on. All the while, questions such as *Who have I been?* and *What have I done with my life?* continuously flooded my brain. But I felt strangely calm. I had not developed my faith in God as I should have, but His spirit sustained me in that terrible hour.

"When we reached the tenth floor, we were inundated with smoke. I began gasping for breath and took off my dress shirt to use as a makeshift mask to filter out the horrific burning petroleum smell. Jet fuel had streamed down the sides of the building and was now burning at the bottom, creating a chimney effect. I could see that the presence of the thick smoke was increasing the level of fear in the eyes of those around me. At this point, I began thinking that I had made the wrong decision. I imagined everyone below me was burning up. I even considered jumping. The math training in me came out as I thought, *If I busted out a window, what would be the terminal velocity from this height? Has anyone ever survived a ten-story fall? What if a car could break my fall?* The stakes were so high that rational calculation was impossible. But these are the thoughts one has when faced with imminent death.

"Around the fourth floor, my breathing became much more labored. I began to lose all hope. And then . . . I saw the first firefighters. One stopped and looked me straight in the eye. I'll never forget it. And just like my mother had in the elevator all those years ago, he told me, 'It's going to be OK.'"

Dr. Harnesty choked up. "The firefighters were afraid too . . . you could see it on their faces. Yet they showed me the way to safety, and their courage, selflessness, and humility saved my life and inspired me to walk a *different* path ever since.

"I entered the building lobby. The place where I had had my picture taken for my ID badge the day before was now a war zone. Bodies had been dragged in from the street. Windows had blown out. There were fires everywhere and debris falling. EMTs attending to the injured. There was no safe place to exit on the ground level of our building because the falling glass outside was literally cutting people in half. That's when I thought to myself, *So I made it all the way down and can't get out.* And then a port authority officer waved us over.

"There was one tunnel they had cleared in a single narrow hallway. It led to the mall that connected the two towers. Incredibly, with no hesitation, every person lined up single-file to calmly walk through the tunnel. Everyone was dependent on the others for survival. This is what I mean when I say that everyone that day was a hero. It was an extraordinary tribute to the human spirit of cooperation and unity under the most difficult of circumstances.

"Once we reached a place we could exit from in the other lobby, an officer said, 'Don't look up—just run.' I put my briefcase over my head and ran into a scene that depicted the very definition of chaos. I ran for fifteen minutes as fast as I could, and then I stopped, looked back, and for the first time I saw the gaping hole in the building. I couldn't believe it. It was the first indication I had of what had actually happened. But I still was fearful because my mind immediately began calculating what would happen if the building should fall. *Would it fall sideways like a tree?*

"I heard a *thut . . . thut . . . thut . . . thut . . . thut. Helicopters,* I thought. *The military is here!* But in fact, it was the floors of the North Tower collapsing. I saw the radio tower sink and literally felt the energy from the concussion caused by each floor flattening the one below it. The smoke and dust billowed out with each thunderous clap. It filled the streets as it rolled relentlessly toward me. I ran as fast as my adrenaline could propel me for three miles—all the way to Central Park—in dress shoes.

"Wandering the streets of Manhattan in both a literal and figurative fog, I eventually found my hotel. I knew I had to contact my family so they would know I was safe. My parents were in Italy, where they were celebrating their twenty-fifth anniversary.

"Somehow, in the midst of the mass confusion, I remembered the toll-free number at my father's company. I had used it only once in my life. I believe it was God's providence that brought that phone number to mind. I called my sister, who worked at his office. She got word to my parents within three hours of the disaster. They were relieved, to say the least."

Dr. Harnesty stepped behind the podium and folded his fingers over the edge. "I will always remember the thousands of heroes from that dark day. I considered myself dead in that stairwell on the forty-fourth floor. But I am here telling you my story for those who cannot tell theirs. I mentioned earlier that I've walked differently since that day. You see, I didn't just escape a burning building. In the days that followed, I came to realize that I also escaped from the 'stairwell' of my foolish pride and ambition as well. I reflected on the example of those heroes and came to understand that while *this was an experience I would never wish on anyone, it's given me wisdom I wish I could give to everyone.* And to receive the wisdom, at age twenty-two, that most never gain even in their sixties and seventies, was truly a blessing in disguise."

Dr. Harnesty nodded at the class. "Thank you for your kind attention this morning."

Dr. John stepped to the front of the classroom and led the applause that lasted almost a full minute. "Are there any questions for Dr. Harnesty?" Dr. John asked when the applause was done.

Jenna Tibbett raised her hand and asked, "Did everyone on your floor get out?"

"Unfortunately, no," Dr. Harnesty answered. "All of the associates made it out, although on the way down each of us thought the rest were dead. But our security officer—Rick— went back to make sure there was no one left on our floor. Sadly, on his way back down, the building collapsed."

"Yes, Kensey?" Dr. John acknowledged.

"Yes. Thank you again for being here today," she said.

"Of course." Dr. Harnesty bowed his head slightly.

"Have you ever been back?" she asked.

There was a long pause. "Yes. I have. I went back fifteen years later." Harnesty took a deep breath. "I married a few years after 9/11. Our lives became incrementally busier as each of our three kids was born. My wife, Cindy, wanted to go on vacation to New York to get away for a long weekend. We went to the memorial and the museum. Then my wife asked to go to the Freedom Tower Observatory. It is on the 102nd floor. I resisted. But somehow I knew this request was for me and not for her, so we went.

"I had had reservations to dine at the Windows on the World restaurant at the top of the tower the Thursday after 9/11. I remember, when I was twenty-two, how much I was looking forward to seeing the whole city from the highest point available. But now, the view had little appeal. I was very nervous. When we reached the top, I didn't want to go near the window. Cindy stood near it, exclaiming over the beauty. I stood frozen. She then turned, reached out her hand, and said with a smile, 'It's going to be OK.'"

Several students were holding back tears. Dr. John sniffled as well.

"That moment was freedom for me," Dr. Harnesty said. "Good had conquered evil. And I finally had closure concerning my own fears."

Dr. Harnesty concluded, "On September 11, 2001, I had an hour to escape death. Many people died that day so that I could have a pathway out of that building. Before I came over to class this morning, I visited Heroes Way, where five of your own Fighting Eagle alumni who helped save lives that day are memorialized. I hope you will take a quiet moment sometime to thank them as well."

Dr. John stepped forward and said, "Christian, that was extraordinary. I can't thank you enough! Let's give Dr. Harnesty another round of applause." Dr. John embraced Harnesty as the clapping continued a few more seconds.

"As you've witnessed today," Dr. John said, "the most important thing about storytelling is *authenticity*. Whether it's a fictional tale like the wise farmer, a true story about a heroic person like Dr. Harnesty, or your own personal experiences, the stories you tell are windows into your values. The stories you tell are the DNA evidence of your character—of *who you are*."

The class tried to focus on Dr. John and the next assignment after Dr. Harnesty's incredible story. "Before you go,"

Dr. John said, "I want to issue your next challenge. Write down a personal narrative—250 to 500 words—based on an experience you've had. It can be job related—perhaps at an internship you've had—or any personal experience that tells something about *who you are*. It is due one week from today—before class.

"Also, for the exam, you will need to review figures of speech in **chapter 5.** My favorite is the *chiasmus*—which would be a good bonus question, by the way. Also review the seven story types and the nine little stories with BIG concepts. And yes . . . 'Rudolph the Red-Nosed Reindeer' and the story of the number-two pencil . . ." Dr. John grabbed the giant writing instrument and raised it above his head. ". . . could both be on the midterm." He waved the pencil at the class in a cheery salute. "Have a great day, everybody!"

Dr. John turned to embrace Dr. Harnesty again as the line formed for the guest speaker. Three dozen students joined the queue. Aaron was last in line and spent ten minutes politely asking Dr. Harnesty questions.

Later, Aaron made his way to study carrel twelve in the main library. He was hoping to catch up on his class material after having taken time to care for Amanda the last few weeks. But the 9/11 story had dazed him, and he already suspected he'd have difficulty focusing.

"Howdy, Aaron Woods!" Aaron was startled as he entered.

Aaron looked up to see Lisa Kosta and her sister already seated in the study area. Lisa smiled at him.

"Hi, Aaron, how are you?" Nicole chimed in.

"Oh, hi, girls. I'm good, thank you. I didn't expect to see y'all here again. Do you use this area all the time?" Aaron answered vacantly.

"Yeah, we have 'connections,'" Lisa said, "so we were able to get it reserved for the semester."

"Oh, I didn't know you had to reserve. I'm sorry." Aaron began to gather his things.

Lisa stopped him. "No, wait. You're fine. It's nice to have a different face in here." Lisa glanced at her sister, who responded to the gentle jibe by jokingly sticking her tongue out.

"How's your girlfriend doing? Is she better?" Lisa asked.

"What . . . Yes, I think so. The doctor wants her to take it slow, though." *Did I tell them about Amanda being sick?* Aaron tried to remember.

"That's good to hear." Lisa turned back to Nicole as Aaron set up to study.

"OK, let's do three blocks of fifty minutes again," Aaron overheard Nicole say.

"How about two? I want to go to lunch early," Lisa answered.

"Whatever, but there will be *no excuses* and *no whining* if you don't pass your math quiz," Nicole chided.

"OK, thanks, 'Dad,'" Lisa snapped back. "Let's just get to work!"

Aaron thought to himself, *That's weird. The whole time-block thing again.*

Then he asked, "Hey, girls, what do y'all know about 9/11?"

TEN

READY RECALL

*Education is what remains
after one has forgotten what
one has learned in school.*

—ALBERT EINSTEIN

Aaron entered Dr. John's classroom five minutes early. He was in a particularly good mood this Monday morning. Doctors had given Amanda a green light for easing back into volleyball, and he was beginning to think seriously about his next move with her.

He also noticed that the lady on the building staff was sitting on the back row again. *Maria, her name was. She comes to class often. It looks like she has a pad out ready to take notes.*

As usual, Dr. John entered just before class was scheduled to start. Today's banner had a photo of Albert Einstein making a silly face with his tongue hanging out. Above the photo was the word *Discovery*.

"Good morning, ladies and gentlemen! What if I could show you a way to never forget?"

Strange question, Aaron thought.

As usual, Dr. John was in a good mood. Aaron couldn't recall ever seeing him in a bad mood.

"First things first," Dr. John said. "I've seen some very interesting stories on the portal this week. Would anyone care to share one with the class? Mr. Cobb?"

Justin began. "I was asked in an interview to give an example of when I was dissatisfied with my work performance—and what I did to improve it."

"Great! Go ahead." Dr. John nodded.

Justin started reading the words he'd written off of his laptop. "'Last summer I worked at a golf course, mowing greens. The hardest thing about it was aligning the mower up *perfectly*. It was a pain because it was heavier and harder to maneuver than a normal mower. Also, the grass is so short that it makes it difficult to see where you mowed previously unless there was heavy dew the night before. I got frustrated when my supervisor would criticize the job I did because I was determined to get it right. On a golf course, the maintenance crew is only as good as the weakest member, and I didn't want to be the guy letting the team down. It was a bit humbling, but I just took advice from the guys who had been there a long time. After a few weeks, my lines were exceptional. I almost hated to go back to school.'"

"Wow. I love it!" Dr. John exclaimed. "Can you tell from this story that Justin is an 'all-in' kind of employee? It not only exhibits his skills and character but shows him to be a capable storyteller too. Couldn't you see the golf course early in the morning when the mowers are getting revved up for the day's work? The dew on the grass?

"If Justin uses this story in a job interview, the interviewer will imagine him telling stories about their great products or services too," Dr. John told the class. "They will reason that pursuit of perfection and determination are part of this applicant's character—as well as commitment to the team. He also is not afraid of hard work, as working on a golf course in the summertime is a hot and difficult job."

Dr. John signaled a thumbs-up to Justin. "Anyone else want to share?" Dr. John asked.

Aisha Wilson spoke. "At my internship last summer, I was on a committee to see what we could do to support the children of veterans whose parents have been stationed abroad for more than one year. We came up with an internal fundraiser that gathered enough funds to send fifty kids and parents to the theme parks in Orlando. At the end of the last day of their trip, we had arranged for each of the children to enter one of the attractions that had a huge HD screen in it. The park set aside time in that attraction so that the kids were able to speak via video feed to their mom or dad overseas. For three of the kids, we were even able to have their deployed parent surprise them at the park. It was quite emotional and wonderful."

"I know it must have been. That's a phenomenal story," Dr. John said. "I hate to sound like a broken record . . . but I will tell you again—there is phenomenal power in your stories. Don't forget it.

"Well, let's move on. Wednesday will be midterm review day, and I want to make sure you remember what you need to know for the exam. How many of you took the How to Get a 4.0 in College workshop as freshmen?"

The majority of the hands went up.

"Good. I would encourage you to go back to **chapter 6** in your text and review the 'Ready Recall' section as a refresher. The memory palace technique is one of the best tools to avoid the test-cramming syndrome. Let me also remind you that all-nighters don't work. What you gain in knowledge with the extra time spent reviewing instead of sleeping is lost to fatigue at test time. You might get away with it once or twice, but in the long run—which is what is most important—it has a net negative effect. My hope is that you took the advice you were given a few years back and have been reviewing my lecture notes five to ten minutes every day to lock in the information so that cramming won't be a temptation."

Several students squirmed in their seats at that remark.

"But today, I would like to continue with the sixth key to professional success: **memory techniques**. It takes the ready recall to a sort of graduate level concept that will serve you well in the years to come."

Dr. John paused. "Why do you suppose some things come naturally and others don't?" he asked. "Why can we do so many things without thinking about it, yet other tasks are so elusive?

"Daniel Kahneman is a Nobel laureate who explains how we think in an interesting way. His research maintains that there are two systems of thinking. **System 1**, or *fast* thinking, operates automatically with little effort required. Examples of this would be riding a bike, driving a car, or playing a musical instrument by ear. **System 2**, or *slow* thinking, requires effort, such as with complex equations or unfamiliar tasks.

"*Everything* we learn starts out in system 2. Riding a bike or driving a car is indeed difficult before you learn how, right? Yet, after you master the basics, they become second nature. In other words, you can do these things fast because you don't need to stop and think about how to do them. They move from system 2 thinking to system 1 thinking over time, when reviewed or practiced."

Dr. John continued, "In my guitar-strumming days, learning to play was painful at first. My fingers never seemed to reach the frets, and I had to concentrate intensely on every note or chord. Remarkably, within a few days, I could make finger changes quickly on simple chords without thinking. I had moved from system 2 to system 1. Practice makes perfect, right?

"Now here is the really exciting part of this concept. *All you ever want or need to learn for the rest of your lives can be moved from system 2 to system 1.* And the more methods, concepts, and procedures you move from system 2 to system 1 in your field of expertise, the more of an expert or master you will become.

"Additionally, the speed at which one can achieve this shift correlates directly to intelligence because it provides you with a greater bed of knowledge from which to draw, which leads to greater innovation and creativity. You've heard things about people such as, 'She is fast on her feet,' or 'He has a quick wit.' While none of us will ever achieve total recall, we can increase our accumulated knowledge. As we do, we have more we can draw upon when we need to use ready recall."

Dr. John noticed that students were very engaged in this topic. He gave them a moment to catch up in their notes.

"By the way, for the record, I must add here that these rectangles we're all so enamored with—" He held up his smartphone—"work directly against moving information from slow thinking to fast thinking. Why do you suppose this is? Ms. Martin?"

"Maybe because we rely on them too much?" she answered.

"Not maybe . . . *exactly,*" Dr. John confirmed. "And I suppose that's OK most of the time, but what happens when you're in the middle of a sales presentation, a speech, an interview? Or just a conversation? Will you have the information you need *when* you need it? That's really the most important thing, wouldn't you agree?"

"Dr. John, I understand what you're saying," Taylor interrupted. "But isn't having a good memory today sort of outdated, like cursive writing now that we type everything or spelling now that we have spell check?"

"That's a reasonable question, Taylor." Dr. John smiled, even as he privately noted that typing was almost nonexistent in his class now. "But no matter how much information swirls around us, the less well-stocked our system 1 knowledge is, the less we have to think with. And if you will apply this *system 1–system 2* concept, your professional advantage can become substantial over the long term. Your reservoir of knowledge will increase while colleagues and competitors rely more heavily on artificial intelligence. The fact that a good memory may in fact become 'outdated,' as you implied, can make it all the more valuable to possess in those occasional—but often critical—situations. It's an opportunity to stand out. Does that make sense?"

Taylor nodded in agreement.

Dr. John continued, "The other area I would like to cover today is what I've labeled *tactical recall*. This is when you make a dedicated effort to commit something to memory in order to recall it in the short term for a specific purpose. As a student, the primary purpose for recall techniques is scoring well on tests. But what if you used ready recall to place all of the words that WOW! or the fifteen influence phrases into your system 1 memory so that they flow naturally through your subconscious, whether you're engaged in conversation, a presentation, or writing?

"Imagine, during a sales presentation, being able to focus intently on your audience while making eye contact the entire time—instead of turning your back on them in order to look at slides on a screen. Anyone can read! But having this level of tactical recall at your disposal—even with only a few minutes' notice—is a powerful tool. As an example of what I mean, let me tell you a story . . .

"When I sold my company several years ago, the president of my firm, Michael Reedy, and I flew to Boston to sign the papers and close the deal. We were stoked! Upon arrival to our suitor's beautifully appointed offices, we were ushered into the boardroom. We expected to meet the CEO of the acquiring company and maybe a corporate attorney for some legal formalities. Closing documents had been thoroughly proofed and final details negotiated a few weeks prior."

Dr. John went on. "Instead, Michael and I watched as six additional people filed quietly into the mahogany-paneled room. We recognized and greeted a few of the folks we knew from previous meetings, but in short order we realized that the entire board had been assembled, and nobody was carrying any paperwork. My first thought was that the deal was falling apart. It was an intimidating atmosphere, to put it mildly.

"After everyone was seated, the CEO calmly turned to our side of the table—where Michael and I sat alone—and said, 'Gentlemen, it's good to see you today. We just wanted to make sure the cultures of our two organizations were the right fit.'

"Obviously, someone with substantial influence on their team had raised the question. In hindsight, I think it was a legitimate one. In corporate mergers, culture may be the most important aspect of the 'marriage.' Acquiring firms rightly want to make sure all are fully aligned philosophically in order to best serve soon-to-be-mutual clients. But the manner and setting in which the question was presented took us by surprise. Michael and I looked at each other with wide eyes. We realized that this meeting was about to determine the fate of our valued clients and employees—not to mention the trajectory of our own professional lives.

"Then, unexpectedly, Michael spoke," Dr. John told the class. "'Ladies and gentlemen, when we first met, you gave us this.' Michael held up a pamphlet entitled *Who We Are*. He continued, 'I read the core values you have published in this document—and on your website. I have to believe what we are witnessing here is a match made in financial services heaven.'"

Dr. John cocked an eyebrow at the class. "Did you notice the halo effect framing in that last phrase?" He chuckled before going on. "Without opening the pamphlet, Michael went on. 'When I consider *integrity*, I see an irreplaceable attribute that invokes honesty and communicates your commitment to always doing the right thing. I see *accountability*, which speaks to a characteristic that not only is universally admired but is frankly all too rare in our culture today.'"

Dr. John paused again. "Do any of these words sound familiar?" he asked.

"Michael went on, one by one. '*Determination* means that you will persevere no matter what. *Authenticity* speaks to trustworthiness and substance.' Michael continued until he had methodically and eloquently gone through all seven of our buyer's values." Dr. John smiled. "Then he said, 'Ladies and gentlemen, these are the same values our firm has aspired to for over three decades. We are humbled that you consider us worthy to be called partners. And we can't wait to tell our clients about the advantages that await them because of our new association with your firm and the extraordinary standard of excellence you've been delivering for almost a century.'"

Dr. John paused. "If a pin had been dropped in that room—even on the carpeted floor—I think everyone would have heard it. Everyone in the room was slack jawed by what they had just witnessed—including me! The board members looked at each other in silence, and then all eyes were on Michael and me."

Dr. John looked intently at the class. "After an extended pause, the CEO calmly asked, 'Does anyone else here know those seven core values by heart?' All hands remained on the conference table. He paused again to see if there were any questions or concerns on the faces of his fellow board members. It seemed like ten minutes, but after about ten seconds, he turned to Michael and me and said, 'Gentlemen, this is going to be fantastic!'

"In an instant, all seven men and women were on their feet and on our side of the table before we could barely even stand up. There were smiles, handshakes, laughter, and pats on backs. 'Welcome aboard!' was the prevailing sentiment in the room."

Dr. John raised his hand. "Oh, and one more thing. It was our company policy for the CEO and president to never fly on the same plane just in case the unthinkable should happen. I had taken a slightly earlier flight, having not slept well the night before. I had tried to read but dozed off for most of the flight. While I was napping, Michael chose to utilize the ready recall technique to commit to memory our acquiring company's seven core values—just in case. I hadn't asked him to do that, but looking back, his initiative and memory skills ensured that the deal went through as planned. That deal allows me to be here with you right now, doing what I love."

Dr. John smiled at the class. "I am proud to say that Michael was offered significant leadership opportunities in the acquiring company. He made a decision to decline those tempting offers and remain in a position where he can work directly with clients. That's where his purpose lies. To no one's surprise, Michael is the top-ranked wealth advisor in the company. He has followed his calling, and it shows! I hope you all will have the privilege of meeting Michael Reedy soon."

All of the students sat silently for a long moment. Dr. John could sense that this was all starting to sink into these sharp young minds. He loved it. "Let me finish with today's witness from history," Dr. John said. "Albert Einstein was born in Germany in 1879. He is best known for his development of the theory of relativity and the world's most famous equation: $E = mc^2$. In 1933, while he was on a visit to the United States, Adolf Hitler took power. Einstein was Jewish, and therefore he did not return to Germany. Instead, he became an American citizen in 1940. He alerted President Roosevelt about the development of powerful bombs by Germany, which led to the Manhattan Project and the development of the nuclear devices that eventually ended World War II. He may have been the most brilliant scientist of all time. He attributed this to 'just being more curious than others.'"

Dr. John smiled. "Yet it is said that once, when Einstein was asked for his phone number, he took out a directory to look it up. When asked, 'Don't you know your own phone number?' he reportedly replied, 'Why memorize something you can look up?'

"This may be a funny—even puzzling—story about one of the most intelligent humans to ever live. He spent no time memorizing trivial bits of information like a phone number. Perhaps by this small act, he unwittingly gave us a clue as to how technology today can be used to unclutter our minds of trivial information. Regardless, I'm confident Albert Einstein knew something about ready recall. His remarkable intellect and love for learning assured that he had an enormous amount of knowledge stored in his own system 1—and therefore could access *what* he needed to know *when* he needed to know it. And fortunately for all of us, what he knew—and was willing to share as a new American citizen—helped free the entire world from tyranny," Dr. John concluded.

He nodded at the class. "Well, that's it for today. A friendly reminder: use those time blocks to focus when you study! See you at the review!"

ELEVEN

The Midterm

Love alters not with his brief hours and weeks,
But bears it out even to the edge of doom.
If there be error and upon me prov'd,
I never writ, nor no man ever lov'd.

—William Shakespeare, Sonnet 116

Aaron headed straight to the library to get an early start on midterm exams.

"Hey, lovebug!"

He turned. It was Amanda.

He burst out into the enormous smile that came to his face almost every time he saw her. "Hey! What are you doing here?" He hugged her tightly.

"I got a walk in my first class, and so I've been lying in wait for you," she teased. "How was class with Dr. John?"

"Unbelievable!" Aaron answered.

"Oh, well, I'm glad to hear it! You're in a good mood," she noted.

"I'm telling you, Dr. Daniels has this unique way of presenting his material. Stuff I haven't learned in any other class," Aaron answered.

"Yes, I know. You talk about him all the time. What did you learn today that you are so excited about?" Amanda asked.

"Well, for example, did you know that pretty much *anything* you could ever learn can be as easy as riding a bike?" Aaron asked. "The most complicated equations, procedures, whatever—like riding a bike! You can remember it without even thinking about it."

Amanda made a face. "Really?"

Aaron nodded enthusiastically. "Yeah, and other stuff—time leadership, using just the right words at the right time, how to tell great stories . . . I mean, the other day, Dr. Harnesty came in to speak. He was fantastic. Everything we've learned in there is so applicable to our career and to life."

"Fascinating," Amanda teased, with dancing eyes and a secret smile.

Aaron turned his head slightly. He looked puzzled for a short moment by her tone. "It's really too bad you can't take Daniels's class," he said. "I'm telling you—it's hands down the best material and professor I've ever had."

"Well, that's OK. I think I'll be fine."

"Just sayin'," Aaron urged. "Every student should be required to take it."

Amanda just grinned at him.

Aaron finally caught on she had something to tell him. "Hey, what do you have up your sleeve?"

'Well, you're still going skiing with your buddies at spring break, right?" she prompted.

Aaron shrugged. "Yeah."

Amanda bounced up and down. "Well, guess who is going to Europe with your beloved Dr. John?!" she exclaimed.

Aaron stared before busting out into a grin. "No way! How did you do that?!"

"Well, you just kept telling me about all the stuff you're learning in his class, and you decided to go skiing instead of—"

Aaron interrupted. "Wow! I can't believe you're going on that trip. You're gonna see what I mean!" He paused. "I'm glad you're getting to go."

Amanda laughed. "Me too! I'll take good notes for you." The two of them entered the library to go study for their midterms.

The next Friday, Dr. John entered his classroom from the back door as usual, but today was not an ordinary day. It was time to learn the results of the midterms. "Good morning, ladies and gentlemen!" Dr. John bellowed.

He stopped behind the podium and spread his hands over the top. "I'm very pleased with the results of your exams," he announced. "Generally." He stopped suddenly and looked over his glasses at Nicholas Berry. Students were unsure whether to laugh or gasp. Berry froze. Dr. John grinned. "But seriously, all, including Mr. Berry here, did an exceptional job. Congratulations! Scores are online now. By the way, how many of you are going on the World War II tour with me?"

Three hands went up.

"Great, we had better get moving! We'll be on our way to London in seven hours! For the rest, y'all go on and head out early, and I wish everyone a safe and enjoyable spring break!"

Aaron knew he had aced the exam. His other midterms had also gone well. He was beginning to get a little sentimental, knowing this would be his last spring break at State U. But he was also excited. It was time to plan the most important proposal of his life!

TWELVE

THE BREAK

*The history of free men is never written by
chance but by choice—their choice.*

—GENERAL DWIGHT D. EISENHOWER

"Ladies and gentlemen, Flight 2371 to London will be departing shortly. Please stow away loose items and make sure your seatbelts are fastened firmly around you."

"I can't believe you didn't get us in first class," Mrs. Daniels teased her husband.

"You just wanted to see me tortured in that procrustean bed they call 'luxury seating,'" Dr. John accused.

"Hey, I can't help that you're two inches too tall," she retorted.

"We'll be fine in 'steerage,'" he said as they both laughed.

Anicia Kosta-Daniels was well into her fifties—a stunningly attractive woman with brunette hair, blue eyes, and a beautiful smile. Her fifteen-year marriage to Dr. John had taken them many places, both geographically and personally.

"Remember when we brought all the kids on this trip?" she asked.

"How can I forget?" Dr. John reminisced. He frowned. "That reminds me, it's been over three weeks now since we've heard from Nate."

"I know. I count the days too. Nothing from Colonel Martin either, right?"

"No. Just that they're in the Middle East somewhere. I'm sure they are fine. I just hate not knowing." Dr. John said, staring out the window. He worried about his younger son.

"How about the girls? They make their flight OK?" he asked.

"Yes. All good. Hey, I met Amanda!"

"Who?" Dr. John asked.

"Amanda Watkins. Isn't she the one Aaron Woods is dating? I met her earlier. She seems very nice."

Dr. John recalled his conversations with Aaron with mild interest. "Oh, yeah. Amanda. I'm glad she's on the trip."

As the plane took to the air, Dr. John dozed off.

Two hours later, Anicia was at Amanda's seat, deep in conversation.

Anicia had been deeply struck by Amanda Watkins. She was a pretty, wholesome, and intelligent small-town girl. Her long amber hair was the envy of many women, but her blue eyes and broad smile were appealing to everyone. She had a calm demeanor and was an accomplished volleyball player, as her slender, five-foot-ten-inch frame would attest. Her number-two class rank in high school and 1520 SAT score had been enough to earn her multiple academic scholarship opportunities, but she had chosen an athletic full ride at State U instead."

". . . Do you really think so, Mrs. Daniels?" Amanda asked.

"I do. And I've seen it in my own marriage. I know it sounds a little old fashioned with the 'hedges' and all, but finding a man who will pursue you and then be dedicated to *fiercely* protecting your relationship . . . I think that's what our hearts truly desire."

"I guess you're right. I just haven't heard it put quite that way before." Amanda pondered.

"Well, it sounds like you have a good one in Aaron. You think he is going to pop the big question anytime soon?" Anicia asked.

Just then, the plane bucked and shivered in the air, and a chime sounded over the two women's heads. "Ladies and gentlemen, we are expecting a bit of turbulence. The captain has turned on the fasten seatbelt sign. Please return to your seats at this time."

Anicia shuddered and pressed Amanda's hand briefly. "I hate this part. We'll talk more later. I'd better head back up to my seat so I can squeeze Dr. John's hand off."

Dr. John awakened to a familiar death grip and a nervous wife. "Distract me," she instructed him, seeing he'd woken up. "Read me something. Did you ever memorize that Longfellow poem like you promised?"

"It would be nice to have some coffee." He ignored the question and looked for a flight attendant.

Dr. John saw his wife go into a semifetal position as the plane shook, her head down with her eyes closed and her shoulders forward—getting as low as possible in her seat.

He broke into his best British thespian voice . . .

A Psalm of Life

Tell me not, in mournful numbers,
Life is but an empty dream!

> For the soul is dead that slumbers,
> And things are not what they seem.

The diversion appeared to work. His bride's eyes widened, and her face lit up.

> Life is real! Life is earnest!
> And the grave is not its goal;
> Dust thou art, to dust returnest,
> Was not spoken of the soul.

"That's all I know," Dr. John finished abruptly.

"Oh, man, you had me going!" Anicia screeched.

"Hey, I'm not Michael. His wife told me that when they went to England, he memorized *Hamlet* on the way over and *Macbeth* on the way back." He teased.

"Oh, stop it." She poked him lightly in the ribs as they laughed.

"I'll keep working on it," he promised.

"I look forward to it." The plane had leveled out and was flying smoothly once again. Anicia stretched back out with a smile. "But now, it's time to go to sleep."

The spring break group arrived at their hotel about 6:30 a.m. and had just enough time to put bags in storage and grab an English breakfast before their first day of touring.

At 8:15 a.m., Dr. John gathered his drowsy flock in the hotel lobby. "I hope you all got some sleep on the plane. If not, you will tonight, but for now, we have a full day ahead of us. We're going to start with Buckingham Palace, then Trafalgar Square, then head over to 10 Downing Street, and finally to one of my favorite spots in London—the Churchill War Rooms. There we'll see where they made the plans and conducted operations that helped save the world from tyranny."

The students managed a cheer, and so the day began.

Despite the amazing sights, the group was understandably dragging a little by lunch time. They ate at a deli on Trafalgar Square and stopped by to see the prime minister's residence on the way to the war rooms. Once they had arrived at the famous bunker, however, Dr. John raised his hand to get the group's attention.

"Interestingly, the rooms we will see below were not completely bombproof. Fortunately, the Germans never hit this bull's-eye."

The students were each given an audio device to learn about each room along the ninety-minute tour. About an hour into the tour, Dr. John raised his hand and asked them to turn off their devices.

He then said, "Those of you who have taken my class, do you remember when I told you that Winston Churchill said, 'Words are the only things that last forever'?"

The students from Dr. John's class nodded.

"Well, this is perhaps the most important compartment in all of these rooms." Dr. John pointed their attention to a small storeroom—about twelve feet by sixteen feet. It contained radio and broadcasting equipment.

He continued, "This now-antiquated technology was used by Churchill to talk to the British people via a connection with the BBC just a few blocks away. The words he spoke from this room during fifty-seven straight days of German bombing onslaught were crucial to victory. In fact, when he became only the third non-American in history to receive honorary US citizenship in 1963, President Kennedy said of him, 'He mobilized the English language and sent it into battle.' Robert, you have a question?" Dr. John asked.

"Yes. Wasn't there widespread panic in London during the Blitz? I mean, how did the city keep it together?" Robert asked.

"Great question," Dr. John acknowledged. "Let me see if I can explain. When the bombing started, you can imagine the reaction. No one knew what to do, and everyone was frightened. After the Pearl Harbor attack on December 7, 1941, President Roosevelt spoke the famous line to Congress and the nation, 'We have nothing to fear but fear itself.' London had already experienced the truth of that statement during the Blitz. When citizens made it through a night of bombing without being hit in London, they gained self-confidence— even an exhilarating feeling that they would be OK. The more times they were missed by the bombs, the more confidence they gained. It's a natural response that was eventually borne out by the statistics: only one out of every two hundred Londoners were hurt or killed in the bombings.

"In anticipation of the attacks, the British government tried to boost morale with a poster campaign that said simply, Keep Calm and Carry On. It became a source of pride and strength. You will see the bright red poster in the gift shop when we leave."

Dr. John gestured down the hall. "Just down and to the left, you will see the phone room where Churchill had a direct line to the White House. There, his well-chosen words eventually won over FDR and gained the support of the United States—which turned the tide of the war. You are standing at ground zero for the defense of freedom in the twentieth century."

Dr. John smiled. "Incredibly, Winston Churchill was voted out of office immediately following victory in World War II. He later explained this irony, 'Those who can win a war well can rarely make a good peace, and those who could make a good peace would never have won the war.' The British people had a do-over six years later and elected him again as prime minister."

Dr. John looked at his watch. "We have about an hour before the bus leaves. There is some interesting memorabilia in the museum, and we'll have about twenty minutes in the gift shop after the tour."

Two days later, after more sightseeing at the Tower of London, St. Paul's Cathedral, the British Museum of Art, and the London Eye, it was time for Dr. John's World War II group to go on to France.

As Dr. John rode the train under the channel, he marveled over the tunnel's construction to Anicia. "This thing is unbelievable. Thirty miles tunneled under the English Channel. I didn't remember it was opened back in 1994."

"You're such a little kid," Anicia said.

"Hey, I'm just sayin'—what a feat of engineering." Dr. John's phone buzzed, and he pulled it out of his pocket to see a text from John Jr. "Wow!"

"What?" Anicia asked.

Dr. John turned to his wife in wide-eyed excitement. "Tech U lost in the conference semifinal yesterday! And State won the South Central tournament and is a number-one seed in the national tournament!"

"Oh, that's great!" Anicia replied. She was not a huge fan, but she knew how much the State U basketball team meant to her husband and her oldest stepson.

"Tech got a one seed in their region as well, even though they lost. That figures—the media loves them," Dr. John grumbled under his breath. Still, he couldn't help grinning as he typed a reply to John Jr.

The train from Calais was late as usual. The group arrived at the Caen train station about half-past noon. A bus was waiting, bound for Normandy. The weather on the south side of the channel on this spring day was exquisite—seventy-four degrees, a slight breeze, a few clouds over the water with an otherwise bright blue sky. It made for a stunning tableau for the tour.

The first stop would be the tip of the D-day invasion spear—Pointe du Hoc. As the students stood atop the cliffs, Dr. John spoke, "There is no way to exaggerate the importance of the D-day invasion. Without success, a German victory may have been inevitable. In the early hours of June 6, 1944, the future of the free world rested on the shoulders of 225 Army Rangers led by Lieutenant Colonel James E. Rudder. This giant sword memorial commemorates the ultimate sacrifice that more than half of those soldiers made that day. They scaled these hundred-foot cliffs on rope ladders to attack the German large guns mounted here. You can still see the pillboxes where these guns were mounted, and these craters were inflicted by Allied gunships, which were among the five thousand ships supporting the invasion from the English Channel. To the west is Utah Beach. To the east is the infamous Omaha Beach. It is estimated that more than forty-four hundred men lost their lives in a matter of hours on that fateful morning."

Students looked down and across the historic beaches in awe. Several pointed. Those that spoke did so in low voices.

"Dr. John, I have a question," said Amanda.

"Yes?"

"Why did all these men do this? How could they? Weren't they scared?"

Dr. John pondered. "I ask myself that question each time I come here, Amanda. The truth is, I don't know how they did it. In all my reading, I can only surmise that there is something about wartime—I mean a war that is for the survival of your homeland—that makes you think of nothing else. And so you do what is necessary. G. K. Chesterton once said that a true soldier fights not because he hates what is in front of him but because he loves what is behind him."

Dr. John let the silence stretch for a moment before he spoke again. "Let's head over to the cemetery."

At the Normandy American Cemetery Visitor Center entrance, Dr. John huddled the group together. "The visitor center will take about an hour for you to go through. You can then enter the cemetery. I encourage you to soak in the history and the sacrifice you see displayed. I also have here some small flags. Half are US flags, and half are State U flags. Mrs. Daniels has a slip of paper with the grave-site locations of the twelve State U alumni who gave their lives at Normandy.

Please pair up, and take one of each flag and a location slip so you can place them at the bases of the markers to honor their sacrifice. I will meet you at the main flagpole at 4:45 p.m. Please don't be late."

Johnathan and Anicia stood holding hands in silence as they considered the beauty of the memorial grounds and the sacrifice it represented. They observed the students moving through the cemetery. One knelt. Another stood. Some sat together in silence. Others hugged and were tearful. Some could only place the small flags and move on uncomfortably.

It occurred to Dr. John as he watched that just as there was no wrong way to mourn, there was no one single way to honor—so long as honor was done in a spirit of awe and humility. He knew this would be a lifelong memory for the students that had come here, whether they realized it or not. Most, he thought, did.

Around 4:30 p.m., students started gathering near the flagpole. At 4:45, Dr. John said, "Before we head back to the bus, I wanted to say a couple of additional things about this place—and also tell you about what happened elsewhere during the D-day invasion.

"General Eisenhower sent a message to the men before they left the British shores that said, in part, 'You are about to embark upon a great crusade . . . The eyes of the world are upon you . . . Our hopes and prayers march with you.' I want you to imagine that at the very same time on that day, in every American town—large and small—businesses had placed signs in their windows that said: 'Sorry, we are closed. We are praying for the success of the invasion.' Churches were open all day across the United States.

"Later that day, President Roosevelt took to the radio airwaves, and after only two opening sentences, he said, 'And so, in this poignant hour, I ask you to join with me in prayer.' His prayer lasted almost six minutes. It was an inspiring and unprecedented occasion of national unity."

As Dr. John concluded his speech, "Taps" began to play as the American flag was lowered at the end of another day. The group turned toward the flag. Veterans in and out of uniform saluted. Afterward, the group walked slowly and silently to the bus. Gravel underfoot was the only sound that could be heard.

On the bus ride to the hotel, Amanda sat alone in a window seat, staring into the green Normandy countryside. "You OK?"

Amanda looked up to see Mrs. Daniels had come down the aisle to sit beside her. "Oh, hi, Mrs. Daniels. Yes, I think so. Just pondering," Amanda answered.

"Tell me more."

Amanda produced a slip of paper from her jacket pocket. "Well, you probably didn't notice, but you know the grave-site location you gave me on this slip of paper?"

"Yes."

"The name on it is Corporal James T. Watkins. He was my grandfather's oldest brother. My dad told me to look for his grave when he heard we were coming here. I had forgotten that he went to State U. He left after his sophomore year to enlist. He was only nineteen years old when he died," Amanda said softly.

"Wow. That's amazing that I handed you his grave-site slip. I had no idea."

"To die so young. It breaks my heart. The life he might have lived." Amanda stared out the window again.

Her new mentor touched her shoulder and said, "Amanda, I wish I could ask God why the young die. But I believe their impact is no less. I once heard, at the funeral of a sixteen-year-old girl who had died in a tragic accident, 'Her light burned brightly before she died; now her brightness shines for all time.' Your great uncle lived a short life, but he lived well. He showed the greatest love by dying for those he loved . . . and for us. He died protecting freedom. And he's having an impact on lives he never knew—even at this moment."

"I know . . . You're right. Thank you, Mrs. Daniels. That means a lot to me."

Amanda, Mrs. Daniels, and the other students sat in comfortable silence for the remainder of the bus ride, exhausted both physically and emotionally. The trip had been an impactful one, and their bus to the airport departed the next morning at 9:30 sharp.

"Ladies and gentlemen, we are about two hours from Houston Intercontinental Airport . . ."

"Hey, wake up."

Dr. John reluctantly uncovered one eye under his mask.

"I've been thinking," Anicia said.

"Am I in trouble?" Dr. John chuckled, moving his sleeping mask to his forehead and rubbing his eyes.

"No, silly. I was just thinking how glad I am we made this move to State U. I'm really enjoying getting to know your students. Amanda is as sweet as they come. You're the best professor at the university, and—"

Dr. John interrupted. "Oh, please. You're biased. I do my best."

Anicia smiled. "Just because I'm biased doesn't mean it's not true. Are you still glad we made the move?"

"I am. You know why?" Dr. John asked, feigning sleepiness.

"Why?"

"Because . . ." He lowered one eyebrow and raised the other for exaggerated dramatic effect.

> Not enjoyment, and not sorrow,
> Is our destined end or way;
> But to act, that each tomorrow
> Find us further than today.

"You didn't!" Anicia exclaimed.

Dr. John grinned. "I did."

> Art is long, and Time is fleeting,
> And our hearts, though stout and brave,
> Still, like muffled dreams, are beating
> Funeral marches to the grave.
>
> In the world's broad field of battle,
> In the bivouac of Life,
> Be not dumb, driven cattle!
> Be a hero in the strife!
>
> Trust no Future, howe'er pleasant!
> Let the dead Past bury its dead!
> Act,—act in the living present!
> Heart within, and God o'erhead!

Lives of great men all remind us
We can make our lives sublime,
And, departing, leave behind us
Footprints on the sands of time;

Footprints, that perhaps another,
Sailing o'er life's solemn main,
A forlorn and shipwrecked brother,
Seeing, shall take heart again.

Anicia suddenly joined her husband in unison.

Let us, then, be up and doing . . .

Dr. John stopped and smiled. They laughed and continued together.

With a heart for any fate;
Still achieving, still pursuing,
Learn to labor and to wait.

They paused. "So your toes are 'Longfellows' too, huh?" Dr. John quipped.

Anicia gaped, then burst out laughing. "Why! I oughta . . ." She shoved her husband affectionately, then leaned her head against his shoulder to wait out the remainder of the flight.

7

THIRTEEN

You're Always Interviewing

I will be prepared, and then
perhaps my chance will come.

—John Wooden

"Good morning, ladies and gentlemen!" Dr. John boomed as he entered the classroom. "I trust you all had a safe and relaxing spring break and are ready to get back to work! How about those Fighting Eagles? First number-one seed ever!"

Sleepy heads awoke, and several cheers rang out through the classroom.

"We'll talk a little more basketball in a few minutes, but first things first, I want to say that I'm pleased with your progress at the midpoint of the semester. Your engagement has been at the high level I was hoping for when we started. That said, it's not how you start that matters—it's how you *finish*. We are now halfway through the twelve keys to professional success."

Students shuffled for pen and paper.

Dr. John started, "Thus far, we've hit the interpersonal communication techniques heavily. Building instant rapport, time leadership, words that WOW!, influence techniques, storytelling, and system 1 thinking. Today, I want to talk to you about a life-changing concept. Key to professional success number seven is: **you are always interviewing.** Shakespeare said it this way: 'Readiness is all.'

"In that regard, this is a good time to introduce today's witness from history—Coach John Wooden." Dr. John pointed toward the banner with Wooden's picture with a basketball net hung around his neck. The word *Vigilance* was emblazoned across the top.

"Coach Wooden was my boyhood hero. I never met him, but I did leave a message on his answering machine once. Remind me to tell that story sometime." Dr. John smiled.

"He was an English teacher by trade and would have been very familiar with all of Shakespeare's works. In regard to readiness, he said it this way: 'I will be prepared, and then perhaps my chance will come.'

"Now, this was a very important concept in Coach Wooden's program because almost every star high school player in the country wanted to play for him. He was the greatest college basketball coach of his day—and in all of history, in my opinion. He won one national championship as a player and then an unmatched *ten* championships in his last *twelve* years as coach at UCLA. Imagine: you could be a great player that could star at any other school but sit on the bench your entire career at UCLA. Yet he instilled in all his players that you have to be ready."

Dr. John leaned up against the podium. "One way he ensured vigilance in his players was to stress the fundamentals of the game on a daily basis. Even when they had a huge game the next day, he took the time to drill on the basics of passing, dribbling, shooting, and defensive footwork in every practice. He even personally showed his players how to properly put on their socks and shoes on the first day of practice each year! And keep in mind, these were the best of the best of Division I–level players. They had all been playing for many years. Now *that's* emphasizing the fundamentals and preparation. Today's key is about applying the fundamentals every day and staying ready—just like Coach Wooden.

"Concerning the actual job interview process, **chapter 7** in your text has what you need to know. The 'Dos and Don'ts' list is important to review before *every* interview you have. Also, review the 'Ten Most Commonly Asked Interview Questions' in your text. Yes, Aaron. You have a question?"

Aaron nodded. "Yes, sir. I usually feel prepared for my interviews, but when they ask, 'Why should I hire you?' I tend to freeze up. But it seems like I'm asked that question in every interview I've had."

Chatter broke out across the room. It seemed most students had experienced the same question.

"Oh, that's a tough one, isn't it?" Dr. John answered. "I've thought about that one a lot over the years. I eventually came up with a three-point answer that seems to work well based on feedback I've received. I'll give you the first point for free. It's 'I believe I'm a good communicator.'

"You are in a business communications class, right? You are learning to become great communicators in every way possible—that means in both word and in deed. And if you can communicate, regardless of your profession or job duties, you're going to succeed."

Heads shook around the room. The class didn't seem convinced. Dr. John elaborated. "Companies are all looking for good communicators—and if you demonstrate this ability during the pressure-packed environment of an interview, your communication skills will speak for themselves. You see what I did there?" Dr. John teased.

Aaron sighed and smiled. *So many dad jokes. Sheesh.*

It was time to move on. "For the second part of this answer, let's think back to our third key," Dr. John suggested. "Words that WOW! What are some of the powerful words we discussed?"

Notes shuffled. "Taylor?"

"*Consistent* and *responsibility*," she answered.

"Good. Others?"

"How about *determined* and *no excuses*," Ryan Dotson piped up.

"Excellent."

"*Let's get to work*!" George Denison added.

Laughter ensued. "Yes, George. Thank you for participating! Do you notice what all of these words have in common?" Dr. John asked. "They describe a team player, and when someone asks you why you should be hired, that should be the second part of your answer: that you are someone who is *coachable*. One who is consistent, responsible, determined, makes no excuses, and has a 'let's get to work' attitude is one who defines *coach*ability. Behind these characteristics is one who has an enthusiasm for their work. This enthusiasm comes from not only their *passion*—which speaks to individual motivation—but cognizance of their *purpose*, which is a larger concept that encompasses team goals. Again, the economy of words is so important. By simply saying, 'I'm coachable,' you indicate that you have the characteristics just mentioned without ever verbalizing them.

"The last part to your three-part answer to this difficult question is 'I love to learn.' With these four words, you are saying, 'I know that just because I have a college degree, it doesn't mean I think I know it all. I'm ready to learn all your fine organization has to teach me.' John Rockefeller said, 'I would rather hire someone with enthusiasm than someone who knows everything.' This attitude further indicates another desirable characteristic—humility.

"We'll talk more about this one later at the very end of the semester, but for now, just know that when you say, 'I love to learn,' it's music to any HR professional's ears."

Dr. John spread his hands wide. "So, Aaron, there you have it: 'I believe I'm a good communicator. I'm coachable. And I love to learn.' One-two-three."

"Thank you, Dr. John. That's very helpful," Aaron said.

"Of course. It's my pleasure."

"Now, while the questions you are asked in a formal interview are very important, the most important time in the interview is the *reverse interview*. When the interview is over, it's really just begun." Dr. John said. "Yes, Natalie?"

"I guess I'm not following. When it's over, it's over, right. That last interview question—'Why should we hire you?'— always seems to be the last question in the interviews I've been in," she stated.

Dr. John replied, "Ah, I understand what you're saying. Yes. You're right. That is the last *official* question many times. But then, more often than not, they will ask: 'Do you have any questions for me?' And once the interviewer asks *that* question, it's game on! It's your time to really shine! And remember this famous Latin phrase when you ask these questions: *fortis fortuna juvat*—'Fortune favors the bold.'

"In a few weeks, another guest speaker is going to come and make you all experts in the art of asking questions. But for now, in the interview context, just know that interviewers get to know you by *the content and quality of your questions—* even more so than by your answers."

Dr. John continued, "When you get this question about 'having any questions,' there are three critical things you must absolutely *avoid*. The first is asking nothing at all. This could give the impression that you haven't seriously thought about working for their organization. Next, avoid asking obvious questions. If the answer is easily found on their website, then it's not a good reverse question. Finally, don't ask yes-or-no questions. Open-ended questions are better because they are information-seeking questions.

"So, with your padfolio still open to indicate your readiness and interest in recording their answers, you should reply, 'Yes, I do have a few things I was wondering about.'

"Now, there are fourteen **reverse interview** questions in your text in **chapter 7**. You probably won't use all of them in a single interview—if for no other reason than that your time is limited. But I want to go over *three* questions you should always ask in an initial interview if time allows.

The first one is, **What brought you to this company, and why have you stayed?** When your interviewer answers this question, you have immediate insight into the culture of the company. If the interviewer's reasons align with your own for wanting to join the company, that's usually a good sign. If they respond, 'Hey, it's a job,' then that's a big red flag."

Dr. John paused. "Just as a side note—see who's in charge of the interview when you ask these types of questions? They give you a chance to build greater rapport. You can subtly weave in questions from the LAVA conversation to find out more about the interviewer by encouraging them to talk about their favorite subject—themselves.

"The second critical reverse interview question is, **How would you describe the company's values?** This question will reveal how well the company instills and publicizes its values *internally*. It's safe to assume that your interviewer is considered a 'face' of the organization, so they should know these corporate values well. In addition, the content of this answer reveals what is important in the company culture so that you may assess whether or not you can be fully aligned with it. Sharing the same values as the company you join could be the most important factor of all. Remember the story I told you about my company's merger? This second question also relays the message that you are a person who cares about values—a person of character.

"The third question you should always ask in a reverse interview is this: **What is the biggest challenge your company faces right now?** This question subtly communicates that you're thinking about how you might add value. The fact that you're already considering the job's challenges makes it easier for hiring managers to visualize you in that position. The answer to this question is also valuable, because if the challenge described seems like something you can't do or have no interest in taking on, you might want to pass on the opportunity.

"Now, back to that 'always interviewing' thing," Dr. John continued. He looked around the classroom, intent. "You have, at most, five to seven seconds to make a first impression. I saw one study that said you have less than one second! Regardless, it's a short amount of time for someone to evaluate you. If your first impression is powerful enough, people will never *forget* you. If not, they will never *remember* you. And because the initial encounter is so crucial, you need to get in the habit of applying the keys to professional success in both formal and informal situations. Formal interviews or client presentations are obvious places to be on top of your game, but if you're to be men and women of influence, you must also consider less formal occasions. Always present yourself well. Informal 'interviews' can include a date, social event, or a casual first introduction. But make no mistake—*you're always interviewing.* These may be situations where you would never consider that an interview is taking place when that is *exactly* what is happening."

Dr. John stood up straight, put on a smile, and walked out from behind the podium, modeling a proper first impression. "People will note whether or not you make eye contact and use appropriate words, your voice tone, body language, and overall demeanor. They also assess who you are based on the content of your stories. Given this, every interpersonal communication has at stake the opportunity of making a lasting and favorable impression. So say it together with me: **I am always interviewing.**"

Dr. John paused and waited as the class chorused the mantra back to him. He smiled. "Now let's talk about our next challenge. The timing is perfect. This week is career fair, as I'm sure you are all aware. Over eight hundred companies will be on campus. Many of you are signed up for interviews. Others are already set after graduation. Regardless, I want each of you to attend the career fair long enough to ask the three reverse interview questions to someone either at a booth or in your actual interview. Try to record your answers as soon as possible after your interaction, and then send them to me through the portal by next Monday before class. Everybody got it?" Dr. John asked.

Tricia Thompson raised her hand. "Back to the interview. What about following up with the company you interview with? I never know what the protocol is on that."

Dr. John nodded. "Excellent question! You're reading ahead in the syllabus, I see. Next time we meet, I will cover the topic of the unforgettable follow-up—both for interviews and life in general. It will include one piece of advice that will help make your efforts *undefeatable.*"

Dr. John noticed a few perplexed looks. "Trust me! Please read **chapter 8** for our discussion next time. Have a great day, everyone!"

FOURTEEN

THE FUTURE

Life is the art of drawing without an eraser.

—JOHN W. GARDNER

Aaron approached Dr. John's desk immediately after class ended.

"Hello, Aaron. How was your spring break?"

Aaron blinked. "What? Oh . . . It was good. I went skiing with some old high school friends. The snow was great, and I can't believe the Eagles are doing so well! I think they might go all the way!" Aaron exclaimed.

"Yes, it is exciting, no doubt! Are you going to Houston if they make it?" Dr. John asked.

"Yes, sir! I wouldn't miss it! By the way, I loved your Coach Wooden story today. Did you know he could have had an eleventh championship, but his team never played the game?" Aaron asked.

Dr. John was intrigued. "Tell me more."

"In his first year as a college head coach at Indiana State in 1947, his team was invited to the final four of the tournament. Coach Wooden declined the invitation because the organizers said he could not bring his only African American player," Aaron said, proud he knew something his mentor didn't.

"That's character in action, isn't it? I'm impressed you knew that story, Aaron. Thank you for sharing it," Dr. John replied. He noticed Aaron was getting fidgety. There was something on the young man's mind.

It didn't take long for it to come out. "Hey, Dr. John, what did you think of Amanda?"

Dr. John feigned a confused expression. "Amanda who?"

Aaron paused.

Dr. John chuckled. "Of course, Amanda Watkins. She was delightful! I didn't have that much time to talk to her, but my wife spent some time with her and liked her very much. By all accounts, you have a good one there, Aaron."

"Well, thank you. She said great things about you and Mrs. Daniels also. She said the trip was extraordinary and that she wished she could take your class. She also said she would love to have Mrs. Daniels as a mentor," Aaron replied.

"Maybe she can do both! We'll see." Dr. John looked at Aaron. "Is she feeling OK after the trip? It was pretty intense."

"She's OK, I guess. She is still having some pretty bad headaches, though. I'm about to meet her to go to the clinic just to make sure." Aaron answered. He shifted from foot to foot, obviously nervous. "Dr. John, can I ask you something?"

"Sure, what's up?"

"I have some ideas on how to propose to Amanda, and I wanted to run them by you."

Dr. John held back a bigger smile. "Of course! I'd love to help!"

Aaron laughed uneasily. "Well, first things first, right?" He pulled out a maroon velvet box. "I have a ring!"

"Oh, nice! Let me take a look here." Dr. John opened the box slowly and half rotated it so the ring caught the light. He nodded, impressed. "Well done, Aaron! She will be very excited. I guess you learned all about the three Cs of diamonds—cut, color, and clarity?"

Aaron shook his head ruefully. "Yes, sir. It gets kind of complicated and confusing."

"Haha, yes, I agree. I've had the lecture a couple of times myself . . ." Dr. John trailed off, looking nostalgic for a moment. "Maybe they should add those two Cs to the process—*complicated* and *confusing*." They both laughed, and Dr. John carefully handed Aaron back the ring. "So how are you going to pop the big question?" Dr. John asked.

"Well, her birthday is May 2—which is the Friday before Dead Week. So, there are no classes that next week, and we won't have to worry about final exams until the next Monday. I figured that's the perfect time. She will always remember it being on her birthday too."

"Good so far." Dr. John nodded. "What else?"

"The Legacy Oak—you know, the huge tree by the bench at the end of Heroes Way?"

"Yes, I know."

"Well, I reserved it for like ten o'clock that evening. So, I can take her to a birthday dinner and then get there like in plenty of time."

Dr. John smiled. The unconscious tics he had warned his students against earlier in the semester were resurfacing. He could tell that Aaron was nervous.

"I had no idea you had to reserve it," Dr. John said.

"I might have been OK without a reservation, but I don't want to take any chances. It's a big tradition to propose there, you know," Aaron explained.

"I understand, Aaron. You're wise to make sure all your bases are covered. This is important stuff! So, you have the ring, and you're getting on one knee, right?" Dr. John asked.

Aaron stared. "Of course!" he exclaimed, as if it hadn't even been a question.

Dr. John summarized. "So, you will be under the Legacy Oak, traditional and meaningful to you both as Eagles, on her birthday, after a nice dinner out to celebrate. Hopefully it will be a clear night with stars out in full force."

"Exactly!" Aaron agreed. "And then there is one other thing I'm gonna do that will make it totally unique."

"Bring it!"

"Well, I can't remember if I told you that I'm a member of State U's acapella group, the HarmonEagles. Have you heard of them?"

Dr. John's eyes widened, and then he went into a full-on belly laugh.

Aaron looked up sharply. "What's so funny?" he demanded.

"No, no, you're fine," Dr. John assured him when he caught his breath. "It's just, that's one clever name for a music group."

Aaron flushed and shuffled his feet. "Yeah, yeah, I didn't come up with it. I know it's cheesy." He recovered and continued. "At any rate, I've asked a quartet from my group to hide in the hedges nearby and, when we get right under the tree, to start singing 'Daisy Bell'—you know, 'A Bicycle Built for Two.'"

Dr. John interrupted, "Wait, let me think of the words: 'Daisy, Daisy, give me your answer, do . . . I'm half-crazy, all for the love of you . . . It won't be a stylish marriage . . . I can't afford a carriage.' You know, Aaron, I never thought of that as a proposal song, but it's perfect! And it has the added bonus of lowering her expectations for fame and fortune!"

"Yeah, right?!" Aaron agreed as both laughed.

"May I ask, what's the story behind that being her favorite song?"

"Well, the first time I met Amanda, she told me a story about her father. When she was a little girl, he brought home a shiny maroon two-seater bike for her birthday. It had those plastic streamers coming out of the handles."

"I remember those!" Dr. John broke in.

Aaron nodded. "And she said he would always take a playing card and a clothespin and attach it to the front wheel so that it would hit the spokes as they rode. He said it reminded him of when he was a boy. The sound of the card in the spokes was his 'motorcycle engine.'"

"I did that too! That's old school!" Dr. John laughed.

"She said they would ride every Saturday morning, and whenever the card wore out, he would pull out a new deck of playing cards and remove the queen of hearts to attach it to the bike. As he did this, he would say, 'Amanda, remember—you're the queen of your own heart. Right now, you've given it to me. But there will come a day when you'll want to give it to another man. And so, when the right man sits on this front seat, I'll be there to push you on your way.'"

It was a sweet story that made Dr. John think of his own two daughters. He looked down for a long moment.

Aaron blushed again. "Well, anyway," Aaron continued, "When the singing starts, I'll take her other hand and break into a waltz as they sing—"

Dr. John interrupted, "Wait—you're going to *waltz*?"

"Uh . . . yeah. I'm not a dancer, but Amanda loves to dance. And then, right as they're finished singing, I'll go to one knee and ask her to marry me. Do you think that plan is OK?"

A slow smile came across Dr. John's face. "I think that it's *unbelievable!*"

Aaron's face lit up as Dr. John raised his hand for a high five. Dr. John added, "I also think Amanda is one blessed young lady. Congratulations, Aaron."

Is he choked up? Aaron thought to himself.

"Now, what about her dad?" Dr. John asked. "Mr.—"

"Watkins?" Aaron filled in.

"How are you going to ask his blessing?"

Aaron frowned. "Uh . . . well . . . I'm not sure, now that you mention it. Isn't it up to Amanda whether she marries me or not?"

Dr. John tilted his head, acknowledging the point. "Of course it is, but asking her parents' blessing is still the classy thing to do."

Aaron sighed. "Yeah. You're right," he admitted. "Do you have any suggestions?"

Dr. John smiled. "Well, let's think about this a moment. This is definitely a time one would want to choose one's words wisely, wouldn't you agree?"

"Yes, sir. For sure."

"Now, I would say you don't want to beat around the bush too much with this conversation, because Mr. Watkins will likely suspect something is up when you ask to meet with him."

Dr. John could tell he had the young man's undivided attention. "Yes, sir."

"You could start by simply thanking him for his time and for meeting with you and then go right for it—something like,

'Mr. Watkins, as you know, I have come to grow quite fond of your daughter. I believe we are both at a place where we want to consider a lifelong relationship—'"

Aaron interrupted. "That's good! I like that!" He pulled out his phone and started typing notes.

Dr. John smiled and continued, "Then, without hesitation, you say: 'And so I wanted to talk to you today to get any guidance and advice you might want to give me . . . and mostly, I'd love to get your blessing.'"

"Wow, that's pretty smooth, Dr. John!" Aaron exclaimed.

"I'm glad I could help, Aaron. Now, one more thing. How will you remember this? You want to be tight with it—and to the point." They both pondered for a moment. Then Dr. John had an idea. "How about a little mnemonic? So your main points are that you've grown *fond* of his daughter, you want a *lifelong* relationship, and you would like his *advice* and *guidance*. F-L-A-G. Flag! There you go. You are a prince bearing your flag to win over the king's *favor*."

Aaron chuckled. "I guess so."

"Hey, if it helps you remember and get the job done, then who cares how quirky it is, right?" Dr. John squeezed his shoulder. "Congratulations," he repeated, with a fatherly smile.

Then he slowly exited with his briefcase in tow.

Aaron watched him go, feeling reassured as he did so. "Thank you, Dr. John."

At the other end of campus, Amanda Watkins had arrived early for her appointment at the State U Student Clinic. The longer she waited in the cold, silent consultation room, the more anxious she felt.

Finally, she was called in to the back. "Hi, Amanda. I'm Dr. Ramsey. How are you feeling today?"

Amanda looked up nervously. "Oh, fine. I think. Nice to meet you."

With her head down and eyes on Amanda's chart, the young physician responded, "Amanda, I've reviewed your file and your blood work, and I just don't see any cause for alarm. There are so many things that can cause temporary, intermittent headaches—and you're so healthy otherwise."

Amanda frowned. "I understand—I guess I was just worried about the fainting spells I had a while back. I just haven't felt like my usual self on the court or in the classroom. I'm kind of a perfectionist, I guess—"

Dr. Ramsey interrupted, "I'll tell you what: I'll prescribe a pain reliever that will give you a little more relief than the over-the-counter options. Why don't you keep me posted if anything unusual comes up—any more dizziness or if the headaches become more painful or more frequent."

"OK, Dr. Ramsey, thank you for your time." Amanda smiled.

"Of course." Dr. Ramsey nodded as she exited. The entire appointment had taken less than five minutes. Amanda headed back toward the waiting room and prescription filing window, uneasy. She understood the university clinic was busy, and it was the most economical option for student health-care issues. *If the blood work says I'm good, though, it has to be right. And if the new medication handles the headaches, that'll help a lot.*

Aaron was waiting for her as she turned away from the prescription window and signed the last of her paperwork. "What did the doctor say?" he asked her.

"She said not to worry. There's a lot of things that could cause my symptoms—so just *keep calm and carry on*," Amanda answered.

Aaron smiled in relief and pulled her close with one arm as they left the clinic.

"Hey, you never finished telling me about your trip," he said.

"Oh, it was so great! The history and scenery were wonderful, but my favorite part was meeting Mrs. Daniels. Did you know she is an attorney?"

"No, I didn't. Nice," Aaron said.

"Yeah, in fact, I've even thought lately that maybe I could take a shot at law school," Amanda told him.

"Really?"

"Sure . . . Why not? I don't have to get caught up in the big money scene. Anicia told me about several nonprofit legal organizations with missions like representing orphans or preserving religious freedom. And she said having my own firm later could provide a flexible schedule for when I wanted to have kids." She smiled, waiting for Aaron's reaction.

Aaron looked over at his girlfriend. "Kids, huh?" he grinned. *One step at a time!* he thought, stomach in knots as he considered how big their future was. He shook his head playfully and tweaked Amanda's nose. She made a face at him. "OK. We'll see."

8

FIFTEEN

Connectedness

Man has no nobler or more valuable possession than time.

—Thomas Jefferson

"Good morning, all!"

The witness from history banner of Thomas Jefferson stood next to the lectern. Class quickly came together as Dr. John exclaimed, "How about those Eagles! One more win, and it's off to Houston and the Final Four!"

Coach Sullivan's team had had no real competition in the first three rounds of the national tournament. The regional final and Sullivan's first trip to the coveted last weekend were within reach. It was their next game against Duke on Saturday evening that would be the real challenge.

Dr. John shook his head, dismissing his dreams of the championship for the time being. "I would like nothing more than to spend all of class talking basketball, but we've got some work to do." Dr. John said. "When last we met, Ms. Thompson raised an excellent question concerning when and how to follow up after an interview. I'm going to answer that question—but as you will see, the answer is going to apply to more than just interviews. In fact, today I'll give you ideas that will apply to all of your relationships, be they business, social, or family. There's a huge and unique opportunity on the table, and I intend to make sure you seize it. But first I want to hear how the career fair went. Who wants to share? Let's start with the first question you were assigned to ask the interviewer: What brought you to this company? Ms. Moore?"

"I asked four people that question, and I think only one gave a good answer. Two of them said, 'I just needed a job,'" Hannah answered.

"Interesting. Was that valuable feedback?" Dr. John asked.

"Yes! It was definitely a clarifying question to ask," Hannah replied.

"How did your interviewers describe their company values? Anyone?"

"One guy told a great story about his grandfather, who walked on the moon!" David Freiberg blurted out.

"Wow. That would be a hard story to beat. I'm curious, how did he relate that to his company's values?" Dr. John asked.

"Well, it was an aerospace company, and their slogan is No Boundaries. He said just like his grandfather was a space pioneer, he wanted to have an adventurous career as well. His company's mission of innovation in transportation resonated with him."

"That's impressive," Dr. John commented. "Anyone want to take the last one? What answer did you get when you asked about the biggest challenge their company faces? Ryan?"

"Yes, sir. I asked at least five people, and four of them told me no one ever asked them that question. All the others said they didn't know."

Dr. John smiled. "All of you, take note: if you ask a question your interviewer can't answer, guess what might happen?"

Aaron raised his hand. "They might call you back?"

"Exactly!" Dr. John exclaimed. "The chances are good they will call you back either with an answer to your question—or, more likely, to ask you in for another interview because you have made a notable impression with such good questions. Nice job, everyone. I look forward to reading more of your answers. Let's move on to key to professional success number eight: **connectedness.**

"Now, there are two things that are certain concerning technology: (1) it has changed our lives forever, both positively and negatively, and (2) it is not going away. Yet, in our highly connected world, it seems we are more *dis*connected than ever. Today we will discuss all the ways we communicate in order to deepen our relationships. Let's take a look."

Dr. John walked to the whiteboard, where he had already written the words "The Scale of Communication Connectivity."

He asked, "What is the simplest way to communicate with someone today that also provides the *least* amount of interpersonal connection? Aisha?"

"Is it a text?" she guessed.

Dr. John nodded. "That's it, and on a scale of one to ten, it gets a one." Dr. John wrote it on the board and continued, "Texting is the easiest and most efficient way to communicate today. It's mobile, instantaneous, and ubiquitous in its usage. I like the word your textbook uses: mobiquitous. A text recipient responds in real time. Yet what texting offers in efficiency, it typically lacks in message length and emotional connection, although I know emojis and other characters enhance that. The risk of miscommunicating how you feel and misinterpreting what other people mean is the main reason it gets such a low connectivity score."

Dr. John looked back at the class. "What communication method would come next on the scale? Ms. Martinez?"

"Email?"

Dr. John wrote the answer on the board. "That is correct. The obvious advantages over texting are the length of message it affords and the ability to copy many more recipients. Thus, the sender can expound on thoughts or instructions and can disseminate messages much more broadly. Additionally, the immediate reply pressure inherent with texting is somewhat removed. This increases an email's convenience factor. Email gets a score of three out of ten.

"What's next?" Dr. John asked.

"Telephone," several voices said in unison.

"Good. Yes." Dr. John wrote a six next to the word "telephone" on the board. "Why do you suppose a phone call gets double the value of an email on this scale?" he asked.

"Maybe because you can hear their voice and can respond quicker?" Aaron answered.

"That's right, Aaron. *Tone of voice* is the most important component of interpersonal communication. And the real-time opportunity for back and forth in a verbal exchange brings more complexity and nuance to the conversation. Digital communication can't deliver that. In my opinion, one way to set yourself apart in this generation is to use the phone more."

A few groans sounded around the classroom. Dr. John ignored them. "Let's keep going. What do you think is next on our scale that brings an even stronger connection than a phone call?"

"A face-to-face conversation?" an unidentified voice from the back hazarded. Aaron looked back for the speaker and saw Maria Lopez taking notes again.

"I didn't catch who said that, but that's correct," Dr. John agreed. "A face-to-face conversation receives a score of nine out of ten. It scores so high because, as studies show, body language plays a critical role in nonverbal communications."

Deron asked, "Wait—what about a video conference. Wouldn't that get the same score?"

"Great question, Mr. Johnson," Dr. John acknowledged. "I would give video conferencing a score of seven. Even though it seems like a face-to-face conversation in most ways, it's not exactly the same for one interesting reason—the whites of your eyes. The eyes are the windows to the soul, right?" Dr. John squeezed "video conference" in between "phone call" and "face-to-face conversation."

"You see, I can tell, for example, that Mrs. Lopez—all the way on the back row—is looking directly at me right now," Dr. John explained.

Maria waved and smiled.

"Humans are equipped with a unique ability to tell where someone is looking even though they may be a good distance away. But the ability to see the whites of someone's eyes is slightly muted on video, even at the highest resolutions. In addition, unlike in a face-to-face conversation, you can't see someone entirely. The screen typically shows only their torso and face, so full body language is mostly hidden."

Dr. John turned back to the class. "So, what do you think might get a ten out of ten? Is there anything?"

The class seemed puzzled. Then Aaron thought he knew, but his front-row companion beat him to it.

"Yes, Natalie?"

"A handwritten note?"

"You got it!" Dr. John wrote "HANDWRITTEN NOTE" in all caps on the board.

"Believe it or not, this centuries-old lost art of communicating sentiments in your own hand is a twenty-first century trump card—no pun intended," Dr. John stated. "With any significant encounter or occasion, with the exception of maybe a marriage proposal . . ."

Dr. John paused to a few snickers and glanced at Aaron. Aaron grinned.

". . . You can make the most positive and lasting impression with a handwritten note. It's a great follow-up gesture and one of the most impactful ways you can communicate, period, because it brings out the best in you."

Dr. John continued, "Electronic communication is a big time saver. However, what we gain in speed, we lose in connection. By taking the extra time to write a card, find an address, and then mail it, you have in effect, said, 'I could have texted in fifteen seconds or less, but time is the most valuable thing anyone owns. I felt like it was worth giving up a few extra minutes of my day in order to make sure you know how important this communication—and our relationship—is to me.' You don't have to say any of that out loud because the mere act of sending the card says it for you. That's powerful.

"A letter's value almost always exceeds the writer's effort. A personal note speaks to authenticity like no other form of communication. It's universally accepted in a positive way," Dr. John said. "Prominent leaders know the influence of their own handwriting. President Lincoln certainly knew this, as a prolific letter writer. And he knew the symbolic power of his written signature as well. So much so that he actually signed an amendment to the constitution. It's not required by law, and he is the only president ever to do so. He knew the significance this simple act would have on the Thirteenth Amendment—which abolished slavery.

"Presidents George H. W. Bush and Bill Clinton are also known for their note-writing proclivity and built their careers on their ability to communicate in this manner. Mozart, Napoleon, Helen Keller, Mother Teresa, and Einstein all followed suit. It's no coincidence. Which brings me to our witness from history for today . . ."

Dr. John turned to his left to the Jefferson banner. Atop was the word *Liberty*.

"Maybe the best summation of Thomas Jefferson's life was provided by President Kennedy, who once said at a White House dinner gathering of Nobel Prize winners, 'I think this is the most extraordinary collection of talent and human knowledge that has ever been gathered at the White House, with the possible exception of when Thomas Jefferson dined alone.'"

Dr. John grinned at the old quip. "Jefferson was only thirty-two years old when he penned the Declaration of Independence—which may be the most important man-made document of all time. But he also used his penchant for writing to pen more than twenty thousand notes and letters in his lifetime. He understood that handwriting is like a fingerprint. It can't be faked. It can't be imitated in print or voice. It has an immutable authenticity.

"In spite of the technology we have available, ink on paper is still the best way to express the thoughts that matter most. The act of writing results in more meaningful words because you don't want to write the card over again—and because you also know that there's a high likelihood it will be kept for a long time.

"People usually don't discard handwritten missives. In fact, I have a 'treasure chest' of cards and letters I keep at both home and office. Many of them are from students like you. Handwritten notes are saved because they keep on giving. When they are reread, they provide the same feelings they did the first time—or feelings even more intense. They're like a gift waiting to be reopened in the future. By contrast, verbal compliments are typically gone in just a few minutes. And by the way, people don't typically print and save love *emails*."

Students laughed as Jake Connors raised his hand. "I see what you're getting at," Jake said, "but my handwriting is really bad. If nobody does this much anymore, does it really matter if we don't do it? What do you even say in a card?"

Several students nodded in agreement.

"Thank you for the questions, Mr. Connors," Dr. John responded. "I had a graduate school professor who said, 'Excuses reduce the uses.' That line has always stuck with me. I want you each to remember it too. Jake just offered up three of the main excuses people use to avoid writing cards and letters.

"My oldest son, John Jr., had the same complaint about bad handwriting. And in his case, he was right. His handwriting was terrible. But he stuck with it, and within six months of his dedicated card-writing effort, he showed me an email that actually complimented him on his handwriting! The point is: you can improve. It just takes practice. But even if your handwriting is poor, it's OK. Whenever people like you, they will like seeing your handwriting. Again, it's like your fingerprint. Everyone's is different, and imperfections are usually seen as marks of individuality—not as flaws.

"As far as the 'nobody does this anymore' excuse—that's the point! That's why it is such an opportunity for you to stand out!" Dr. John exclaimed.

"And you *do* know what to say. Remember the LAVA conversation you likely had with this person at some point? It's teeming with things you can refer to in order to connect with them.

"There are two other excuses I often hear for not writing handwritten notes. Neither of them fly with me either.

"Some say notes take too long to arrive in the mail. To that, I say, it's OK. The mailbox surprise is worth the wait. It's been said that we don't remember days; we remember moments. The opening and reading of a handwritten note is often one of those unforgettable moments. And by the way, it's fine to send an electronic thank-you *and* a card. In fact, it's even more of a surprise then because they considered your gratitude already expressed, right?

"Others claim they don't have the time to write cards and take them to a mailbox. When people say this, I reply that time is the most precious gift we can give. It's the 'great equalizer,' as they say. We all have twenty-four hours in a day. When you give up ten minutes to write a card instead of ten seconds to send a text, it speaks volumes on the value you place on your relationship with the person to whom you're writing. Mark this down: *if you will send one handwritten card five days a week for the rest of your career, you cannot fail.* As technology continues to encroach on our lives, handwritten notes will become even more valuable. Emerson said, 'Good manners are made up of petty sacrifices.' Sacrificing a few minutes for this daily endeavor is worth it. Trust me.

"Here are a few additional pointers to *make a note of.*" Dr. John cocked an eyebrow at the class.

He always looks up for a reaction to even the lamest of puns, Aaron mused.

"Use good materials for your cards and envelopes." Dr. John held up samples. "I like a rough-edged parchment card that reminds people of our founding documents and old grocery store paper sack material for my envelopes. Nostalgia connects, remember? There are several ideas for cards in **chapter 9** of your text. I would suggest that you make your personal notecard say something about *who you are.* Think of your own LAVA. Maybe you love horses or fishing or playing guitar. It works well to have these interests displayed on your personal cards. I have two designs. Both are simple." Dr. John held up the first.

"For personal messages, I have one with a sketching of quill pens and an open book, which shows my love for reading and writing. For business, mine has only my name in a typewriter font in the lower right-hand corner. No one uses typewriters anymore, but it lends to the idea that I believe in the fundamentals—*the things that don't change.* You can develop your own style that conveys subtle messages. Note that including your middle initial can be a good trick—research shows people with middle initials are deemed to be smarter." Dr. John grinned.

"You will also notice that my cards fold. This allows me to put a quote or passage on the top section and my message on the bottom. Yes, Joy?"

"How do you know what to put on the top of the card? What quote should you use?" Joy asked.

"Thank you for bringing that up. Once again, this is where LAVA comes in handy. You can place a quote that connects with the recipient based on your small-talk conversation. If they're a big golf fan, then maybe a quote from golfing legend Arnold Palmer would make a connection. If they are a spiritual person, then perhaps a verse or proverb will resonate. You get the point. Before this class is over, I'll supply you with over a thousand quotes you can use for any card you would ever need to write."

"Wow, thanks! That's great!" Joy exclaimed.

"As far as the bottom of the card, as I was discussing with Jake earlier, you'll know what to say. But whatever you say, include at least three sentences. If you want a classic look, then a fountain pen is hard to beat. I like to use brown ink because it's unique and it reminds people—even if only subconsciously—of some famous documents. Which ones do you think?"

"Our founding documents," James said. Dr. John looked at the shy student near the back. It was the first time he had ever spoken in class.

"Ah, you were listening, Mr. House. Thank you.

"Send thank-you cards as soon as possible," Dr. John told the class. "Even if you've offered a verbal or electronic thank-you. Always include a *date* on your card. Remember, people will read these again. And as I emphasized earlier, they will often have an even greater connection when they are read a second and third time. Handwritten notes are also the best way to say, 'I'm sorry,' and to express condolences."

Dr. John paused. "Let me end with a little secret sauce."

Students leaned forward.

"As I pass around some samples of cards that I use, what do you notice on the envelope?"

"A wax stamp?" Natalie answered, passing a sample to Aaron.

What the heck? Aaron thought, remembering Nicole and her little glue gun. *So weird.*

"That's it, Natalie. A wax stamp has been used throughout the centuries to certify the contents and to identify the sender of important correspondence. I would encourage each of you to make this a practice. Your contemporaries will not do this. Therefore, you will stand out. Furthermore, I would take it one more step.

"Anytime you are complimented on this unique approach, send that person a wax stamp of their own. It can simply be their last initial. These are inexpensive and make great and lasting *impressions*."

Dr. John continued, "Another idea to make you stand out is to use actual postage stamps. Never use a postage meter for handwritten notes. And when you choose your stamps, look for more than the standard flag stamp. Look for unique stamps that give the recipient a pause in their day. Old, classic pickup truck stamps, comic strip superheroes, historical figures . . . you get the idea. Maybe a stamp that resonates deeply with someone. My youngest son once met a gentleman who had been awarded two purple hearts for his service in action. Well, they make purple heart postage stamps. When my son sent this gentleman a card, he sent not just one stamp—all that was required to mail the card—but *two* purple hearts to represent and honor this patriot for his service.

"Finally," Dr. John said, "you may be wondering how to end a card or a letter. What valedictions are most effective? The answer: those that express gratitude. *Thanks, Thank you, Thanks in advance, Many thanks,* all work well if the note calls for it. *Warm regards, Sincerely,* or *Respectfully* nearly always work well. And believe it or not, the worst way to close a note is with the word *Best.*"

Dr. John collected his samples from the class. "I want you to understand that the power of the personal note will never be diminished. It's an invaluable tool to help ensure your success in business and enhance both your current and future relationships. And I will say it again—write one note every day, and you will be astonished at the doors that will open for you. So guess what we are going to do for our next challenge? We are going to send some notes.

"This challenge is due two weeks from today, but you need to get on it right away. I want you to send out three handwritten notes. They can be either thank-you notes or 'thinking of you' notes. Perhaps you have a specific occasion to thank someone who has helped you lately—maybe an interviewer, or someone to whom an expression of gratitude is long overdue. A friend, family member, mentor, professor . . . it doesn't matter. Follow the guidelines we talked about, and try to get them in the mail no later than this Thursday. That will give you ten days or so to get any feedback. I realize you may not get responses in time to report them to me, but try to get them out so you have a chance. If you get a response by the deadline, then report it. Otherwise, I want you to at least tell me about the three cards you sent. I don't need names; just a description.

"In closing, I have one more thing to share with you." Dr. John reached into his left inside coat pocket and pulled out a well-worn greeting card. He slowly put on his reading glasses, then carefully opened the envelope.

Students were silent.

Dr. John held up the card to show to the class. "At the top, it says, 'If your actions inspire others to dream more, learn more, do more and become more; then you are a leader.' John Quincy Adams." He smiled and began reading.

Howdy Dad,

First things first, I miss you and the family so much! Thank you for the book and the awesome shirt! I love it! Thus far, our time in-country has been very challenging but rewarding. My job as a platoon leader is sixteen to eighteen hours a day with hard—sometimes brutal—never-ceasing work. While it is stressful, it is also humbling. I know I'm gaining invaluable experience and perspective. The locals here work so hard, and with a smile on their face. They are so appreciative of what we are doing for them. I've definitely started to get close to them.

Well, it's almost time for another patrol. I just wanted to tell you that I thank God every day (Dr. John paused) *for having such an incredible dad as a mentor and a role model. While I'm here doing what I love—serving my country and protecting freedom— not a day goes by that I don't recall something you or Anicia taught me through the years. Love y'all a ton. Hope everything is going well with your mission too. Tell the family hey for me.*

As ever—your son,
Nate

PS: Where can I get more of this cool stationary? I'm
running out!

Several students laughed at the postscript . . . some in
order to give Dr. John a few more seconds to collect himself.
Dr. John casually touched a corner of his eye, wiping away a
tear. Clearing his throat, he said, "I'm sorry. This card is from
my youngest son, who is serving overseas. I never fail to get
a little choked up when I read it. And even though he used
the word 'awesome'"—there was more supportive laughter at
this—"it means more to me every time I read it."

Dr. John looked up. He swallowed. He nodded once.
"That's the power of the perfect ten of *connectedness*. That's
the power of the handwritten note! See you next time!"

Students exited class earlier than usual, as the awkwardness of the situation dictated. Dr. John stood over his desk,
staring at the card he had just shared. Aaron suspected that
Dr. John carried that missive next to his heart everywhere he
went, so he could think and pray about his son. As Aaron was
leaving, he suddenly stopped and turned around. "Excuse me,
Dr. John?"

Startled from his thoughts, Dr. John responded, "Oh . . .
yes. Hi, Aaron. How are you today?"

"I'm fine, Dr. John. You OK?"

"Yes, I'm fine," he answered as he carefully placed the card
back in his jacket.

"May I ask you a personal question about Nate?"

"Sure, I suppose. What is it?"

"Why did he join? Why did your son decide on a career in the military? It seems like such a sacrifice. Do you see him often?"

Dr. John sighed and looked long at Aaron before he answered. "You're right. It's difficult not seeing him. The truth is we rarely get to even hear from him. He's in Special Forces, which means his activities are usually kept secret. It's been twenty-seven days since our last contact. But you asked why he joined?"

"Yes."

"Well, he certainly didn't need to. He has an advanced degree from State U, and his career prospects are strong. But since he was a little boy, he wanted to be a soldier. I suspect 9/11 had something to do with it. He was just nine years old when it happened. When he asked me about a military career, I told him, 'In this life, you don't get many chances to make a difference.'" Dr. John's voice cracked. "We just pray for his safety and his mission each day and trust that God will provide a hedge of protection around him. He's our Psalms 91 kid."

Aaron could see that Dr. John was getting emotional again.

"Thank you, Dr. John."

"Of course."

As he reached the classroom doorway, Aaron looked back. Dr. John was leaning on the lectern . . . weeping.

Outside of the classroom, Aaron pulled up Psalms 91 on his phone.

> You will not fear the terror of the night,
> nor the arrow that flies by day . . .
> A thousand may fall at your side,

Ten thousand at your right hand,
But it will not come near you . . .
No harm will overtake you,
No disaster will come to your tent.
For He will command his angels concerning you
To guard you in all your ways . . .

As he left the building, Aaron said a prayer of his own for Nate, Dr. John, and their family.

SIXTEEN

THE GAME PLAN

*We rarely forget that which
has made a deep impression
on our minds.*

—TRYON EDWARDS

Dr. John picked up his ringing phone. "Hello?"

"Johnny!" Coach Joe boomed through the speaker.

"Coach, congratulations! What a win! Did you ever think this day would come? The Final Four!"

"Honestly, Johnny, no. It's a dream come true, as you can imagine. And to have it in our home state—one hundred miles away, with Tech U in the other semifinal? The stars seem to be aligning for quite an event," Coach Joe said.

"Well, I could not be happier for you, Coach. You deserve this," Dr. John assured his old friend.

"Thank you, Johnny. In fact, I called to tell you I have two tickets with your name on them for Saturday's game. Here's the only catch—no locker room speeches this time!"

"Yeah, I figured I was done after last time," Dr. John laughed. "You're thirty-five and one, and I'm the *one*." As Coach Joe laughed, Dr. John hesitated. "Uh-oh." He stared at his phone. "Is Saturday the second?"

"That's right! Saturday, April 2. Why?" Coach Joe asked.

Dr. John's heart sank. "I have a wedding to go to." Dr. John grimaced.

"A wedding? Whose wedding? Who schedules a wedding during the Final Four?!" Coach Joe wanted to know.

"My niece. And the irony is, she and her fiancé are both State U alumni. I haven't reached out, but I'm sure they feel terrible about it. But in fairness, Coach, who would have thought you would make this kind of run, right?" Dr. John tried to soften his disappointment.

Coach Joe sighed. "I guess you're right. Can you miss it?"

From his tone, Dr. John could tell the coach already knew the answer. "No, I'm sure I can't. Plus, I wouldn't if I could. Family and all."

"Gosh, I'm sorry, Johnny. I understand. I'll tell you what I will do. I'll find some big donors to give these two tickets to, and if we make it to the final, you and John Jr. are behind the bench. I'll find a way to get two extra press passes. How does that sound?"

Dr. John smiled wide and punched the air. "That sounds *unbelievable*, Coach! Thank you!"

"One more thing, Johnny," Coach Joe said.

"Yes. What is it?"

"If we play the Ugly Orange in the final, I'm going to need your help," Coach told him.

"How so?"

"Just stay ready, Johnny."

"I'm always ready, Coach!" Dr. John promised.

April 2 was a beautiful spring evening for a wedding. The grounds of the iconic Hotel El in Austin provided an enchanting atmosphere that any bride would cherish, and as Dr. John sat in the audience before the event, he thought his niece, Marcella, looked magazine-cover radiant.

While Dr. John and his eldest son were pleased to attend the event—Marcella had been a friend as well as a cousin to John Jr. his entire life—both men lamented that the wedding had landed on the same day as the Eagles' semifinal! The game started about an hour before the ceremony.

Dr. John and John Jr. took turns watching the game on their phone—usually as they hurried off to the men's room. A casual observer might have suspected they had accidently doubled up on their diuretics. State U was a two-point favorite and had a comfortable nine-point lead over Indiana at the end of the first half. Marcella's wedding began a few minutes after the second half started.

The minister stepped to the lectern and said, "Dearly beloved, we are gathered here this evening to bear witness to the holy matrimony of Marcella and Douglas. For any basketball fans in attendance today, I understand there is an extraordinarily exciting event occurring—even as I speak. The bride and groom would kindly ask that you not refer to any electronic devices—at least *during* the ceremony."

Several heads suddenly popped up in the crowd, and the audience let out a collective chuckle. But thirty-five minutes later, the "I dos" were said, and they were off! Not the happy new couple—the Eagles fans! They dashed in every direction—ten or fifteen small groups of people engrossed in their phones to catch the end of the game.

With fifty seconds remaining, State U was up five points, with Eli Driver shooting two free throws. He made them both. Indiana instituted the conventional strategy of fouling to make State U earn the victory at the line. The eleven-point victory at the end was deceptive—it had been a close game. Coach Joe was calm and humble as he shook hands with the opposing coach. He knew his job was not complete. His players celebrated, but they did not go overboard. They had the final to win yet, and it wasn't certain yet who they'd be facing.

Marcella and her new husband went off on their honeymoon celebrating like the rest of the State U fans—and praying State U went the distance.

On Sunday, as Dr. John and his family drove back home after spending the day with Marcella's family in Austin, they talked about Tech U's game with North Carolina. It had been a thriller! Tech U overcame a ten-point, second-half deficit to prevail by two with a shot at the buzzer in double overtime.

As Dr. John and his family rolled into their driveway at midnight, the stage was set for what every Texas basketball fan had hoped for—a showdown in Houston between the Lone Star State's two largest public universities. Dr. John and John Jr.'s exhaustion was tempered with a suspended sense of anticipation. "See you tomorrow, son," Dr. John said to his eldest.

Anicia gave her stepson a kiss on the cheek as he shuffled sleepily off to his own car.

What a day, Dr. John thought as he threw his keys on the kitchen island.

His phone rang. *Who could that be at this time of night?* Dr. John wondered. When he picked it up, he knew. "Coach! Congratulations!"

Coach Joe didn't waste any time getting down to business. "Thanks, but you saw the second game? Tech is next, and they *know* us. Johnny, I need your help."

"I guess you know each other pretty well by now," Dr. John agreed.

Coach Joe interrupted. "No. I mean they know our plays, our sets. We need new signals, new nomenclature for Tuesday night. Can you help us?"

Dr. John's head cleared as he understood what Coach was asking him to do. "Of course, Coach. It will be my pleasure."

"Meet me in Houston tomorrow at noon, and we'll talk. We practice at 3:00 p.m. And Johnny?"

"Yes, Coach?"

"This will be it for me."

Dr. John feared he knew what Coach Joe was saying. He hoped he was wrong. "Excuse me?"

"This will be my last go-around," Coach Joe confirmed. "Whether or not we win tomorrow—this has been an epic season. All I'd ever dreamed of. Best to go out on a high note. I'll tell the team in pregame." Coach Joe hung up.

Dr. John stared at his phone, torn between sadness and pride.

"OK, everybody up!" Coach Joe said in his "command and control" voice. "Gentlemen, I know you are as excited as I am about our opportunity tomorrow night. It's the rubber match we wanted with Tech, and there's nobody I would rather beat to bring home State U's first national championship."

Players jeered at Tech's mention and then cheered, anticipating their victory.

"We have a big job ahead of us, and I've invited Dr. Daniels here to help." Coach Joe motioned to Dr. John to speak.

"Thank you, Coach," Dr. John answered. "Men, we just spent the last two and a half hours discussing the concern Coach has expressed about the familiarity that Tech has with your playbook. You've played them twice, and they have scouted you almost every game this season. So it's time to change things up. How many of you took my How to Make a 4.0 in College seminar as freshmen?"

Nine of the twelve players raised their hands, and Eli said, "I've used it my whole college career to study; made me look smart!"

"Well, looks aren't everything, Driver," Coach Joe teased his star over the ensuing laughter.

Dr. John smiled and continued. "I recognize most of you," he told the team. "Our strategy here is simple. We are going to use the ready recall system and implement the classroom and president memory palaces. I will go over them both in the next twenty minutes, and then I'll provide worksheets that will enable you to have them in your subconscious by tomorrow afternoon."

"Any questions?" Coach Joe asked. When none were forthcoming, he nodded at the team. "OK. Let's get to work!"

Dr. John took the Eagles' offensive sets—numbered one to twelve—and changed them to corresponding objects found in a classroom. He then slowly and methodically taught the team the ready recall system that would enable each of them to instantly remember the play being called. Fortunately, for most of the players, it was just a refresher.

1. Whiteboard
2. Light Switch
3. Carpet
4. Chair
5. Book
6. Telephone
7. Door
8. Window
9. Table
10. Bottle
11. Marker
12. Filing Cabinet

In a similar manner, each defensive set would now correspond with a US president.

1. Washington
2. Adams
3. Jefferson
4. Madison
5. Monroe
6. Quincy (as in John *Quincy* Adams)
7. Jackson
8. Buchanan
9. Harrison
10. Tyler
11. Polk
12. Taylor

The players committed the plays to their worksheets to study over the next night and day. They would have them memorized before the final. As they finished learning the new names for their plays, Coach Joe remarked, "I like 'light switch' and 'door.' I believe Tech U may subconsciously think about our 'switching defense' or 'back door' plays. Also, two of our starters have presidents' last names, so we can use that to confuse them at an opportune moment, if it should come."

Coach stepped up in front of his team. "Now, we figure that by halftime, their assistant coaches will have broken the code. So, at that time, we'll switch. Offensive calls will become presidents, and defensive sets will become the classroom. The bottom line is that we will still need to execute tomorrow night if we want to cut down the nets on national TV. But this may at least throw them off in certain situations to give us an advantage. The game is going to come down to a bucket or two. Does everyone understand?"

The Eagles nodded. "Yes, sir!"

"I know Coach wants to use these today in practice," Dr. John said. "It won't be perfect yet, but take the sheets this evening so you can drill yourselves and each other. By lunch tomorrow—or, at the latest, by the shootaround tomorrow afternoon—you will have them down perfectly. The main concept to remember is that all of these are *synonyms*. 'One,' 'whiteboard' and 'Washington' all mean 'one.' 'Two,' 'light switch' and 'Adams' all mean 'two,' and so on."

Practice went well. Both Coach Joe and Dr. John were impressed by what quick studies the players were in learning the new call signs. After Coach Joe dismissed the players, Dr. John asked him, "Are you sure about this, Coach? Is this your last lap? Really?"

"It is. I've given it all I've got," Coach answered. "We will do our best tomorrow night, and then I have the fourth quarter of my own life to plan. It's about *legacy*, Johnny. Our children and our grandchildren need me and Nell. Basketball has been great to me. I've lived my career dream no matter what happens. But if I don't do all I possibly can to leave my family with the wisdom they need to carry on, then I will have accomplished nothing."

"I understand, Coach. Believe me. I understand."

SEVENTEEN

DRESS FOR SUCCESS

You never get a second chance to make a first impression.

—WILL ROGERS

"Good morning, ladies and gentlemen. Please be seated. Thank you," Dr. John greeted the class. He was dressed more formally than usual, with a matching maroon tie and cardigan that showed his school spirit. The campus was electric with excitement on this Monday morning with the National Championship game just ten hours away.

As the class came to order, an extraordinarily well-dressed couple was standing near a full-length mirror at the front of the classroom. The gentleman was dapper, tall, and lean. He looked like he had played college quarterback. He was wearing a charcoal gray suit and sporting a State U Eagles tie. The woman with him was striking, too, exquisitely attired in a black pencil skirt and a maroon business jacket to commemorate the big event. Students were attentive as they took notice of the guests.

"Today, we are going to be presenting our ninth key to professional success," Dr. John announced. "I'm thrilled to welcome not one but two guest speakers today.

"Chris and Sharon Kotten are the founders of Kotten Clothing, Inc. For more than three decades their associates have been advising professionals on **how to dress for success**. They have been featured in numerous radio and television interviews and in over 350 publications—including the *Wall Street Journal*. They have also been honored as distinguished alumni here at State U. Ladies and gentlemen, I present Chris and Sharon Kotten."

Applause filled the room.

"Thank you, Dr. John," Chris Kotten said. Suddenly, he whipped an Eagle towel out of the pocket of his suit and began swirling it in above his head. "Go State U! Go State U! Go State U!"

The surprised class quickly joined the chant, pumping their fists and stomping their feet. "How about those Eagles?" Chris cried over the class.

The students cheered and applauded. Dr. John clapped and gave Chris a thumbs up.

As the class settled, Chris grinned. "It's always so great to return home to State U."

"I agree!" Sharon added. "Now let's get to work. We're excited to be with you today to talk about presentation. We've all been told that you can't judge a book by its cover, but some of you may have already begun to realize that's not true in the real world! People *definitely* make assessments of you based on how you dress—especially in job interview or client situations."

Chris eyed the students. "I'll bet Dr. John has already told you that you only get one chance to make a first impression."

Heads all nodded.

"Yeah, well, he's right. And not only that—like it or not, you're always interviewing." Chris gave a nod to Dr. John as he smiled back.

Chris looked back to the class. "Did you know that people will make an evaluation of you fewer than seven seconds after meeting you? And like Mark Twain said, 'Naked people have little or no influence in society.'"

A roar of laughter filled the room. Dr. John just grinned and looked down. It was not an unexpected comment coming from Chris. He was always good for a crazy line or two when he spoke.

"But seriously," Chris said. "If you wear the wrong outfit in an interview, you can go from candidate to reject instantly. It's not fair. But like we tell our kids, 'The only kind of *fair* that's real is an amusement park with rides.'" He laughed at his own joke—just in case no one else did.

Sharon rolled her eyes at her husband. "Think of it like this—with cover letters, it's the opening paragraph that gets their attention. With a face-to-face encounter, it's how you dress and look that sets the tone." She then took a seat on a stool set up near Chris.

"There are three principles to consider when dressing for success," Chris went on. "The first is this: **dress for the position to which you aspire**. Not everyone wants to be a CEO, and that's OK. But if you do, *then you must dress like one*—even at the entry level. Remember, if you're in a large corporate environment, you are competing for the top positions. If a good first impression is important, then avoiding a bad or even average impression is also important. So you should maintain a reputation of *always* being presentable. Yes. A question?" Chris asked, catching sight of a raised hand.

"So are you saying we can't ever wear jeans again—ever? Almost all of my friends work in companies that have casual Fridays," Matt Williams said.

"Excellent question," Chris answered. "I'm saying just because you *can* dress down like everyone else doesn't mean you *should*. In my professional opinion, the casual dress trend we see today is another opportunity to be a cut above. Again, that's just me—and I sell clothes for a living. But I would still play it safe. With that said, there may be a cultural atmosphere in some companies where *not* dressing casual could be seen as strange—or even noncompliant. In that case, play along. But when you wear jeans, wear *nice* jeans. Here is a general rule of thumb—it's always better to be overdressed than underdressed.

"In general, make a *commitment* to being your best, no matter what. Whether it's your clothes or whatever—throw yourself into things. Especially when you're young and you don't have responsibilities like kids and stuff, get to work early, stay late, and add value. Even work a weekend now and then. If you do these extra things, you'll be amazed at how fast you rise. Your friends may brag about how much freedom they have at work, but they won't be developing the strong work habits they will need to be the best they can be. You will. If you are an individual who commits to excellence, you can write your own ticket to anywhere you want to go."

Chris looked at Dr. John. He rubbed the back of his neck. "Sorry about that, Dr. John. Sometimes I get off on a tangent."

Dr. John smiled and said, "No worries at all, Chris. I loved it."

Chris glanced at his wife, and she stood up. He took her place on the stool as she came up to speak. "My mom used to say, 'Life is 10 percent latitude and 90 percent attitude,'"

Sharon told the class. "Looking great helps your attitude—there's no question about it. Our company doesn't just build wardrobes, we build *confidence*."

Sharon held the projector remote in her hand. She flipped it on and began displaying photos of different professional wear. "Attention to detail is paramount in all of your business dress," she instructed. "Any of these colors in a wool blend—black, navy, gray, or brown—projects professionalism. Ladies, I would suggest minimal jewelry—either small, delicate pieces or one large piece. In official interviews, don't chew gum, and keep the perfume light as well. Interviewers or customers may have allergies. Chris, for example, is allergic to *everything*. I can't wear perfume at all." Sharon glanced and chuckled. "Look at him. He's about to sneeze just hearing the word *perfume*."

Chris made a sour face, and laughter ensued.

Sharon flicked the slides ahead. "Let's talk about skirts. Hems should extend below your fingertips when they are at your side—and preferably to your knees. A pencil skirt is a foundational item in any smart business wardrobe, and if you want to mix it with a mismatched jacket for a smart modern update occasionally, that's OK too.

"Keep patterns simple, like houndstooth or pinstripe," Sharon advised. "Solids are the safest bet. I know many women prefer pants. If you do as well, then go with cotton, silk, or a blend. Again, a solid in navy or black is perfect.

"I also like blazers because they always fit in a business situation. Those neutral colors like navy, black, brown, and tan all blend well with other colors. They're just hard to beat as good wardrobe staples. A blazer and a skirt are a good alternative to a suit."

Sharon clicked the remote, and pictures of several cute women's shoe styles came up on screen. "Shoes should be low enough to walk comfortably. No one wants to see you trip. It's also a good idea to have flats or sneakers with you in case you have to park and walk a ways. You can switch in the restroom before your meeting. A larger purse or briefcase is well suited for business meetings." Sharon flipped the presentation ahead another slide, and attractive, professional women came up on screen from the front and in profile. "Lastly, keep your hair neat, and make sure it's not in your face. Nothing fancy on the nails, and don't overdo the makeup, and you should be good."

Sharon saw Calli Clark raising her hand. "A question here?"

"Yes, ma'am. What about carrying a leather padfolio?"

"That would be fine, although I would still carry a purse if you go that route. The padfolio does not have to match your shoes or your purse. I prefer either black or brown. Burgundy is also OK."

Chris stood again and took the remote from his wife. "Thank you, Sharon. Excellent advice. The second principle of dressing for success is that **there is a difference between being stylish and being trendy**."

There were some confused looks around the classroom.

Chris flipped the remote ahead to a side-by-side comparison of two men's jackets. "For instance, men's jackets slowly switch back and forth between three-button and two-button as the *style*. They also go back and forth between narrow and wide lapels. Again, these are traditional aspects of men's jacket styles that change over the long term." He flipped ahead again. "But going from a regular fit to an extra-tight jacket is *trendy*.

And by the way, gentlemen, never button the bottom button on any jacket.

"Remember this: classic dress is *always* in style, but trends, by definition, come and go more quickly. If you enjoy trendy clothes, by all means, enjoy them in your social attire. But use discretion when deciding to wear them to the office or a business function. We want you to exude confidence and come across as wise beyond your years in every way. We know for sure that traditional style in your clothes is one way to communicate this.

"Let's talk about proper dress for the gentlemen," Chris said. "A guy's first impression starts with a foundation of clean and polished shoes. That's the first thing many look at when they see you in a suit or jacket. I like leather-soled shoes versus rubber—and I don't like to wear black shoes during the day. Some good folks in my business may disagree, but generally, black suits and black shoes are for weddings, funerals, and after six o'clock. Brown or burgundy shoes go with every other color of wool suit—be it navy, gray, olive, brown, etc. It's OK to wear a black sport coat, but still wear brown shoes with the pants. That said, always make sure your belt and your shoes are the same color."

He went on, "Earlier, Sharon said that attention to detail is paramount. That's true even down to something as seemingly trivial as the color of the buttons on your coat sleeves. Yes, that's right. For the record, suits should have buttons that are the same color as the fabric. Sport coats can have different-colored buttons.

"Doing these small things just right in regard to your wardrobe gives an important indication of how you will attend to other details in your job—and in your life. Dr. John often says it's about the fundamentals—in our business, we've found that's just right!"

Dr. John nodded and smiled in agreement.

Chris brought up a slide with a selection of neckties. "As far as ties go—and, for that matter, scarves for the ladies—anything within the blue or red color spectrum, including our beloved State U maroon, works well." Chris held up his tie and grinned. "Solids, stripes, or small patterns are also good. But an interview is not the time to wear your hot sauce or team tie. Button-down collars are OK with sports coats, but I would avoid wearing them with suits. And finally, don't wear a blue shirt with a black suit."

Chris and Sharon switched the stool once again, and Sharon shut off the projector and looked intently at the class. "The third and final key is this: **make an investment in yourself—and your wardrobe**. This one is pretty simple. What you do is one thing. Who you are is another. And how you present yourself says something about *who you are*."

Man, it's so easy to tell who Dr. John's disciples are, Aaron thought.

"It's been such a pleasure for me and Chris to be with you this morning," Sharon finished. "Thank you so much!"

Dr. John led the applause.

"Thank you, Chris and Sharon. You are true professionals and clearly born to do what you do." Dr. John checked his watch. "We have time for one or two additional questions." He surveyed the class. "Rachel?"

"Yes. Thank you for being with us today. I really enjoyed it! I was wondering . . . this all sounds good, but when you said to make an investment, that sounds like code for 'expensive.'"

A few murmurs of agreement were heard.

Sharon smiled. "Thank you for that insightful question. Let me ask you—anyone—what kind of car are you going to buy after you get your first job?"

"A Range Rover!" someone said from the back row.

"A Beamer!" another said.

"I hear some nice car brands being thrown out here. It may be a while before you can get that nice car, but you can dress well right away. And admittedly, high-quality apparel is not inexpensive. But don't stress too much. When you're starting out, you can get away with one suit and then some items that you can mix and match. Jackets, blouses, scarves, skirts, etc. Men can do the same with a sport coat or two, different ties, and shirts."

Chris interjected. "My dad taught me that you will never regret buying the best of anything. Quality lasts—and is therefore the better bargain in the long run. So when you begin your professional life in earnest, you must think in terms of making an *investment* in your wardrobe as opposed to just spending money on clothes. You will not regret it.

"We recommend you set a wardrobe budget. Oftentimes, professionals won't keep up the quality of their clothing because they tend to think of it as a big buying decision to get a ton of clothes at one time. And we all tend to put off big decisions. However, if you lock in a quarterly amount, for example, then it becomes a budget item, and you're always up to date and looking good!"

"Let's give our friends another round of applause!" Dr. John boomed. He glanced at the Kottens. "I believe Chris and Sharon are able to stay around for a few minutes after class?" They both nodded.

"Thank you again." Dr. John smiled as he shook their hands.

"You may have noticed, I did not bring a witness from history today," he told the class. "That's because *you* are the witness today." Dr. John motioned to the mirror. "Like it or not, how you dress and present yourself to the world will be a significant factor in your future success.

"Before I let you go today, I wanted to get back to Ms. Thompson's question from a while back about *when* to follow up after an interview or presentation. We talked last week about following up with handwritten thank-you notes, but there's a bit more to it, and while we're talking about presentation, it's a great time to address it."

Dr. John explained, "The first mistake people often make when following up is *failing to set the follow-up protocol* before you leave the interview. Simply ask at the end of the meeting, 'When can I expect to hear back from you with any further questions you may have for me?' This shows your eagerness to cooperate and also that you are interested in taking the business relationship to the next stage. If the answer to this question is three days, then feel free to call on day four if you haven't received any communication."

He continued, "The second follow-up mistake people often make is *hesitating to call back* at the established time for fear of being a pest. People get nervous. But as Cato said, 'He who hesitates is lost.' If you don't follow up in a timely and predetermined manner, you may well get lost in the mix because everyone is so busy. Don't see calling back for details as demonstrating impatience—instead, you are demonstrating enthusiasm for the offered opportunity.

"A follow-up time of three days almost always allows you time to get that handwritten note to them via snail mail before they get your follow-up call. As I've emphasized, write the card the same day—or the next at the latest. Like we talked about last time, this can set the table for much success. Especially now that you're so well dressed!"

Dr. John grinned at the class. "Our next key will focus on a method of making decisions through your life. I can't wait to tell you how to make life's big decisions next time we get together. No office hours today—I'm heading to Houston to see our Eagles BEAT THE HECK OUT OF TECH!"

The class cheered again and dispersed, and at the front of the classroom, a line formed to meet the Kottens.

After class, Aaron made his way to the library. He didn't feel motivated to study; he was as excited about the game as everyone else. But the ninety-minute time block was on his schedule, so he figured he should go ahead.

He entered study carrel twelve to see Lisa and Nicole Kosta had been using it today as well. "Oh, hi, girls. I haven't seen you in a while. How's it going?"

"Don't you look dressed up! You got a date?" Nicole teased, noticing his button-up and slacks.

"Yes, my girlfriend and I are going to the game," Aaron told her. "Can't wait! Are y'all going?"

"No, I'm going to the watch party at Metcalf Arena with my roomies," Nicole answered.

"I'm going to Metcalf with Chi-O, my sorority. It should be a blast!" Lisa added. "Hey, I met your girlfriend. Amanda Watkins? Plays volleyball?"

"Yes. She is—and she does," Aaron replied. "How do you know her?"

"I met her at a Chi-O meeting the other night. She's my roommate's little."

Aaron shook his head. "Oh. How about that?" *The world gets smaller every day.*

"She seems pretty sharp. My roommate said she goes on and on about you." Lisa smiled.

Nicole perked up. "Do tell!"

Lisa's phone beeped, and she looked down to see an alert. "Oh, shoot! Listen, I've got to go. I'm late for another meeting." She gathered her things.

Nicole slouched, disappointed at missing out on the girl talk. "Oh, too bad." Her eyes wandered over to Aaron, and she sat up again and propped her chin up on her hand to look at him. "So, Aaron, what do you feel is the biggest issue in your relationship with Amanda?"

"Nicole!" Lisa screeched.

Nicole looked back at her older sister innocently. "What?"

"You're not a counselor yet!" Nicole just batted her eyes at Lisa, and Lisa sighed. "Sorry, Aaron. I hate to leave you with this inquisition. Good luck!"

Aaron laughed nervously as Lisa left him alone in the carrel with Nicole. "No worries," he muttered. "Hah! Uh . . . she's a busy bee, isn't she?"

"Always!" Nicole answered. "But back to the question. What can I help you figure out about Amanda?"

Aaron ran his hand through his hair. "Well . . . uh, I don't know." Truthfully, everything was going great with Amanda, but Nicole looked so intent and eager to help he felt he had to say something.

"There's got to be *something*," Nicole urged him.

Aaron considered. "Well, I guess maybe I wish I could just help her more?"

Nicole latched onto this immediately. "How so?"

Aaron shrugged. "Sometimes, it's like she will be having a bad day, and I'll try to do what I can to get the answer to her problem or fix it, and she gets even more frustrated. Sometimes at me, and I haven't even done anything!"

Nicole started laughing even before Aaron could finish. Aaron frowned. "Why is that funny?"

"It's the old 'don't worry, honey. I can fix anything' syndrome. Every man has it," Nicole told him.

"What do you mean? How do you know?" Aaron narrowed his eyes. "How old are you, again?"

Nicole snorted. "Old enough to know this one. Let me give you some advice. Take it or leave it. When a girl tells you what is bothering her or that she had a bad day, she's not necessarily saying she wants you to fix it. More often than not, all she wants is for you to just *listen*. It's called having *empathy*. Just say, 'I'm sorry to hear that. If you would like to talk about it, I would be glad to.' Or just remember it this way: Your ears won't ever get you in trouble. But your *mouth* . . . different story."

Aaron blinked. He found himself strangely without a rebuttal. "OK . . ." He was always irritated when Amanda, his mother or sisters—or other female friends, for that matter—vented about a problem when they weren't asking for help. *Wow. This girl is like nineteen going on thirty-five. I hate to admit it, but her advice might be worth noting. After all, I guess listening CAN help.*

"Well, Nicole. What can I say? I think you're headed in the right direction with your career for sure!"

Nicole smiled back at him. "Thanks. And I gotta say, if that's the worst you've got, Aaron, you and Amanda are probably in pretty good shape." She made a face down at her chemistry textbook. "Back to work?"

"Back to work," Aaron agreed without enthusiasm.

EIGHTEEN

The Game

*A person does not become whole until they become
a part of something bigger than themselves.*

—Jim Valvano

James Nelson, play-by-play announcer for the college basketball national championships, was as excited as the roaring crowd as he began his opening remarks for the Tech U–State U game. "Howdy folks! WE ARE LIVE from Greatest Generation Stadium in Houston, Texas! Welcome, everyone, to the National Championship game, deep in the heart of the Lone Star State, where the biggest crowd in college basketball history will witness the two top-ranked teams—and the biggest rivals in all of college sports—go at it tonight! I'm here with my esteemed colleague, Billy Hacker. Billy, welcome. How do you see this contest tonight?"

Billy Hacker had to shout to be heard over the noise of the crowd, even with the microphone. "Well, Jimmy, I've been doing this game for thirty-three years, and I've never seen anything like this! There hasn't been this kind of excitement for basketball in Texas since the University of Houston's Phi Slamma Jamma back in the 1980s. The combined student enrollment for these two schools is well over one hundred thousand, and I think they are all here tonight. Tech comes in with just two losses, and of course, State's only loss was to Tech at Metcalf Arena."

"But it's bigger than this one game, isn't it, Billy?" Nelson asked.

"Yes, it is, Jimmy. These two have been going at it for over a hundred years, and tonight will be their 250th meeting. Tech has mostly dominated with, 164 wins to State's 85—and State has largely taken a back seat to the more dominant Tech program and Coach Clark Thorn's three national championships. State, on the other hand, has never come this far. All-Americans Sterling Sharper for Tech and Eli Driver for State will obviously be the key players. They both will have to stay out of foul trouble for their team to win. But the real story behind the scenes tonight may be on State's bench . . . and I don't mean the players. It's been reported that legendary Coach Joe Sullivan has decided this will be the last game of his forty-five-year career. He is telling his players of his decision as we speak."

And in fact, in the Eagles' dressing room, that was exactly what was happening. The State U team was unusually subdued. Cotton mouth and butterflies had come upon them like no other pregame before. Outside, the players could hear *BEAT THE HECK OUT OF TECH!* reverberating time and again at an almost deafening level. It wasn't a life-or-death situation by any means. But the looks on their faces told a different story.

Dr. John and John Jr. were against the back wall, trying to hide their urge to smile ear to ear. It was a serious moment, but what a moment! And what a privilege to be here!

Coach Joe held up his right hand to signal he was about to speak. He looked across the room and made eye contact with each player before he began. "Gentlemen, we are one of two teams left not just because of what you have done but because of *who you are.* We have already made history by making it this far. But tonight, we will be defined and remembered for our effort, our character, and our ability to handle adversity. And there will be plenty—from both our opponent and the referees. They will miss some calls, guaranteed. But we will get our share of breaks as well. So don't worry about them—that's my job. It will be physical out there because the refs don't want to determine the outcome of a championship game—especially down the stretch, if it's close.

"Visualize your free throws, talk on defense—I want the lady eating nachos on the top row to hear you. Eli, you have to pressure Sharper. Get under his chin. Make him use his left hand when possible. We will be starting with an offensive tip, and I know you have your ready recall play lists locked and loaded."

Coach Joe exchanged a nod with Dr. John before turning back to the team. "Trust your teammates! Be disciplined. Every loose ball is ours. When this is over, have no regrets. Be able to look yourself in the mirror and say, 'I gave it my all . . . and that's all that matters.' And one last thing . . ."

Coach paused. "I want you to take a moment and look at each of your teammates."

The team did as he said. No one spoke.

"This group of men will never be together again. This is it. Life and its circumstances take us away from each other eventually, and that is why this moment is so special. For me, it is particularly so . . . because . . ."

Coach Joe swallowed, uncharacteristically emotional. "Nell and I have made a decision that this will be the last game I coach for the Eagles. It has been a glorious ride. And there's no team I would rather it end with than this one! Win or lose—I hope you know I love you."

Players sat stunned. Dr. John looked down. Tears welled up.

Eli Driver broke the silence, standing. "This one's for Coach!" he shouted. "Everyone in here! 'Coach Joe' on three!"

"COACH JOE!" the team shouted, hands clasped together above their beloved leader's head.

As Dr. John and John Jr. made their way down the narrow hallway leading to the arena, John Jr. placed his hand on his dad's shoulder and said, "I wish Nate could see this!"

Dr. John replied "Me too, son. Me too."

As they squeezed into their seats behind the bench, Nelson boomed out over the stadium, "Here we go, folks: the game the college basketball world has waited for!"

"That's right, Jimmy—word is even Vegas couldn't decide a winner. The betting line is EVEN for the first time ever in a championship game."

State lined up with Driver—their only senior—Cade Carson, Matt Hall, and "the presidents," Steven Jefferson and Patrick Quincy. Tech countered with their own all-American, junior Sterling Sharper, a sophomore, and three freshmen. This crowd was almost five times larger than the last time the teams had met—evenly divided between Eagle fans and Tech U Steers fans.

Much like the contest that brought State its only loss of the year, the game started at a faster pace than Coach Joe had hoped. Tech took the lead early and then held an eight-to-ten-point margin for most of the first half.

This looks all too familiar, Coach Joe thought.

"Jimmy, I'm surprised at how easily Tech is getting into the basket," Hacker remarked. "Sharper is cutting through their defense at will. We knew he would get his points—but he's got twenty-two, and we are not even at halftime."

"I know what you're saying. Uh-oh. Look there, Billy," Nelson said. "We've got an injury on the floor. Oh my—that doesn't look good at all."

It was Eli Driver. With thirty-two seconds remaining before intermission, he had come down perfectly wrong on his left leg, pinning it across another player's shin with his full body weight. It was a compound fracture of the tibia—the type made famous by Washington Redskins quarterback Joe Theismann, who had suffered the career-ending injury on Monday Night Football in 1985. Like Theismann's, Eli's injury was so grotesque it was not shown on the replay screens above the stadium. All they saw was the knot of medical personnel around Driver, waving frantically for a stretcher and to get an ambulance ready.

The record crowd of 82,012 was silent. Coach Joe paced around the huddle of doctors. Head down.

After a few minutes, Coach Joe made his way back over to the bench. Eleven worried faces looked up. "Men, it looks pretty rough for Eli. Let's say a quick prayer for him and the doctors."

As they knelt in a circle, Dr. John walked over and put his hand firmly on Coach Joe's shoulder.

"Amen!" The team stood and applauded with the crowd as Eli was lifted onto a stretcher. He was in obvious agony.

He reached out for Coach Joe.

"Coach, listen! You can do this! I'm only one guy—"

"It's OK, Eli." Coach Joe clasped his hand. "You get well. We'll be fine."

Driver looked up again as they began to move him off the court. He lost sight of Coach Joe. "COURAGE!" he shouted. "COURAGE, guys! COOURAAGE!"

Dr. John, back in his seat, shook his head. *Courage indeed, Eli. Thank you.*

Play resumed, and State held the ball for the final shot of the half. Matt Hall drove to the basket and was fouled as he scored. He made the free throw, which brought the Eagles within seven points of Tech.

State U coaches considered their options at halftime. The new ready recall play codes had worked reasonably well in the first half, and they changed them as planned. That was at least one thing to make sure Tech was kept off balance. But without their star player, they knew this was going to be a tall order. Coach Joe gathered the team.

"Men, I knew we had a tremendous opportunity here this evening. I just had no idea it would be *this* big." Players looked around, puzzled. Eli Driver's injury was a real blow, and their faces reflected that reality.

Coach continued, "It was going to be a great victory . . . with Eli leading us. But *without* him"—he looked into the eyes of each player one at a time—"it will be a victory of proportions we could never have imagined. Now let's go win this thing!"

Eleven players jumped up shouting.

"'Eli' on three!" Coach Joe screamed.

"ELI!"

"We've got a subdued maroon section as the second half starts, Billy," Nelson commented as the players ran onto the court again.

"That's OK, Jimmy. This isn't Coach Joe's first rodeo."

"We'll see."

Freshman Kit Potter ably filled in for Eli Driver as the second half began. He scored eight points in the first five minutes, but then Tech took control of the tempo again. The Eagles clawed back to within four points with eight minutes on the clock. Then two successive foul calls went against them, with starter Matt Hall fouling out. Coach Joe was now without two starters in the last and biggest game of his career. Sterling Sharper was leading the Steers with thirty-six points and playing perhaps the best game of his career.

But as the teams traded baskets back and forth with Tech only able to maintain a narrow four- to six-point lead, the amazement in the stadium grew. "You know, Jimmy, on paper you certainly wouldn't expect State to even be competitive right now," Hacker remarked. "But the longer they stay in this game, the more confident their younger players will become."

"I agree, Billy . . ."

With fifteen seconds remaining, Steven Jefferson made a layup to bring the Eagles to within six. Tech called a timeout.

"All they have to do is hold the ball and wait to be fouled here, Jimmy. There's no need for Tech to take any unnecessary chances," Hacker said.

Tech inbounded to Sharper. He dribbled down, unguarded. He then inexplicably took a shot from behind the arc—no good.

State got the rebound, passed to Quincy—he took a three-point shot. Good!

"That's crazy!" Hacker cried. "I know Sharper has had the hot hand, but you don't shoot a three in that situation."

"I agree, Billy—wait, look at this!"

Tech's lead was down to three. With no timeouts left for either team, State double-teamed the Tech guards and forced a pass in to Tech's tallest player. He dribbled down court. Kit Potter—the freshman who had cost State their only loss of the season—poked the ball free from behind. Jefferson retrieved the ball and passed back to Potter for another three-point shot—good!

BUZZZZZ!

The crowd was screaming. "This is unbelievable, Billy!" Nelson yelled. "Tech had this game won! Now we are going to overtime."

"It's just so unusual to see a Thorn-coached team lose their bearings like that," Hacker observed.

"I'd still give Tech the advantage in overtime given State's loss of two key players," Nelson observed. "But it's not bedtime yet, America!"

"We're gonna be stayin' up late in Texas!" Hacker added.

In the first minute of the extra period, Tech took a six-point lead on successive three-pointers. State fought back to within three on a Jefferson three-pointer. Then Potter stole an inbounds pass, took the ball to the basket for a dunk, and was fouled.

"What a performance by this young freshman tonight, Jimmy," Hacker said. "For him to have to fill the shoes of their star player Eli Driver like he has; it's just remarkable . . ."

Potter missed the free throw.

With a one-point lead and the shot clock off, Tech passed the ball around in a keep-away fashion to avoid getting fouled.

Finally, Sharper was fouled and awarded two free throws. He made the first.

Getting ready to take the second shot, Sharper dribbled. The Eagle student section counted them off in unison: "*One . . . two . . . three*." No good! State's Quincy got the rebound and passed to Potter. Potter passed to a streaking Jefferson. The ball was deflected out of bounds. State, down by two, had the ball, with only 2.9 seconds remaining.

"Time out!" Coach Joe screamed.

"OK, men. We've been here before. They are right where we want them. We're running 'Jackson'—that's underneath out-of-bounds play number seven. Everyone got it?" Coach Joe spoke slowly and deliberately.

"Brae, I want you throwing the ball in. Now, we *don't* need to call 'Jackson' because you all know that's what we are running, right?" Heads nodded. "But Brae, I want you to call 'Jefferson' and then 'Quincy' to try and get them to subconsciously react to Steven's and Patrick's names. Steven and Patrick, when you hear your names, take a jab step to sell the idea. Kit, you're doing such a great job that they are all over you right now, so I want you to pop out as a decoy, and then we'll get the ball to Cade off a high screen. Cade, you're going to hit the three for the win. If we can get just a split second of hesitation because of the names, you should have the time you need to get off a clear shot. 'Eli' on three!"

"We knew it was going to be a good one, Billy," Nelson said as the players made their way to their positions.

"Yes, we did! We just didn't know the scenario was going to play out like this. Jimmy, no matter what happens now, State U has put on one of the grittiest performances I have seen in all my years covering the game."

Freshman Braelon Browning took the ball from the referee. "Jefferson!"

Steven feinted.

"Quincy!"

So did Patrick.

It worked! For a split second, the Tech players leaned slightly in the direction of the presidential players. Cade came around a perfectly set screen at the top of the three-point circle. His teapot wrist follow-through was textbook. Every fan was on their feet. This was the moment—one that would last forever for the State U Eagles and Coach Joseph D. Sullivan.

SWIIISH!

"It's gooood!" Nelson howled. "That's it! The Eagles . . . have . . . landed. State University of Texas—you're the National Champions of college basketball!"

Coach Joe jumped into the arms of his assistant coaches. Dr. John and John Jr. embraced, hopping up and down, crying tears of sheer, unadulterated joy. Maroon-and-white confetti filled the stadium. The State U student section filled the court.

After a few minutes, game commentator Billy Hacker caught up with Coach Joe.

"Coach Sullivan, how does it feel? What did you tell your players a moment ago in your celebration huddle?"

"You know, Billy . . . I just told them again how much I loved them . . ." Coach Joe said. He was sobbing.

"Take your time, Coach. I know this is an emotional time," Hacker said.

Coach Joe regained his composure and continued. "I also told them that no matter how good this feels, my hope for them is that this will not be the greatest moment of their lives and that they will go on to do great things and have many more extraordinary moments . . ."

As Coach Joe wiped away another tear and stepped away from the interview, the State U band began to play. The music echoed in the cavernous arena. Coach Joe soon recognized the tune. Forty thousand Eagles fans swayed back and forth, singing a familiar and poignant song:

> Should old acquaintance be forgot,
> And never brought to mind?
> Should old acquaintance be forgot,
> And days of auld lang syne?
>
> For auld lang syne, COACH JOE!
> For auld lang syne,
> We'll take a cup of kindness yet, for auld lang syne . . .

NINETEEN

MAKE GOOD DECISIONS

*The only thing worse than being blind
is having sight but no vision.*

—HELEN KELLER

"Good morning, ladies and gentlemen! Is anybody tired of being national champions yet?" Dr. John yelled out on Wednesday morning.

The class's cheering lasted almost thirty seconds.

Dr. John grinned, still living the high he'd felt at that championship game. "Me neither! But we have to get started, and it's key number ten today, and it's a big one! So let's get to wor—" Dr. John broke off and whistled. "Oh, my! Aaron, how was the photo shoot?"

The class caught sight of Aaron, wearing a shirt and tie. There was laughter all around.

"You're looking dapper this morning," Dr. John remarked. "The Kottens made quite an impression, did they?"

Unabashed, Aaron retorted, "Well, like he said, 'If you are going to be a CEO—you've got to look like one.'"

"Good for you! I notice many of your classmates look a little more presentable today also. With all these communication skills and now all of you dressing for success, you will be unstoppable! Soon, you'll have every interviewer thinking to themselves, 'I just can't figure out exactly what it is about him, but all I know is that he has what we want, and I want him on this team!'

"Now, before we get into our next key—I wanted to talk about your latest challenge assignment. I've seen some of the reports on your handwritten cards. There are some outstanding ones! Anyone want to share a quote they used in a card?" Dr. John asked. "Mr. Martaug?"

"Yes, sir. My uncle tells a story of how he caught a touchdown pass from Roger Staubach—"

Dr. John interrupted. "Oh, wow! He played for the Cowboys?"

"No, it was just at a summer football camp when he was in the sixth grade, but he likes to tell the story all the time anyway," Wes explained.

"Ah, OK," Dr. John chuckled.

"Anyway, I sent a card to him with this quote at the top: 'There is no traffic jam along the extra mile,' by Roger Staubach. He called me right away. I hadn't seen him in a couple of years." Wes finished.

"I love that quote." Dr. John said. "Natalie, did you have your hand up?"

"Yes. I thought I already knew what I wanted to do after graduation, but then I went to the career fair for this assignment. I talked to a guy that had a huge Wile E. Coyote balloon behind his booth, and I asked him why it was there, since it had nothing to do with his company. He said it was there to get attention—and it worked! He also shared during our LAVA conversation that he was a comic book junkie. He answered all three of my reverse interview questions well, and now I'm actually interested in his company. So when I went to get stamps for the thank-you card, I noticed the post office has Road Runner cartoon stamps."

"So it's not hard to guess what happened next," Dr. John offered.

"Yes!" she said. "He called back. Raved about the stamp, and now we're talking about compensation packages."

"Well, there you go. We have time for one more," Dr. John said. "Mr. Berry?"

"I was skeptical, but I went with the wax stamp," Nick said.

"Tell us more," Dr. John encouraged him.

"I burned my thumb the first time, and it took about four tries to get it melted just right on the envelope—" Dr. John smiled in amusement—"but it did get a reaction. I sent it to my high school football coach, and he gave me a call the day he got it. I hadn't talked to him in four years, but that's how he reacted," Nick concluded.

"That's very cool, Nick. Thank you all for sharing.

"Well! Now . . . it's *decision time*," Dr. John declared, spreading his hands out across the podium. "We make thousands of decisions each day. Most of them are mundane. Yet all of our choices help shape *who we are*. It's been said that decisions are the fulcrum of life, and there are a few *big* decisions that have profound implications. One of those is which organization you should join once you've earned your sheepskin. This choice should not be left to your gut. You need a *quantitative* process to eliminate as much subjectivity as possible.

"Today, our tenth key to professional success is about **how to make life's big decisions.** The tool I will give you today is called a decision matrix. It was developed by American corporate leaders almost a century ago. But first, let's start by looking at five barriers that can prevent good decisions. Ready? Here we go."

Dr. John turned to write on the whiteboard. "**Too rushed.** This first one is easy. You've heard it before: haste makes waste. My Grandma said, 'The hurrieder I go, the behinder I get.' Take your time."

Dr. John listed the next one as he spoke it. "**Too much information**. When we're overwhelmed with data, paralysis by analysis sets in. This can freeze you into indecision, which actually *is* a decision—to do nothing.

"**No process**. Without a quantifiable process, many things come down to a coin flip. I'll make sure this doesn't happen to you.

"**Overconfidence**. This one is sneaky because we often don't know what we don't know. Being humble when making big decisions can help eliminate this danger."

Dr. John closed the marker and tapped it against the whiteboard as he finished the list. "**Groupthink**. We've talked about the tyranny of the majority before. This is when you take the 'everyone is working there' approach to finding a place to start your career. Decide what is best for you and your unique talents and aspirations. That means asking: What is my *purpose*?"

Every head was down, writing. It was apparent that the course had turned serious. It was about real life now—making a living rather than simply making a grade. That attitudinal turning point gave Dr. John satisfaction every semester.

He continued, "The good news is that each of these barriers can be removed by applying solid decision-making principles. The first one we're removing right now by simply planning ahead for this process. The other four will be removed systematically by using a criteria-based model that organizes your thoughts and optimizes objectivity. And that is the key—*objectivity*. I call this process Seven Steps to Wise Decisions. Yes, Ms. Moore?"

"I'm not sure what you mean by *objectivity*," Hannah said. "I guess we can look at their financials, but it seems like most of my friends have just taken a job because it feels right to them, and some of them have taken the first offer because they're afraid of the tight job market. I don't understand where else we can get data to make finding a job that objective."

Dr. John grinned. "Spoken like a true accounting major. Thank you for that question, Hannah. Feeling is important. You have to feel good about your decision and where you decide to start your career. But if you'll hang in there with me for just a moment, I'll show you how the data fits into the equation of landing an exceptional career entry opportunity."

Hannah nodded.

Dr. John walked back to the podium and turned on the projector for the day's presentation. "Step one." Dr. John paused as students readied pens in hands.

"**Identify the question**. The obvious question seems to be: 'Where should I work?' But be more specific. 'How should I spend the next two years?' is a better question. This leaves room for those of you who may be considering graduate school or other options.

"Step two is to **prioritize your objectives**. And these objectives fall into two categories: *must-haves* and *want-to-haves*.

"*Must-haves* are nonnegotiable items. If an opportunity doesn't include a must-have on your list, then that opportunity is immediately discarded. Period.

"*Want-to-haves,* on the other hand, will be scored on a scale of one to ten—with ten being the highest priority. But note this is not a *ranking* of the list of want-to-haves but a *relative* score. So you can have more than one category that scores a ten. For our case study, I've preloaded categories and scores collected over the last few years from former students."

Dr. John brought up a table on the screen and discussed each one, using his laser pointer.

Must-Haves	Want-to-Haves	Rating
Culture Fit (Values)	Compensation	5
Warm Climate	Benefits/Perks	7
Faith Community	Grad School Funding	8
	Team Atmosphere	10
	Strong Career Ladder	7
	Good Reputation	9
	Cost of Living	7
	Car-Friendly	9
	Vibrancy/Beauty	6

"Now, given these scores, what might we ascertain is important to this job seeker?" Dr. John asked.

"They don't like cold weather, and they attend church regularly," said David Freiburg.

"Good. What else?"

"Money is not that important to them, but they want to have a fun place to work," said Aaron.

"Aaron, I think that's true—they want a great team atmosphere. In fact, based on the '10' it was given, it's the most important want-to-have listed. Anything else?" Dr. John asked.

Deron Johnson answered, "They hate traffic!"

The class laughed.

"Yes, Deron, that appears to be the case. Having lived in the big city for decades, I can empathize! So, Hannah, can you see how the numbers here can help you be objective?"

"Yes, sir. It's making sense now," she agreed.

Dr. John smiled. "Good. Step three of the decision matrix is easy. **List the alternatives**. I suggest continuing your search to find three good alternatives before you can begin this quantitative analysis in earnest. Note that this does not mean the *first* three opportunities you come across. You now have the skills to be confident and selective.

"Imagine that you have received three offers. Let's call them Alpha, Inc., Omega, Inc. and State U. Let me reiterate that all three of these options meet the must-have requirements. Otherwise, they would not be on the chart. I included working at an academic institution—in this case, our beloved State U—as the 'something completely different' option.

"Step four is to **assign the numbers to each alternative**. In this step, we want to focus on facts—not opinions—as much as possible."

Dr. John went through each category, placing values in corresponding boxes for each.

	Rating	Alpha	A	Omega	Ω	State	U
Want-to-Haves:							
Compensation	5	8	40	9	45	5	25
Benefits/Perks	7	9	63	7	49	10	70
Grad School Funding	8	5	40	6	48	10	80
Team Atmosphere	10	7	70	9	90	10	100
Strong Career Ladder	7	6	42	9	63	7	49
Good Reputation	9	7	63	8	72	9	81
Cost of Living	7	6	42	7	49	8	56
Car-Friendly	9	4	36	6	54	9	81
Vibrancy/Beauty	6	7	42	8	48	6	36
TOTAL			438		518		578

"In step five, we do the math and **get a total score** for each of the three options. Here are the results." Dr. John clicked to the next chart.

"As we compare the two private companies under consideration, Omega, Inc. comes out ahead *in the end.*"

"We see what you did there!" an unidentified voice rang out.

Dr. John chuckled. "Thank you. But the surprise comes in option three, as State U emerges as the clear winner overall—primarily because of the importance of things like lifelong learning opportunities and a team atmosphere. Perhaps without this objective comparison, the academic career track may not have been considered. Your hand is up, Mr. Seigel?"

"How can we find out enough about these three alternatives to accurately score each of these categories? It still seems kind of vague to me," Brandon said.

"Great question! Remember the fourteen reverse interview questions in **chapter 7**? We talked about three of them already."

Brandon nodded.

"While we can never be completely objective—either because of bias or a lack of a full set of facts—those reverse interview questions are critical to providing as much information as possible to help us to complete our chart.

"Now, about step six—" Dr. John looked slowly across the room, making eye contact with several students. "**Seek wise counsel for confirmation**. This is a good time for a story."

Students leaned forward.

"A good friend of mine named Dave implemented a unique method of seeking mentors when he turned twenty years old. On each of his 'zero' birthdays, Dave finds a new advisor at least *ten years older*. Someone he considers to be wise. He then interviews this person about their own life journey. He starts with the simple question, 'What did you learn in the decade I am entering that would be a lesson you could pass on to me?' Not only does Dave get good advice for what is to come, he also has accumulated multiple counselors, enabling him to build a substantial mentor network. And by the way, my friend Dave will turn *eighty* next month, and he told me that he's already identified a ninety-six-year-old new mentor.

"Why is it so important to seek counsel from those who are older and wiser?" Dr. John asked. "Because they have the ability to see a situation from a different perspective. They have dealt with many of the challenges of life that you have yet to encounter. They likely have also learned not to take themselves too seriously—something we all tend to learn with age.

"If you have multiple trusted advisors, show all of them your decision matrix. Seeking this wise counsel will either cement your choice or help you consider aspects of the decision you might have overlooked or misunderstood. A good mentor will always say to you, 'I have high expectations for you, and I know you can meet them. And when you experience failure along the way, I'll help you recover.'"

Dr. John stepped out from behind the podium and leaned up against it. "Step seven is to **set a timetable for implementation.** Once your mentors have signed off, it's time to inform your new employer of your decision and get into the logistics. The excitement of your first career position begins! Justin, you have a question?"

"Yes, sir. I can see how this matrix will be helpful deciding on our first position out of college. But as life gets more complicated with kids and all that, does the method work well as you get older? Wouldn't you be simply comparing your current position to another you're considering? Seems like it would be easier when there are only two choices."

"You know, I'm not sure I've had that question before. Thank you. It's a good one," Dr. John acknowledged.

"First of all, this method probably becomes *more* valuable as life gets *more* complicated. Even if only two employment options are under consideration, life's variables become more numerous. You mentioned children—which are definitely a huge variable. And because you're all going to be great communicators and always strive for excellence, I predict many career suitors will come calling. The complications of life will multiply; you're right.

"I used the decision matrix method when I decided with which company we should merge," Dr. John said. "I was blessed to have more than one interested at the same time. I used it again when I decided how to divide my time between corporate consulting and the university. So I guess you can thank—or curse—this method for me being here with you today.

"I used it yet again when choosing which university I should align with. Although, I admit, in my case the matrix served as more of a confirmation than the deciding factor. But it really is a method that will help you make good decisions your entire life. You can use the decision matrix when determining when and how to make a move, when debating a decision like buying a home or school choices for any kids that come along—ad infinitum," Dr. John assured the class.

"I add one more step to my process that is not in your text," he added, "and that's *prayer*. With life's big decisions, in my opinion, we need wisdom from above."

Dr. John noticed some pensive stares and nods.

"I'm wondering if any of you know the name of our witness from history today," Dr. John asked. No hands went up, and Dr. John nodded, unsurprised. "She is not as recognizable as most. Her name is Helen Keller."

The word *Vision* was written above her picture portrait.

Dr. John continued. "She was a wise lady who once said, 'Character cannot be developed in ease and quiet. Only through experience of trial and suffering can the soul be strengthened, ambition inspired, and success achieved.' This quote is even more impactful when you consider that Helen

Keller was born both blind and deaf. In spite of her inability to see or hear, she became the first deaf-blind person to earn a bachelor of arts degree. She was a prolific author and lecturer who inspired a classic movie, *The Miracle Worker*. But most of all, she was a visionary known for this quote: 'The only thing worse than being blind is having sight but no vision.' She is our witness for this lesson because *vision* is what the decision matrix is all about—allowing you to *envision your future*: something that, out of all of creation, only humans can do."

Dr. John paused briefly to refocus the class.

"Now, here is a new challenge for you. I assume most of you have narrowed your first career move down to two or three options. The challenge is to create your own career decision matrix. Even if you have made a decision already, the decision matrix will confirm it—or not. Be deliberate about it so that you can see the full value of this method. There is a template on the class portal you can use. It's due in two weeks."

Dr. John folded his hands behind his back. "Well, that's it for today. Our next class will be memorable, trust me. We'll have another guest speaker, and I can't wait for you to hear what she has to say about the three most important questions you can ever ask. Please review **chapter 11** for next time. Have a great day, everyone!"

Dr. John collected his items as Aaron approached his desk. "Hello there, Aaron. How are you? You've been scarce lately."

"Oh, just busy, I guess. Just trying to get everything lined up to graduate."

"I understand. I vaguely remember those days!" Dr. John agreed.

"You know, Dr. John. I did some research on you," Aaron said.

Dr. John looked over his glasses. "Uh-oh."

"No, I mean, you were very successful. When I looked at your firm, you had a significant and growing company. You won awards, had a radio show, wrote several books—and you were relatively young. I'm just wondering why you would give all that up. It seems like you kind of had it made. Why would you choose this gig over that one?" Aaron asked.

Dr. John laughed. "You know, I've asked myself that as well, Aaron—and so has my wife." Aaron was focused, waiting for an answer. Dr. John considered. "I don't have time to tell you the whole story. Maybe I can someday. Just know that life on paper and real life are two different things. Real life has twists and turns that we don't expect or understand—especially at the time they are happening. I certainly could still be doing what I was doing. They were important things. I would certainly be making a lot more money and all that. But life comes in stages—first a job, then a career, and then—"

Dr. John trailed off, reflecting. "Then there comes a time for a fortunate few of us when talent, opportunity, and purpose all meet in one place and time. That creates a *calling*. That's what happened in my case. It's rather ironic, really. I spent over three decades teaching and coaching people on how to retire and take it easy when I never had any intention of ever retiring myself."

"What do you mean?" Aaron wanted to know.

"I've always had a passion for teaching and coaching of a different sort—with you and your generation, the generation of my own children, and their children. I believe circumstance—no—*providence* has allowed my purpose to be here in this place, at this time, with you and your classmates. And with all that I might be reaping now in my former profession, I know I'm gathering even more treasure now. I must tell you that I could not be happier or more fulfilled. I've really never looked back. As I told my players way back in my coaching days—always have a *next-play mentality*."

Aaron stood silent. He was intrigued by the depth of Dr. John's answer.

Dr. John broke the awkwardness. "That may be a different answer than you expected, Aaron. But I'm glad you asked. Amanda doing OK?"

"Oh, yes, sir. She is. Thank you for asking." Aaron smiled.

"Well, gotta scoot. I have office hours. Take care, Aaron."

"See you later, Professor."

Later, at the end of his office hours, Dr. John turned the corner out into the corridor and saw a familiar sight. He spread his arms wide. "Hey! Look who it is! My two girls!" he exclaimed.

"Johndee!" Nicole gave him a big hug.

"How are you, Noodle?" Dr. John asked.

"I'm good!" she replied.

Nicole turned to Lisa. "Don't worry, sis, I'm not trying to push in on y'all's special time."

"It's your turn, right, Sunflower?" Dr. John asked.

Lisa grinned. "Yes. And I'm starving!"

Dr. John hugged his eldest stepdaughter in turn. "Where are we going today?" It was time for their monthly "What's Up" session. Dr. John had one with each of his children . . . when they could work him into their busy schedules.

Nicole interrupted. "I've got to run, but I wanted to tell you that mom's gift is in." She tried to contain the urge to hop up and down.

Dr. John smiled wide. "The Gonzales? It's here already?"

"Yes! And it's perfect!" Nicole confirmed.

"She's going to be so surprised!" Lisa enthused.

"You know she's teaching my class next week on her birthday, right?" Dr. John reminded his daughters.

"Yes. We will both be there for it," Lisa confirmed. "See you later, Nicole."

"Have a great day, Noodle," Dr. John said, waving at Nicole as she headed out to her next class. Lisa fell into step with him and they headed together out of the building. "Sunflower, I'm ready for some scoop! Tell me how everything is going."

Dr. John put his arm around Lisa, and she began to tell him all her news as they headed off for lunch.

TWENTY

ASK GREAT QUESTIONS

*When you study definitions accurately,
you plumb the depth of ignorance.*

—SOCRATES

Aaron sat down and placed his backpack underneath his desk, staring at the witness of the day. *Who is the guy in the toga?* he thought. The large *"What do you mean by that?"* banner from the first class was also hanging over the front of the room. Then he heard a familiar giggle. *Nicole?* Sitting to his far left near the door were Lisa and Nicole. *What are they doing here?* Aaron half waved, and they smiled back.

"Good morning, ladies and gentlemen! This is going to be extraordinary!" Dr. John announced. "Our speaker today is Anicia Kosta. She will be presenting key to professional success number 11—**asking great questions**."

Kosta, Aaron recalled. *So they came to hear their mom. This should be interesting. I guess I never finished their LAVA conversation like I should have.*

"Originally from Cuba, Kosta received her undergraduate and master's degrees from State U before heading to law school—"

Anicia's presence in front of an audience was regal. She had the distinct appearance of an accomplished professional in a conservative business suit it was not difficult to imagine her wearing while giving a closing argument in trial. At the same time, she had a rare sense of joy and a disarming humility about her.

"It is my great and personal pleasure to introduce our distinguished guest, Anicia Kosta."

Did Dr. John just wink at her? Mmmm . . . This is all coming together. No wonder the girls know all Dr. John's tricks.

"Thank you, Dr. Daniels. It's always an honor to be with you and your fine class," Anicia said. Despite her Cuban origins, she spoke without an accent. "I would like to start our discussion with a question: What is *truth*?"

There was a long pause.

"Logic?" Mary Wright answered.

"Yes. Good. What else?"

Rachel Anderson raised her hand. "Conclusions based on facts?"

"Excellent. That is certainly an aspect of truth. Anyone else?" Kosta encouraged the class.

"Is it the same as reason?" Aaron hazarded.

"Yes. Thank you. Logic, facts, and reason are all features of truth. But it's more than that. Have you ever heard that it's more important to teach someone *how* to fish than to *give* them a fish?" she asked.

Most heads nodded.

"One of my favorite proverbs says, 'Buy the truth, and sell it not.' Today, it's the *process* of finding truth that I want you to know." Anicia looked around the classroom. "We live in a generation where many are trying to persuade you that truth is *relative.* 'You have your truth, and I have mine,' they say. But I would ask, 'If truth is relative—is *that* statement true? Or is it relative?'"

Anicia paused to let that statement sink in. "The ability to see through illogical statements like this will equip you to learn the truth of any matter for yourself—and to persuade others as you develop sound arguments full of logic, facts, and reason. The ability to use these tools to uncover truth is tantamount to learning to fish for *wisdom*. It is the single most important skill I can teach my children. And I want you to have it as well.

"About 150 years ago, there lived a scholar who understood how important the pursuit of truth was. John Stewart Mill was a British citizen with a great admiration for the US Constitution and the principles of freedom—particularly free speech. He wrote a book in 1858 called *On Liberty*. In it, he explained how important it is to engage in classic argumentation.

"To paraphrase, he said, 'If your opinion is right, then a discussion will confirm it. But if wrong—you gain a clearer perception and livelier impression of *truth* produced by its collision with error.'" Anicia hit her fists together lightly to emphasize her point. "The British always know how to put things, don't they?" she laughed. "All of us believe that the view we hold on any particular issue, at any particular time, is the correct one, right? Otherwise, why would we hold it?

"Mill is saying that civil discussion in the arena of ideas either corrects a wrong view or substantiates a correct one. So there is nothing to fear when truth is objectively sought with pure motives. Wrong ideas gradually yield to fact and argument. Facts can't tell their own story. The only way to know the whole of a subject is by hearing what can be said about it by every variety of opinion. This is how we acquire wisdom."

Aaron noted that Anicia was speaking entirely without notes. *Impressive.*

She paced in front of the classroom. "Another well-known proverb says, 'Give instruction to a wise man, and he will be still wiser.' We all need more truth and wisdom. Wouldn't you agree?"

Heads nodded.

"But what if no one argued anymore? What if all we did is go on social media and cast anonymous aspersions at one another without the civility of a polite exchange of ideas? What happens when citizens are under constant surveillance— whether active or passive? What happens when technology is developed to a point that we're intimidated into silence and compliance with the politically correct dogma of those in power? What happens?"

Anicia waited until she had every eye in the room.

"Hitler happens," she said, quietly and clearly.

Silence.

"Did Dr. John assign you to read *How Do You Kill 11 Million People?*" she asked.

"Yes," several students responded.

"And what was the answer to that question?"

"You lie to them," Jake Connors answered.

"That's right. And not just little lies. In fact, in *Mein Kampf*—the infamous book he wrote while in prison— Hitler even explained that the *bigger* the lie, the *more* believable it was. It's counterintuitive, isn't it? But he took advantage of the good nature of his citizens, who typically didn't even tell many small lies. So there was no way they could believe he would tell such big lies as he did. And Hitler told the same lies again and again because he knew that if he told a lie enough times, it would eventually become truth.

"As you read for yourself, his lies led to at least 11 million deaths directly under his reign of terror—plus an additional 30 to 40 million throughout the world. If you add in Stalin and Mao, in the last century, more than 100 million people have been lost to tyranny—more than all of previous human history *combined*. And all because of big lies and the muting of free discussion—and therefore truth. So you see, finding truth is a serious endeavor indeed!" Anicia exclaimed.

"I want to give you some critical tools in the lifelong pursuit of truth today. They're simply three questions that you must use continually. Remember this: *truth always survives scrutiny*. Therefore, your job is to develop the ability to analyze the arguments of others and also to formulate your own. And it starts with these three questions. Are you ready?" she asked.

"Yes," sounded all around the room.

"Let's get to work!"

Wow. She's been around Dr. John too much also, Aaron thought.

He watched Anicia's hands as she spoke—they were in constant synchrony with her words. "I love the witness from history Dr. John has displayed today. The word *truth* above Socrates is so appropriate. As you can see, his clothes were a little different than what we wear today."

A few students chuckled.

"Socrates never wrote a book, nor was he ever paid for a speech, yet he is known for the technique of pursuing truth via questions—known as the Socratic method. I became quite familiar with this in law school. He spent his entire life in

Athens, where he developed this form of inquiry to promote critical thinking and to clarify ideas. It was a simple yet seminal idea.

"Today, any successful person understands that if they ask better questions, they get better answers. Furthermore, people come to understand *how much you know and care by the quality of your questions*—and far less by the quality of your statements or declarations. Asking the right questions at the right time puts you in an exclusive category of those who optimize their personal influence.

"The three questions I'm about to offer will allow you to defend yourselves when necessary—and go on the offensive in an *in*offensive way. You must learn to never make a statement when a question will do. Here's question number one." Anicia looked up and pointed to the banner above her.

"**What do you mean by that?** Socrates said, 'When you study definitions accurately, you plumb the depth of ignorance.' He knew that life is about *definitions*. The same words have different meanings for different people. Often, disagreements are simply the result of a misunderstanding of what is meant by the words that are used. This first question is telling someone, 'Please define your terms for me.'

"This question is also a perfect bridge to a more extended conversation. If someone truly is an expert in their field, you'll get an education. This question conveys that you don't want to misinterpret the meaning of their statements. You're also making sure they know what they are talking about and are not just spouting off a bumper sticker they read or arguing a purely ideological position."

Anicia spread her hands. "Wouldn't you agree that if someone makes a statement, they should be willing to defend their position if they're interested in knowing what is true? When we don't ask 'What do you mean by that?', people may espouse ideas that could turn out to be false. This first question can also buy you some time to think if you need it."

Anicia paused to give students time to catch up in their notes. She gave a quick glance and a smile to Dr. John.

She continued, "By the way, feel free to keep asking this first question until you're satisfied your companion knows what they are talking about. Socrates always did! However, you may want to change it up to maintain an engaging atmosphere. Alternatives such as, 'That's interesting, can you tell me more?' or, 'Please expand on that idea,' work well. And remember, the illusion of knowledge is powerful. Many arguments have seemed reasonable until they come up against the simple yet powerful question of 'What do you mean by that?'

"Once someone has answered question number one to your satisfaction, it's time for question number two: **How did you come to that conclusion?**

"Just because someone has proven they have a cursory understanding of a topic doesn't prove that understanding to be true," Anicia explained. "In legal circles, we call this second question the 'burden of proof' question. While the first question deals with the *what* of their topic, this question deals with the *why* for their position. In other words, they must provide sufficient evidence to back up their claim. Please write this down and then highlight it: *Whoever makes an assertion must also defend it.* Don't fall into a trap of defending against what the *other* person claims. This second question keeps you out of that situation.

"At its core, this question also gives the benefit of the doubt that the person who made the claim also researched it adequately. You are making sure they aren't saying something just because they believe it or just *think* or *feel* that's the way it is. That's not good enough. Confidence does not equal truth. Again, they must provide evidence. This second question will make them do so. *Beliefs cannot change facts*—regardless of how sincerely they are held. Truth is not affected by the attitude or the feelings of the person professing it. Contrary *beliefs* are possible. Contrary *truths* are not.

"Other variations of question number two are, 'Please share with me more about the reasons you believe that,' or, 'I'm wondering. What makes that so compelling for you?'"

Anicia continued, "Questions one and two will show that you are an agreeable person—even though you have not necessarily agreed with their position. You will also show them that it's safe to discuss issues with you because you are genuinely interested. You'll then be in the midst of a meaningful and productive conversation. But now, it's your turn. This next question provides an opportunity to also start providing some answers of your own."

Anicia smiled. "Question number three is: **Have you ever considered . . .** ? This question is known in a court of law as a *leading question*. I know that sounds like someone should now stand up and shout, 'Objection, Your Honor!'" She flourished dramatically with her hand like an actress, and the students laughed.

"But unlike the negative connotation in a courtroom where a witness is being intentionally led to answer in a way that might be detrimental, this leading question is an honest attempt to find truth," Anicia explained. "The goodwill you have created in the discussion so far will hopefully carry the day. Of course, there is always a chance this last question comes across as offensive. Softer alternatives to this question can be, 'Would you be surprised to know . . .' or, 'Imagine what would happen if . . .' Then you simply fill in with your argument."

Dr. John stood up and raised his hand, "If I may interject here, Anicia, there are about a dozen more forms of this last question in **chapter 4** of your textbook under the heading 'Influence Phrases.' You can simply make them into a question and then use any of them as the third question, as Ms. Kosta is suggesting."

Anicia nodded. "Thank you, Dr. John. I would also like you to make a note that a fourth question is available if needed. It is a rhetorical question. Rhetorical questions are asked for the sole purpose of making a point—not to elicit a reply. This additional question can be used to make a powerful final point. It is simply: **What if you are wrong?**

"This question forces someone to make an immediate assessment of their position. They may come back with an answer, but regardless, the attention is moved from you, the questioner, to them, the answerer. Dale Carnegie said, 'Someone convinced against their will is of the same opinion still.' Rhetorical questions begin opening the doors in a mind for a person to begin searching out the truth for *themselves*."

Anicia smiled. "I have so much more I would love to tell you, but Dr. John is giving me a signal over there. In conclusion, let me quote Augustine, who said, 'We love the truth when it enlightens us and hate the truth when it convicts us.' Either way—if we are to live in a free society, the pursuit of truth is vital and will aid you in your journey after wisdom your entire lives. Thank you for your kind attention," Anicia concluded.

"Thank you, Anicia!" Dr. John started a robust round of applause. "I cut you off a little early there because I know how many questions you always get. I hope that's OK," Dr. John explained.

"Of course!" she agreed.

"Great! Who has a question for Ms. Kosta? Yes, Ms. Martin?"

"Do you still practice law?" Taylor asked.

Anicia shook her head. "No, I don't. I loved it when I did, but I sold my practice a few years back so that I could concentrate on my four children and also have time to be with great students like you. Like Dr. John, I had a successful career, but I feel that my calling is now here—trying to make a difference in this generation. The generation of my children—and maybe their children, God willing."

Aaron looked up suddenly from his notes. *Where have I heard that before? "Calling"?*

He was distracted from his thoughts by his neighbor's raised hand. "Natalie?" Dr. John asked.

"Thank you. Yes, Ms. Kosta, you mentioned you were from Cuba. The United States has normalized relations with them now. Are you planning to go back any time soon?"

Anicia's expression froze. She looked at Dr. John directly and paused. "Well . . ." she muttered.

Dr. John nodded as if to say, *Go ahead.*

Anicia took a moment to collect her thoughts. "What is your name again, please?"

"Natalie Nguyen."

"Thank you, Natalie. That's a good question. Let me tell you the truth about Cuba."

Every student leaned in.

"When I was born, Cuba was the jewel of the Caribbean. We had a freely elected president—and it was a tourist paradise with a free market economy like the United States. Higher education, technology, and health care were all thriving areas of our economy. Poverty was very low, and the middle class was large and strong. Then, General Fulgencio Batista came into power through a coup d'etat. He was a corrupt dictator who tortured and imprisoned anyone who would oppose him.

"Fidel Castro came in with many false promises of freedom and ousted Batista. He was a compelling public speaker who hid his socialist ideals. He said all the right things when he came into power, and then one day there was a knock on our door. I will never forget it. '¡Abre! ¡Ahora! ¡En el nombre de la revolución!' They stormed in aggressively, screaming at my father. 'This clinic is no longer yours! It belongs to the people!' He was told he had one week to vacate the medical practice he had spent fifteen years building. We would soon be simply trying to survive."

Anicia continued. "Castro destroyed the fertile fields of the Havana fruit belt and planted *gandules*—a kind of bean popular in Puerto Rico. Over time, there were few useful food crops available for the Cuban people. Food shortages were rampant. It was horrific. We ate ground-up banana peels, which we pretended were ground meat, and pressed grapefruit peels together to cook with spices and become our 'steak.' My father's breakfast was a half cup of weak coffee. There was little else. Years later, Castro even took his centralized government theories and destroyed Cuba's cash crop of sugar cane."

Anicia's fingers clenched over the top of the podium. "The surveillance was suffocating. It was very similar to what you read about in the classic dystopian novel *1984*—a book that is outlawed in Cuba, by the way. It was oppressive in every sense of the word. Lifelong friendships ended because no one could be trusted. Families were torn apart. I had an older cousin—Fernando—who was part of the resistance at the Bay of Pigs. He died in prison."

She stared at the floor for a moment. "My Uncle Fernando was brought to court on false charges—what the government called 'subversive' activities. When you live under tyranny, the minority is always considered 'subversive,' regardless of the truth. The farce of a trial lasted fifteen minutes. Before his family even knew what was happening, they watched as he was executed on live TV by a firing squad. *Tío* was a hero. He has a street named after him in Miami."

Dr. John looked around the room. Every student sat frozen, eyes wide open, glued on the speaker. "Finally my father had had enough. He had been forced to work in a government hospital under terrible conditions for subsistence-level pay. One afternoon, Castro's henchmen came to his clinic and announced that all workers—regardless of position—would be bused to the sugar cane fields in the morning for a 'day of solidarity.' In spite of the urging of his friends, Dr. Sebastian Kosta refused to participate. That night, we all hid in the basement of the hospital for what would be five days of fasting and fear. He arranged for us to make our way to Tampa by way of a daring escape in the hull of a fishing vessel. I don't have time to provide all the details now, but it was a story of survival that any Hollywood producer would be quick to embrace.

"To return to *your* question, Natalie, in my opinion, the normalization of relations between the United States and Cuba has only made things worse for my people. There is still no freedom of assembly. Anyone—even women and children—who protests the abusive policies of the regime can be imprisoned without a trial. Property rights are very restrictive. And for seven decades, the island's famous and beautiful architecture has crumbled into disrepair. US normalization takes away any incentive to make things better for the citizens of Cuba. The increased tourist dollars go straight into the pockets of the tyrant now in charge and his soldier bullies. So do I want to go back? No. I want to stay here and tell students like you my story—let them know what freedom is truly about. I hope one day your generation and others will rise up to fight tyranny once again—in their own lives and around the world. It is my mission, and it is *infinitely* more important than anything I could ever do in a courtroom."

Anicia saw some surprised looks in the audience. Dr. John started to get up, but Anicia was not yet finished. "You know, it staggers me when I hear that over 50 percent of your generation romanticizes socialism. Yet I can show you so many Cubans who escaped the horrors of a socialist regime to America with only their lives. They are very successful now because of *freedom*. Freedom is about equal *opportunity*—not equal outcomes. You all have an opportunity to make an A in Dr. John's class at the beginning of the semester. However, if you make an A, are you OK if he *donates* a letter grade from you to a C student so that everyone can have a nice B? No! The only thing socialism eventually equalizes is misery, as standards for achievement go down because no one has an incentive to excel.

"No country has ever experimented with socialism to a successful end. It always deteriorates into a communist regime. That's because socialism takes away the invisible hand of individual choices and innovation that a free economy depends on. Socialism depends on the state's visible fist to force its will on the people." Anicia held her own clenched hand up for effect. "That's why I will be here, fighting fiercely for truth, because I know firsthand how freedom can disappear in just one generation. I've seen it. Well, not on my watch . . . *Not here!*"

A tear rolled down her right cheek. She dashed it away quickly.

It was now one minute until class was due to end. No one had looked at the clock. The students seemed stunned.

Catching herself, Anicia said, "Oh, Dr. John, I'm afraid I got carried away there. I apologize."

Dr. John smiled and nodded as if to say, *No worries at all.*

Anicia paused and looked down. Then, in a much softer tone, she said. "Last evening, my sweet family gave me a gift that I will always treasure at a special dinner to celebrate my birthday. It is a colorful painting of a rooster by famed Cuban artist Salvador Gonzales. It is called *Cantando.* It is such a special gift, because when I was a little girl there was a rooster that would crow every morning outside my window. My father said he was *contando al amanecer*—which means 'singing at dawn.' While it sounded the same every morning, it signaled a new day. A day always full of possibilities. A day full of freedom. I long to see the light of freedom shine again in my Cuba. And I pray it never goes out here in my blessed America."

Anicia raised her right hand in benediction over the entire class. "May you all become champions of truth and surround yourselves with honest people who are willing to argue with you! Thank you for your kind attention this morning, and may God bless each of you."

A standing ovation rippled through the classroom. Aaron noticed tears in the eyes of Lisa and Nicole, proud to have a mother like that—one whose life's goal was to seek truth and pass it on.

As the applause faded, Dr. John said, "Thank you again, Anicia. I know your birthday is actually today, so thank you for spending it with us!"

A few cheers and thank-yous rippled through the class at this. "See you next class, everyone," Dr. John said, turning to smile again at his wife.

As a line formed to ask Anicia more questions, Aaron made his way toward her daughters, who were quickly exiting the room.

They were almost to the exit at the top of the stairs. "Hey!" Aaron called. He caught up to them just outside, and they both turned and said hello.

Out of breath, Aaron said, "So your mom—she's unbelievable!"

Lisa smiled. "Yeah. We're kinda proud of her."

Nicole nodded.

Aaron looked behind him. "The line to talk to her is out the door!" He sighed regretfully. "I have a lab today. But I hope I get a chance to ask her more questions someday."

Lisa looked thoughtful. Her lips twitched up. "Maybe we can make that happen," she offered.

"That would be great. Are y'all going to study later?"

Lisa shrugged. "Maybe. See you soon!" She and Nicole turned to head toward the Student Union, and Aaron waved goodbye as he headed to his lab.

TWENTY-ONE

LIFELONG LEARNING

The best way to predict your future is to create it.

—ABRAHAM LINCOLN

"Good morning, everyone!" Dr. John exclaimed in his usual tone. The witness from history banner today had the word *Leadership* across the top with a famous portrait of Abraham Lincoln beneath it.

"Let me begin by saying that I am impressed with the decision matrices I've seen from the latest challenge I issued two weeks ago. This one is really going to pay off for many of you. The career opportunities you're telling me about are extraordinary! I would love to hear what your experience was like as you developed your matrix. Who would like to go first?"

Joel Simpson raised his hand to speak first. "There were so many areas I had not thought to evaluate. I was mainly thinking about the location and the salary. The intangible categories you taught us, like team atmosphere, career ladder, and corporate reputation, made a difference."

"What do you mean they made a difference?" Dr. John asked.

"Well, the scores confirmed that I had made the right choice, but I was surprised that it was a blowout. When I was making the decision with my gut, it was closer in my mind," Joel explained.

"Interesting. Good. One more. Yes, Ms. Schmidt?"

Maggie nodded. "It changed everything for me. I made my choice at the end of last summer. I was feeling good about it, even though it was a hard decision. After I ran through the numbers on the matrix, it completely reversed my thinking because the other company's score was so much higher than the company I chose. It kind of scared me. So I ran it by my parents and another mentor, and they agreed I should change. So I did."

"Wow. How about that?! Thank you both. I think those are two excellent examples of how objective data can provide clearer vision to make important life decisions."

Dr. John paused, waiting for everyone's attention. "I have a story for you. In 1832, a farmer in Kentucky who had given up on the land packed up his family and headed back home. He stopped at a general store along the way and was greeted by a tall twenty-four-year-old storekeeper standing outside on the covered wooden porch. This awkward young man had only one year of formal education, and he was deeply in debt, with no real prospects.

"The farmer asked the storekeeper if he would like to have any of the items on his wagon. He promised to 'make him a good deal.' The storekeeper waved him off. The farmer persisted, offering a large barrel for just fifty cents. 'You could use it for storage,' the ex-farmer told him. Noting the traveler's resolve, the young man finally relented and gave the farmer his price. The storekeeper figured he *could* use the barrel for storage at some point. He rolled it out of the way into a corner of the store and went about his business.

"Months passed. One day, the storekeeper decided to empty the barrel for other uses. When he turned it upside down, trash fell out—and also a book. It was *Blackstone's Commentary*, published in 1769. The tome was long held to be the leading work on English law, which led to the development of the American legal system.

"The storekeeper read the book," Dr. John said. "And from then on, he read every law book he could get his hands on. He became a successful attorney in Illinois—and eventually the sixteenth president of the United States."

Dr. John nodded at the witness banner. "Abraham Lincoln's dedication to lifelong learning allowed him to eventually reach the highest office in the land. We should be thankful for the persistence of that failed farmer, because without the barrel he sold Mr. Lincoln, that twenty-four-year-old shopkeeper might never have discovered *Blackstone's Commentary* and embarked upon a law career. If Lincoln had not first become a lawyer, he would never have had the opportunity to become president and turn the tide of the Civil War with his address at Gettysburg. Without Gettysburg, there would be no United States. And if there were no United States, all of Western civilization would have long been lost to tyrants."

Dr. John spread his hands atop the podium. "Just one book can change the world," he concluded. "And in this case, it did. Now, with that in mind, you're in for another treat today! Our final guest presenter for the semester is Mr. Michael Reedy."

Echoes of "sweet" and "nice" rippled across the room from a few students.

Dr. John smiled. "Ah, so some of you remember the story involving Mr. Reedy that I told you earlier? Michael is here to present our twelfth and final key to professional success: **lifelong learning**."

Dr. John's introduction for his friend was effusive, overflowing with WOW! descriptors like *exceptional, extraordinary, above and beyond,* and even *awesome.* Reedy was well dressed and exhibited a humble but confident demeanor as Dr. John wrapped up his introduction: ". . . Once again, it is a privilege to present my good friend, Michael Reedy."

Applause filled the room.

Reedy waved in appreciation. He waited an extra second for the room to fall completely silent. "Let me start with a question: How many of you read books other than textbooks?"

About half of the class raised their hands.

Michael raised an eyebrow. "Not bad. Now, did you know that 33 percent of high school graduates never read another book after they get their diploma?"

Michael paused. "And *42 percent of college graduates* never read another book after college."

A few students whispered in surprised tones.

"Furthermore, 70 percent of American adults have not been in a bookstore in the last five years!" Reedy let the statement sink in, then turned back to his friend and former colleague. "Thank you, Dr. John. It is indeed a pleasure to be with you today. I love that story about Lincoln, and every time you invite me, I can't wait to get here and get to work!"

Of course, every guest we've had says that, Aaron thought, laughing to himself.

Reedy took his place at the front of the class. "As a culture, we seem to think that once we have our career training, we don't need to learn anymore. When I reflect on my own life, there was a time when I could have been described that way as well. I believe that reading as part of continuous improvement is so critical that it's the difference between those who will be wildly successful and those who will dwell in mediocrity their entire career. Coach John Wooden said, 'It's what you learn *after* you know it all that counts.' President Truman—who also lacked a formal college degree—said, 'Not all readers are leaders. But *all leaders are readers.*' When I see the word 'leadership' over Lincoln's portrait, it reminds me that the simplest test of leadership can be boiled down to one question: 'What are you reading now?'

"I've heard it said that reading one hour per day in your chosen field will make you a subject matter expert in seven years. And because of the age of distraction we live in, the opportunity gap for success has never been wider."

Michael continued, "Cervantes said, 'The journey is better than the inn.' Knowledge is a journey—not a destination. Einstein said that he was not smarter than anyone else—just constantly curious. I pray I can make at least this one impression on you this morning: *if you will read, you will succeed.*

"When I was a boy, my mom would often say, 'Youth is wasted on the young.' And as I get older, the meaning of that statement becomes clearer. Our energy and physical capabilities are at their peak when we're younger, but our experience and wisdom are lacking. Another ancient proverb says, 'Knowledge in youth is wisdom in age.'"

That sounds mighty familiar, Aaron thought.

"Now, this speaks to the way it *ought* to be. But oftentimes, knowledge is not synthesized into wisdom as it should be. I want to show you an equation Dr. John taught me many years ago."

Reedy wrote on the whiteboard:

$$(I + K) \times E = W$$

"Now, in this equation, the *I* is for 'intellect' or 'IQ.' It is the mental capacity that you were born with. It's essentially a fixed factor. *K* is for 'knowledge,' which comes from information and therefore is potentially unlimited. Greater knowledge is that which allows innovation, which is the fuel of our incredible free market economy. *E* is for 'experience.' Finally, the *W* is for 'wisdom.' So intellect *plus* knowledge *times* experience *yields* wisdom. This is called the Wisdom Factor."

Pens were moving as Michael spoke.

"Let's look at an example. Here is someone with a genius-level IQ who just graduated from college with no working experience. This person could have a wisdom factor that looks like this . . ."

$$(10 + 4) \times 1 = 14$$

"Here's another person with a high intellect who just earned their college degree, does a fair amount of reading, and has held jobs since they were a young teenager. They would score higher." He wrote on the board:

$$(8 + 5) \times 2 = 26$$

"The score of the second is almost *double* the first even though the intelligence quotient is lower. This comparison shows the effect on the wisdom factor when a person has an increased drive to learn through extra reading or they have more experience. In this case, the experience was gained in jobs they had when they were younger.

"Here is what person number two might look like after ten years of consistent reading and work experience:

$$(8 + 7) \times 6 = 90$$

Again, notice that *I* doesn't change, yet wisdom soars. You see what is going on here?"

Students nodded.

Michael continued, "These examples show the enormous leverage that is available when a commitment to aggressively acquiring knowledge is heightened in its application through experience.

"By the way," Michael added, "experience is not just *time*; it's also affected greatly by good positioning decisions. That means finding work environments, mentors, and companions who make you better. It also means having the proper perspective to learn from your experience—especially your failures.

"I ask my kids every night at dinner, 'What was your biggest success and biggest failure today?' And then my wife and I share our own. Learning from the experiences of others is important. In fact, one of my favorite maxims says, 'Learn from the mistakes of others. You don't have the time or money to make them all yourself.'

"Let me give you one more example. Here's a person who did not have the opportunity to get a formal education but who has above-average intelligence and has been an avid reader his entire life. He has also surrounded himself with wise people and has twenty-five years of experience in the workplace:

$$(7 + 9) \times 9 = 144$$

"What do you notice about this Wisdom Factor?"

Aaron raised his hand. Michael acknowledged him. "Yes?"

"Even though he didn't get a degree, his wisdom factor is crazy high."

"That's right, Mr. . . . ?"

"Woods, sir. Aaron Woods."

"Thank you, Aaron. And while my first advice to my children, and anyone else, is to absolutely get a college degree if you have the opportunity, many famous achievers throughout history did not: da Vinci, Galileo, Beethoven, Rembrandt, Lincoln, Truman, Disney, Winfrey, Jobs, Gates . . . to name a few. But I can promise you this—they were and are dedicated lifelong learners.

"Let's examine more closely the *K* part of our equation —*knowledge*.

"Academic studies have shown that time spent in 'deep reading'—in a quiet setting—gives us more attentiveness, better memory, and improved cognition. Our brains become calmer and sharper because we aren't overstimulated. We can relax. The result is a state of contemplation. This leads to *deep thinking*. Books calm the mind."

Michael went on. "Seventeenth-century French philosopher Blaise Pascal once observed, 'The sole cause of man's unhappiness is that he does not know how to stay quietly in his room.' Maybe in our frenzied information age, a back-porch swing could be one of the best career-advancement tools you can have.

"With that said, I'm going to recommend to you the same thing Dr. John did for me fifteen years ago: create a lifelong learning game plan."

Michael looked around the classroom, waiting for students to catch up in their notes. "The first step is to identify categories of learning areas, such as history and government, economics and finance, psychology and sociology, faith, self-help, fiction—and, of course, your own field of professional expertise. Having these diverse categories provides a 360-degree perspective.

"Now, I suspect Dr. John has mentioned how important it is to write things down on paper in order to learn them and make sure they get done. Am I right?"

"Yes," several students chorused. Some gestured to their notebooks expressively.

Michael nodded. "Well, it's the same *story* here. When you put your lifelong learning game plan in writing, you're making a commitment, at least to yourself. And that, in turn, increases the chances of consistent behavior.

"As an example, let's say you're determined to read twenty-four books for the year—that's two per month. Here is what your plan might look like if you're a financial professional like me."

Michael wrote on the board:

Economics/Finance	9
History/Government	5
Psychology/Sociology	4
Faith/Fiction/Misc.	6

"This simple plan will provide ample emphasis in your area of expertise and also give you a good balance of knowledge in other areas. This will create a *crossover effect*. For example, because economics is affected by government, history, and sociology, this crossover gives a broader perspective and keener insights into your *primary* field of knowledge. By being well read in so many areas, you'll be able to connect on a personal level with anyone, anywhere, at any time.

"And check this out—" Michael rubbed his hands together as if he was about to reveal a big secret. "Each book you read affects *who you are* because reading is not just informational; it's *transformational*. Each of the authors you choose has read hundreds of books themselves in order to write their own. It's another way this plan provides a positive multiplier effect. The Inspired Text says, 'A wise man is surrounded by a multitude of advisors.' Guess what? Those advisors can come not only from live humans with whom you surround yourself; they can also come in the form of books from wise authors of every age. Isn't it remarkable to think that there is an unlimited source of mentors who can enrich your level of success and significance? 'Though they are dead, they still speak.'

"Let me show you something." Michael walked over and placed a laminated poster board on an empty easel. It was about three feet by four feet and appeared to have colored rectangles in a grid. He smiled as if he were holding the blue-ribbon science fair project. "A gentleman by the name of Charles Tremendous Jones once said, 'You will be the same person in five years as you are today *except* for the people you meet and the books you read.' About ten years ago, I started keeping up with the books I read in the form of this chart. It's called a PTB, or a 'periodic table of books.' In a way, it tells you *who I am*."

The class focused intently on the chart, trying to read some of the titles.

"It's also an invaluable tool when I need to remember where I read something if I'm presenting, writing an article, or just making book recommendations to a friend or associate," Michael added. "As you can imagine, I'm the guy people ask, 'Have you read any good books lately?' I update it every January and currently have about five hundred books on it. It also looks pretty cool on my office wall."

Michael smiled. "I've heard that an author invests about two years of life experience, on average, into every book they write. If that's true, then I've gained a thousand years of experience I would not have otherwise had! So what will *your* PTB look like in five years? Who will *you* be? Imagine not just the enjoyment the books will provide but the enormous advantage they will afford you—because I can tell you that most of your peers are *not* reading consistently."

Michael looked at his watch. "I know Dr. John wants me to save some time for Q & A, so let me end with this story. I was valedictorian of my high school class. I earned a scholarship to State U. But I still had to get a part-time job to make ends meet. After a successful academic career, I married the love of my life—also a mighty State U Eagle. We since have been blessed with three wonderful daughters. My professional trajectory was on a steep climb in the first decade of my career. But the rigors of that corporate ladder climbing wore heavily on my family life.

"I was always diligent at scanning articles and industry publications to keep up with my profession, but as I mentioned, I was not a reader per se. Maybe three or four books per year at most. With Dr. John's encouragement, I enrolled in his firm's lifelong learning program. Again, I will stress that I was not very enthusiastic at first, but I trusted my mentor and kept reading. And then something happened. I liked it."

Michael walked out from behind the podium to lean against it—one of Dr. John's own mannerisms, Aaron noted. "I came to understand the power of the *crossover effect*. I realized that the habit of continuous learning had equipped me to feel comfortable in any conversation. The payoff for my effort came one evening when I was on the road visiting a client in Florida. I found myself at a dinner party arranged especially for me in order to meet a dozen of my client's closest friends. It was a great opportunity to meet some extraordinary people. The trouble was that the average age of the guests at the gathering was about seventy—with the youngest still being around sixty. A generation and a half is a big gap. Most people my age would see this as an intimidating situation. But you know what I did?"

Michael paused. "I relished it. I seized it. Upon arriving back at the office the next afternoon, I went straight to Dr. John's office and related the experience to him, exclaiming, 'I have never felt more comfortable in a business or social situation! I had complete command of the room. I did a LAVA on every person there, and there was *no topic* of conversation that I was not totally comfortable engaging in. All the books I have read in the lifelong learning program prepared me beyond anything I could have ever imagined.'

"In just a few years my Wisdom Factor went from this—" Michael wrote on the board.

$$(9 + 4) \times 3 = 39$$

"To this—"

$$(9 + 8) \times 7 = 119$$

He circled the "119" with a red marker. "And it can only go higher from here," Michael concluded.

Dr. John stepped to the front of the room. "Who has a question for Mr. Reedy?" he asked.

"Here, in the red sweater." Michael gestured.

Dr. John identified the student for his friend. "Calli Clark."

"Yes, I understand that reading books is good," Calli said. "But can't we just be diligent about keeping up with things online and get the same effect over time? It's much more convenient than reading an entire book, plus we can check out a lot more topics."

"Thank you for that question, Calli. When I was your age, I felt exactly the same way. What you said makes perfect sense, especially when we're all so busy. Sitting down and reading a book takes planning and time, doesn't it?" Michael asked.

Calli nodded in agreement.

"It's important to realize that books are different than articles or blogs because of the level of vetting involved. Articles and blogs are more prone to error because of deadlines. But a book—while not immune to this—is much more likely to contain information that's been researched more thoroughly. It's been read by editors and other collaborators and has gone through multiple iterations by the time you open it.

"When I wrote my own book," Michael explained, "the version I finally turned into the publisher was version 18.0.

Books are subject to more scrutiny—and thus more reliable information. And keep in mind, I'm talking in general. There are exceptions.

"The other thing is that reading other materials is often 'shallow reading.' That's because you are prone to many more distractions since you most often read them on your devices. Hard-copy books, on the other hand, are separated from those distractions, though many avid readers will read e-books after they have developed enough discipline to ignore those distractions. That's great if you can do that."

Michael looked around the classroom. "Another question?"

"Jake?" Dr. John called.

"I did the math when you were showing us your book chart. How can you read fifty books per year?!"

Michael laughed. "Well, some years I read a hundred and other years only twenty-five or thirty. But I believe reading one book per month is a must to even be in the game. And if you'll read two books per month for the rest of your career, you will be either a business owner or an executive level manager—probably C level. But it's not as hard as it might seem. Here is the math." Michael went back to the board.

$$MPD = n \times 2$$

This guy really likes his little equations, Aaron mused.

"If you wanted to read twenty-five books per year, for example, then that's fifty minutes per day (MPD) which equals 25 books (n) times two."

$$50 = 25 \times 2$$

"Another way to put it is this: take the number of books you want to read each year, and then read that many minutes *twice* per day. One book per month—twelve per year—is only twenty-four minutes of reading per day, or twelve minutes twice per day. That's not much. Who can't do that? And this math is based on an average book size of 250 pages at a reading pace of only one page every *three* minutes. That's plenty of time to highlight, make margin notes, or stop and contemplate."

"We have time for one more question. Right here: Mr. Cobb," Dr. John said.

"You mentioned that balancing your work and personal life was important to you. How do you do that and still maintain such a high level of performance?" asked Justin.

Michael stared at the back of the room for a moment. "It's not easy," he said. "I would say you must first *learn your lessons well.* What I mean by that is putting into practice the usable life lessons Dr. John is teaching you in this class. I have the extraordinary blessing of having him as a *personal* mentor. You're getting the next best thing by having him as a professor.

"After that, three things come to mind. The first is to become an exceptional time leader and learn that it's OK to say no. If you don't, the demands of others will eat your schedule up. You can do almost *anything*, but you can't do *everything*. Einstein said, 'I am thankful for all those who said no to me. It's because of them that I'm doing it myself.'

"Secondly, master the art of asking great questions and telling impactful stories. Both of these tools make your communication more efficient—so they're big time savers.

"And thirdly, and most importantly, know your *purpose*. My life is prioritized in the following way: faith, family, friends, fitness, and financial stewardship. My relationship with our Creator comes first. Then my wife and kids, and good friends that will 'be real' with me are invaluable. I try to maintain my physical health so I'll be around a while, and I never put money first because I believe if you follow this sequence, all the 'stuff' we need will come along."

The class was silent as students pondered these words.

"Well, I hope that helps. The twelve keys to professional success changed my life. They will do the same for you. I want you all to call my office in five years, make an appointment, and come by and show me your periodic tables of books. Remember: if you read, you succeed! Thank you for your kind attention today," Michael concluded.

Hearty applause rang out for the second week in a row.

Dr. John hugged Michael. "Great job, brother." He turned back toward the class. "A couple of things before you head out," he said. "There is a free app that goes along with your text-book. You can download it by typing **theoldschooladvantage**. It has the twelve keys we have learned this semester on it so that you may refer to them long after the ink on your diploma is dry.

"But!" Dr. John raised his forefinger until he had every-one's attention. "The app won't do you any good on your exam! Remember to review your notes and go over everything we've learned independently."

After a brief pause, Dr. John continued. "It's time for your last challenge of the semester, and you can easily guess what it might be. I want you to create a lifelong learning game plan of your own. It should be a twelve-month plan and have a min-imum of twelve books on it. Be sure to mark the categories of your selections to show a balance to optimize the crossover effect Michael talked about. The template is on the portal, and it's due the Friday of Dead Week by normal class time. We will review for your final next week, but for now, have a great day!"

The line to talk to Michael Reedy after class formed quickly. To Michael's surprise, John Daniels Jr. was first in line.

"JJ! It's been too long! How the heck are you?" Michael laughed, giving John Jr. a hug.

"It's great to see you, too, Michael," John Jr. said.

"I had no idea you were going to be here!" Michael exclaimed.

"I couldn't miss my mentor's speech," John Jr. responded. "I'm also in town for the week. We have a symposium, and I was asked to speak and then serve on a panel."

"Wow. A chip off the old block if I've ever seen one. Congratulations. I'm so proud of you! How's your bride?" Michael asked.

"She's amazing! Thanks for asking. Hey, maybe we could catch a quick cup of coffee?" John Jr. smiled.

"Sure! Let me answer a few questions for these fine students, and then we'll head over to the Union."

"Great!" John Jr. replied.

Aaron stood by, watching the exchange. As he turned to leave, he felt a hand on his shoulder and heard Dr. John say, "John, I want you to meet Aaron Woods. He's one of my star pupils this semester."

"*Star pupil*"? Aaron smiled.

John Jr. shook his hand. "Oh, great! Nice to meet you, Aaron. Where are you from?"

The LAVA conversation proceeded from there, and afterward, Aaron asked, "How do you know Mr. Reedy?"

Michael was my mentor for the first five years of my career," John Jr. answered.

"Really? That must have given you a real advantage." Aaron said.

"Oh, absolutely!" John Jr. exclaimed.

"May I ask you one question about that experience . . . working with Mr. Reedy, I mean?" Aaron asked.

"Of course." John Jr. allowed.

"What was the most important thing he ever taught you?"

Without hesitation, John Jr. answered, "The only way to succeed is to fail as often as you can."

Aaron considered this for a long moment. Then he replied, "Thank you. It was nice to meet you, John."

"The pleasure was mine, Aaron. Take care." John Jr. said as Aaron headed out the door.

He turned back to his dad. "You want to join Michael and me at the Union?"

"No, you enjoy. We're going to meet later for lunch," Dr. John replied.

"OK, I'll catch up with you later," John Jr. said, hugging his father.

"Love you, son."

"Love you, too, Dad."

TWENTY-TWO

THE REVIEW

You can learn more about a person in an hour of play than a year of conversation.

—PLATO

"Good morning! Please take your seats so we can have some fun!" Dr. John exclaimed on the day of the review.

He paused as the class settled in.

"Life is *this* close, ladies and gentlemen." He held up his right thumb and forefinger a quarter inch apart to demonstrate. "Let me show you what I mean. Are there any baseball fans in here?" he asked.

Half the class held up their hands. Dr. John picked up a baseball from the front table.

"Oh, good. Baseball season is upon us, and you know baseball is the Great American Game. In fact, it's so ingrained in our national culture and psyche that I would challenge you to go an entire day without using or hearing a baseball term. Think about it:

"'He struck out.'

"'I'll touch base tomorrow.'

"'They're out in left field on this one.'

"'She hit a home run.'

"'They are playing hardball.'

"We use these phrases every day. Did you know that there are 162 games in a major league baseball season?"

A few heads nodded.

Dr. John held up the ball for emphasis. "A baseball season is a marathon. If your team wins ten out of every twenty games they play, they are *guaranteed* to *miss* the playoffs. If they win eleven out of every twenty games, they are all but *guaranteed* to *make* the playoffs. One more win out of every twenty games makes the difference between 'wait until next year' or a chance at baseball immortality as World Series champions. And it's that way in every aspect of life. It's *that* close. That's why we've been learning the twelve keys to professional success—so that you will consistently win *eleven* games or more and not just ten."

Dr. John looked around the room. "Any baseball players in here?"

Wes Martaug raised his hand from the fourth row. "Right here."

"You got skills, then, right?" Dr. John said as he lobbed the ball softly to him underhanded.

Wes caught it. "Thanks!"

"You're welcome. Now it's time to play a little game of our own," Dr. John said.

Maria Lopez came forward to stand beside Dr. John at the front of the classroom. Behind her, the scoreboard from the first day of class was ablaze with red numbers on a table at the front.

Dr. John began, "As you know, classes don't meet next week, and then the following Friday is your final exam. Today is review day, and I thought we might take a nonconventional approach. No doubt you've noticed my scoreboard. I've asked my good friend Maria to do the honors of operating it for us—and also to act as our official referee."

Referee? Aaron thought. Students sat up in anticipation.

"Everyone from Aaron over to the left will be on Team Maroon, the 'home' team on the scoreboard. Everyone from Natalie over this way is on Team White, or the 'visitors.' Maria will help me monitor the room, looking for the first hand up as I ask review questions. All clear?"

All heads nodded.

Dr. John grinned and said, "Here we go! First question: What does the first *A* in the acronym LAVA stand for?"

There was a moment of hesitation as everyone tried to collect their thoughts. Then Natalie raised her hand.

"Natalie?"

"Associations?" she answered.

"That's it! Two points for Team White, please," Dr. John said, glancing at Maria.

"Next question: What question did Ben Franklin ask himself each day on his written schedule?" Dr. John asked.

"'What good shall I do this day?'" shouted Nick Berry, raising his hand.

"Thank you, Nick. Keep calm, now," Dr. John said as the class laughed.

All now understood the contest at hand. *Game on!* Aaron thought.

"Here we go. Next question: What is one characteristic that is implied when you use the words 'first things first'?"

"You are organized," answered Rachel.

"Yes!"

Dr. John picked up the pace. "What phrase did the wise farmer from China use—"

"We'll see!" Mary squealed.

"That is correct!"

"Next question: Which system is known as 'fast thinking'?"

"System 2," Calli said.

"No! Team White, for one point?"

"System 1!" Deron exclaimed.

"Your deductive reasoning skills are exceptional, Mr. Johnson!" Dr. John teased.

The class teams were tied at fifteen each and going strong. Back and forth the questions and answers flew. "Name one of the three things companies are always looking for in good employees."

"Good communicators!" Madison said.

"Thank you, Ms. Taylor. That is correct!"

Students were beginning to *anticipate* the questions. "What is the most connecting form of communication?"

"A handwritten note!" boomed Robert Harris.

The competition had reached a fever pitch. *As it always does*, Dr. John thought gleefully. The contest proceeded for another fifteen minutes, until both teams were tied at forty-one points and Dr. John only had one more question to determine the champion.

I bet this always comes down to the last question, knowing Dr. John, Aaron thought as he smirked.

"Here we go! Are you ready?" Dr. John perused his notes, tormenting the students. "Let me see here—which one should I ask? For the class championship . . ."

"Come on!" Brandon exclaimed from the back.

Nervous laughter ensued.

Dr. John looked up over his glasses and asked slowly, "What is one of the three most important . . ." Then, quickly, he barked, ". . . reverse interview questions? Yes, Aaron!" Dr. John pointed.

"'What do you mean by that?!'" Aaron cried.

"That's *not* it!" Dr. John screamed. "Natalie—for the win?!"

"'How would you describe your company's values?'" she answered.

"That's it! Team White wins the championship!" Dr. John said in his best excited radio play-by-play voice.

"What?!" Aaron clasped both hands behind his head. Dr. John, amused, thought he resembled an angry cobra. "No way!" Several of Aaron's teammates booed jokingly. Some threw crumpled-up pieces of notebook paper. Dr. John's belly laugh showed he was quite pleased with the trick question. Aaron, of course, had defaulted to one of the more recent important questions he had learned, failing to think further back.

After the class was brought back to order, Dr. John thanked Maria for her assistance.

"What do we win?" called Jake Conners.

Dr. John answered, "Something no one can ever take away from you: bragging rights."

Guffaws and laughter filled the room.

"Maria, please . . ." Dr. John motioned for her to return to the front of the classroom. "I want to formally introduce to you my good friend, Maria Lopez," Dr. John told the class.

Maria was clearly embarrassed by the attention.

"Maria is one of the most extraordinary people I've ever known. You may have noticed her sitting in the back for most of our classes this semester. She arrived an hour early on those days to get a start on her work here in the building so that she could sit in. She earned her business communications degree in December and is auditing the class as she wraps up translating the 12 Keys to Professional Success into Spanish."

Maria looked down with her hands folded in front of her.

Wow! That's impressive! I guess it makes sense now, Aaron thought.

"Maria has an incredible story," Dr. John continued. "She came to America several years ago from Guatemala on a student visa. She found the love of her life here at State U and is now married to David. He's a real prince of a guy too."

Maria smiled as she looked up at Dr. John.

"David is the minister of a small church near campus, and the two of them now have two children: David Jr. and Concepción. You call her Conchita, right?"

Maria nodded.

"I love that name. She's such a doll," Dr. John said. Maria beamed. "Their dream is to distribute the material you've learned in this class and use it in their ministry. They have set a goal to travel and teach in every Latin American country—starting with their beloved Guatemala. And after seven years of waiting, both Maria and David recently became United States citizens, right?"

"Yes," she said, as tears pooled up in her eyes.

"Thank you for your help this semester and for your example of diligence." Dr. John began to clap but was interrupted as Maria raised her hand with a serious look on her face.

She paused. A tear streamed down her left cheek. She quickly wiped it away and said, "Dr. John, I want to tell these students something." Her soft, firm tone was clear through her heavy accent. The students subsided to listen.

"Ever since I sat on my grandfather's lap and he told me how President Reagan described America as a shining city on a hill, I dreamed of coming here. And the proudest moment of my life was on March 14, my *abuelo*'s eightieth birthday. On that day, I raised my hand and swore allegiance to the Constitution of the United States of America. And then I sang 'The Star-Spangled Banner' for the first time as an American citizen. I love this country. Thank you."

Maria wiped away more tears. Dr. John lightly put his right hand on her shoulder to comfort her. He did not need to lead the clapping. The ovation came naturally and immediately.

As Maria returned to her seat, Dr. John gathered himself. "I'm not sure what to say after that." His voice cracked slightly. "I hope you will all get a chance to know Maria. We wish you Godspeed."

After an extended pause while Dr. John pretended to rearrange his notes, he continued. "I know today probably wasn't the comprehensive review you expected, but sometimes we have to have fun.

"Now, if you'll remember, I promised you all a copy of *The Day Book* at the end of the semester. I'm excited, because today you get those books!" Dr. John exclaimed. "If you remember, going all the way back to our second key to success on time leadership, *The Day Book* is designed to align with the first principle of reviewing your schedule every evening on paper. It's kind of interesting. I'm seeing more and more articles lately on the subject of returning to analog daily planners.

"Now, I know that paper planners have limited space to write—which some might see as a disadvantage. But the unlimited space that apps provide may cause you to hoard tasks—and forget about them. This causes the short-term *urgent* items to constantly bubble up at the expense of the long-term *important* items. Remember, prioritization is the key to time leadership. Limited space *helps you prioritize.*

"*The Day Book* is a special analog planner that super-imposes the twelve keys to professional success over your schedule. As we pass these out, please open your copy to the first page, and I'll show you what I mean."

Dr. John and Maria picked boxes of the planners up from where they had been sitting inconspicuously against the wall, and passed them back to every student in the class. The class was silent except for the sounds of rifling pages as the students examined their new planners.

When each student had a copy, Dr. John returned to the podium. "On the opening page, you will see a place to put your contact information in case it gets lost and then that stanza from one of my favorite poems, 'Normal Day.' Next are the seven time leadership concepts you learned. They are here as a reminder.

"On the first calendar page, located just over the date, is the 'National Day.' Did you know that January 8 is 'National Clean Your Desk Day'? March 2 is 'National Dress in Blue Day,' and March 29 is 'National Viet Nam Veterans Day.' You can use these 'National Days' as an excuse to reach out to someone who has a messy desk." Several roommates pointed at each other. "Or have your team at work all wear the same color. Or honor a veteran for their service," Dr. John added.

He turned a page in a sample planner he held above the class to demonstrate. "On the left, you see the to-do list with a place to rank each task. There's also a place for the GMAD—if it has one. At the bottom left is a quote of the day, ready to go for your daily handwritten note. Of course, the hourly schedule is aligned on the same page, adjacent to your task list for ready reference. Finally, on this left-hand side is a WOW! word or phrase of the day to keep you sharp and to plant them deeper into your system 1 thinking.

"On the opposing page on the right is an area for meeting notes, without lines so you can draw mind maps if you wish. Remember mind maps from your freshman How to Make a 4.0 workshop?" Dr. John asked.

Heads nodded.

"And here is one of my favorite parts. Oftentimes, either we're too tired or we just forget to journal about our lives each day. So at the bottom right, there is a space to write a short daily entry. Ben Franklin's famous question 'What good have I done today?' is there to motivate you to take just a few minutes to reflect.

"Now turn to the back tab, please," Dr. John instructed. "Here you will find what I call the 'Crib Notes Section,' which contains lists and ready reference of all the concepts you've learned this semester: WOW! words, ready recall memory palaces, influence techniques and phrases, a place for your story vault, steps to big decisions, a lifelong learning blueprint you can fill out . . ." Dr. John smiled. "Well. You get the picture. It's all there at your fingertips for everyday usage. I'm excited for you all to start using this tool. So please enjoy!"

It looked like a room full of kids on Christmas Day. Many students said low thank-yous as Dr. John paused again. "Remember, we won't meet next week. That means you have plenty of time to ace the final! Now go get to work!"

A line of students hung around after class to express their appreciation to Dr. John, knowing that, the way things usually went when the school year wrapped up, it might be their last chance.

Aaron noticed Maria standing by herself. "Excuse me, Mrs. Lopez?"

"Yes?" Maria smiled.

"My name is Aaron Woods, and I just wanted to say congratulations on all your achievements. Your story is very inspirational, and I know you and your husband are going to do great things. Thank you for sharing it."

She graciously bowed her head and accepted his compliment, then said, "I know who you are, Aaron. Dr. John has talked much about you."

"Really?"

"Yes. You're from Fort Worth, aren't you?" she asked.

Aaron smiled, and the LAVA conversation flowed for several more minutes. Aaron wished Maria well and then turned to take his turn to talk to Dr. John.

"Howdy, Aaron! What can I do for you?" Dr. John asked.

"Dr. John, I—I just wanted to thank you for this semester."

"Well, you know it's absolutely been my pleasure—" Dr. John replied.

Aaron interrupted. "No, I mean it. I've never had a professor who had more of an impact on me and the way I think about life. I feel so confident and excited about the future. You've equipped us well, Dr. John. In fact, I wanted to come to you for confirmation concerning a decision I've made—using the decision matrix, of course."

"Of course." Dr. John smiled. "Tell me about it."

"I have to admit, over the winter break this year, I didn't think any company would hire me. I was panicking. But I've since applied the things I learned in your course, and they all work. Dressing for success, handwritten notes—and one of the companies interviewed me for two and a half hours! When they offered me the position, they said they had never had a candidate ask *them* so many questions. I probably used all fourteen reverse interview questions and then some."

"That's great, Aaron. That may be a record!" Dr. John replied.

"Yeah . . . maybe. Anyway, I had two job offers from exceptional companies. But then a third option came into play. You inspired me to consider an academic track for a third option after graduation. I hadn't really thought about anything but business until . . . until, I guess, I met you," Aaron said.

Dr. John smiled. "Well, I'll take that as a compliment, Aaron."

Aaron continued, "I compared the two great job offers I've received with the partial scholarship offer to stay in school and work on a graduate degree while Amanda finishes up. Ironically, just like in the example you showed us a few weeks ago, the matrix scores I ended up with have me leaning heavily in the academic direction. What do you think?"

Dr. John looked at Aaron for an extended moment, smiled, and then asked, "What if I asked you to work with me?"

"Wha . . . What do you mean by that? Teach?"

"Yes. That could be part of it. Starting in the fall, I've been allotted a stipend for a teaching-assistant position—it isn't much," Dr. John added.

"Oh, I understand," Aaron responded quickly.

"But I also do consulting work for various companies and organizations," Dr. John told him. "The twelve keys curriculum fits corporate audiences, obviously. And I teach other courses on advanced storytelling, the extraordinary client experience, and becoming a life-changing mentor to various teams and executives. It would be a unique opportunity for you—and I think you would be a phenomenal protégé. Maybe you can even carry the baton for me one day. I won't be around forever, you know."

Aaron was stunned. Both men stared at each other.

"Yes," Aaron blurted. "It sounds good. I mean, can I sleep on it?" He flushed. "Maybe I can tell you after finals?"

"Of course. There's no hurry. It's just a thought. It would be fun. Just let me know. Hey, by the way, I almost forgot—are you ready for Friday night?" Dr. John asked.

The mention of his upcoming proposal made Aaron smile. "Yes, sir. I'm nervous, but ready."

"All your HarmonEagles are in place?" Dr. John laughed. "Your reservation at the Legacy Oak is in order?"

"Yes. All is ready to go."

"And Amanda. She's still doing OK?"

"Yes. She still has an occasional moment of dizziness now and again. The doctors just think it's the meds. It limited her off-season practice time. But she always just tells me she has to keep calm and carry on."

Dr. John recognized the reference and grinned. "Does she, now?"

"Well, again, Dr. John, I just wanted to say thank you for the class—and now for the offer to work with you. I'll think it over and let you know."

"Fair enough, Aaron. You don't have to wait until the final exam to let me know how things go with your big proposal, OK?"

"Yes, sir. I'll be in touch," Aaron promised

How can things get any better than this?! Aaron thought. *I just received a proposal for my dream job, and I'm about to issue a proposal to my dream girl.* He felt like skipping as he left the classroom. He refrained. Barely.

TWENTY-THREE

THE CALL

Grief is the price we pay for love.
—QUEEN ELIZABETH II

Dr. John settled into his favorite time of the day. Early morning coffee, quiet time, and reading. *Another excellent semester is almost in the books*, he thought to himself.

He extended a hand beneath the table to a sleepy yellow lab. "Come over here, girl. How's my puppy dog? Yes, sir. She's a good one." Dr. John scratched Sadie, his son Nate's twelve-year-old dog, behind her ears and accepted her affectionate lick of his fingers. With a happy sigh, she sank down to sit by his feet.

Dr. John had just finished scanning the *Wall Street Journal* when the phone rang. He looked at the grandfather clock as he answered. It was two minutes after seven.

"Hello?"

"Professor Daniels?"

"Yes, this is he."

"This is Barbara Woods, Aaron's mother."

"Yes, Ms. Woods. How are you?" Dr. John said, curious.

"Not so well, I'm afraid. We've received some bad news."

Dr. John's pulse quickened. He had heard that statement before. His eyes closed tightly for the worst.

"Aaron wanted me to call you . . . and let you know that his girlfriend, Amanda . . . passed away suddenly late last evening." Ms. Woods's voice was trembling.

Dr. John's heart sank. *No, God, no!* He found himself unable to speak.

Ms. Woods continued, "You may know that she had been having periodic fainting spells—which had largely subsided of late."

"Yes. I know," Dr. John replied vacantly.

"Well, it appears as though the spells were a result of microstrokes, but this time a larger vessel in her brain ruptured, and there was nothing that could be done. It's a rare condition but is often the explanation for the cause of death when an otherwise healthy young athlete dies suddenly. The condition was congenital." Ms. Woods tried to speak in a physician's monotone in an effort to make the news easier to deliver. Her voice broke, and over the speaker, Dr. John heard a woman who had loved the girl she'd hoped would be her future daughter-in-law sob. "I'm sorry to have to be the bearer of this terrible news. But Aaron wanted to make sure you knew."

In shock, Dr. John softly said, "Thank you for letting me know. I'm not sure what to say. How is Aaron?"

"He is currently here with us. I'm sorry, I must go now." She was weeping.

"Is there anything I can do?" Dr. John asked.

But Mrs. Woods had already hung up.

Johnathan Daniels sunk to his knees, dropping the phone beside him. He felt like raising a fist and screaming at God. He had done it before. But he knew it wouldn't help. He also knew it wasn't God's fault. But would Aaron know that?

Dr. John prayed silently for the comfort of Amanda's family and for Aaron, and he prayed that he might also have a chance to do the hardest job of a mentor: provide hope after tragedy.

But for now, it was a time to mourn.

Amanda's teammates decided to hastily organize a candlelight vigil for Friday evening to honor their friend. It would likely be her family, close friends, and teammates, but it would still provide some small modicum of closure on what would have been her twenty-first birthday.

A crowd of about one hundred gathered in the central commons around "Bart"—the statue of the university's first president, Bartholomew J. Morton. The blustery spring evening made the candles challenging, yet dozens were lit. And then scores more. Word had spread quickly. They shone from all directions in the dark. Hundreds and finally well over one thousand students came to pay their respects.

It's just that kind of place, Dr. John thought as he witnessed students stream to the center of campus. The outpouring of sympathy confirmed again that his university was like none he had ever seen. The character. The confident humility of the type of student who came to this unique place filled with tradition. His profound sadness was mixed with an indescribable pride in his alma mater. He struggled to contain his emotions, but he was determined to remain strong in case he saw Aaron.

As the crowd settled in, there was total silence. Campus lights were off. Even dorms closed their curtains to douse unnatural light. This provided an unusual atmosphere of darkness on campus. The gathering was illuminated only by the candles that survived the breeze and by the Milky Way, which hung like a chorus of peering angels. All stood motionless.

Amanda's father stepped forward to give an address. Then he heard a lone bugle softly playing.

Daah . . . dah . . . daah . . .

Mr. Watkins stepped back to the inner rim of the circle. Another bugle joined in.

Daah . . . dah . . . daah . . .

Finally, a third bugle.

Daah . . . dah . . . daah . . .

The melancholy notes of the traditional student memorial ballad floated into the moist spring air. Not a word was uttered. The harmony was simple and breathtaking.

Daah . . . dah . . . daah . . .

All in attendance were familiar with the tune, but many were surprised. The bugle call was a normal occurrence at the official student memorials, but with finals coming up, no one had expected the instrumentalists to play tonight.

Daah . . . dah . . . daah . . .

Dr. John had called in a favor. He still had a friend or two in the band at the university. They had agreed to provide the dulcet tones for this unscheduled occasion. The beautiful and haunting rendition ended, and the notes wandered off, as if blown away by the cool evening breeze. Suddenly, the wind subsided. A calmness overcame the assembly. No leaves turned. Candle flames burned unstirred.

Then another faint sound came out of the distance.

Riiing . . . ring . . . Riiing . . . ring . . .

What is it? A bell? Dr. John wondered.

Riing . . . ring . . . Riiing . . . ring . . .

Faintly, Dr. John began to hear another sound, like a fan or a click.

Clikclikclikclikclikclikclikclik . . .

The outer part of the crowd circle began to stir.

A bicycle built for two rode slowly up the walkway.

Riing . . . ring . . . Riiing . . . ring. . .

Clikclikclikclikclikclikclik . . .

Aboard was Janet Simpson, volleyball captain and Amanda's best friend. She rode slowly, ringing the bell softer and softer. The back seat was empty. The mourners parted as she made her way to the center of the assembly.

Clikclikclikclik . . . clik . . . clik . . . clik . . . clik.

Janet dismounted and quietly rested the vehicle on its kickstand. She then slowly reached down and unpinned the playing card attached to the spokes. Tears streaming down her face, Janet held the card out toward Amanda's grieving family.

Mr. Watkins stepped forward again. This time, Amanda's mother and sisters followed. Heads down. Tears flowing. Mr. Watkins took the card and whispered, "Thank you."

When he looked at it, he was overcome. On the back, at the top, was scribbled in a little girl's handwriting, "From my dad. May 2." It was the original queen of hearts. Unknown to him, Amanda had kept it to tell the story again and again to all who were close to her—a story she had treasured all her life.

Mr. Watkins turned, trying to control his own emotions with limited success. He motioned to Aaron, weeping silently off to the side. Aaron walked over to join the family, and Amanda's mother hugged and consoled him.

And then, Dr. John heard voices in the distance . . . singing softly.

Male voices.

> Daisy, Daisy
> Give me your answer, do

The rendition was a full beat slower than normal.

> I'm half-crazy, all for the love with you
> It won't be a stylish marriage

It was the HarmonEagles. It was ten o'clock—and they had been scheduled.

> I can't afford a carriage
> But you'll look sweet upon the seat
> On a bicycle built for two

Then female voices began singing along in perfect harmony.

> Daisy, Daisy give me your heart to do
> I'm half-crazy, hopeful in love with you
> It won't be a stylish marriage
> I can't afford a carriage
> But you look sweet upon the seat
> On a bicycle built for two

The mixed chorus joined together for one last stanza, slower still.

But you look sweet upon the seat
On a bicycle built for two
On a bicycle built for two
On a bicycle built for two
For two, for two, for two, for two . . .

Complete silence fell over the assembled students, family, and friends at Bart's statue. Two thousand eyes. Not one dry.

TWENTY-FOUR

THE MEMORIAL

Friendship multiplies joys and divides griefs.
—H. G. BOHN

Amanda Leigh Watkins's funeral on Sunday afternoon was in her hometown of Brenham, a small, quiet community less than an hour's drive from campus. It was a beautiful sunny day and a more beautiful celebration of her life. More than eight hundred mourners were in attendance.

Young people who die out of season have the largest funerals, Dr. John thought as he stood in the back of the sanctuary with his family.

Amanda's father gave her eulogy.

"... Amanda was a diligent student. A loyal teammate. A doting granddaughter. A devoted sister. A loving daughter. And a woman of high character and purity, who looked forward to 'leaving and cleaving' to the man of her dreams one day."

Mr. Watkins paused and gave a nod to Aaron.

"I know that Amanda would have demanded that this day be one of celebration. She was a person of deep faith. And in spite of this tragedy and the pain it has wrought on our family, God is still good. He is still generous. He still loves us. He is still full of grace. That would be the story Amanda

291

would want you to know and remember . . . and now . . ." Mr. Watkins fought to maintain his composure for a few seconds more. "Now she sees her Lord face to face."

As Amanda's father sat down, a full contingent of HarmonEagles stood. They sang a heavenly acapella rendition of "Amazing Grace." Afterward, State U president Dr. Sid Allen closed the memorial in prayer.

Amanda's casket was opened to allow mourners to pass by and pay their respects. Then the pallbearers rolled her closed casket slowly down the center aisle, followed by family and close friends.

Dr. John exited the church and stood on the porch facing the doorway. He had not had a chance to see Aaron since Amanda's death. As Aaron came outside, he saw Dr. John and collapsed toward him, tears flowing.

Dr. John enfolded the young man in a strong hug. "I'm so sorry, Aaron."

A funeral director gently asked Aaron to continue with the procession as the pallbearers neared the waiting hearse.

"Come see me this week," Dr. John said softly.

Aaron nodded.

Lisa and Nicole, near their stepdad, were emotional as they watched their friend go, and as the family made their way out to the car, Anicia took Dr. John's hand in hers and put her head upon his shoulder.

The following Friday, Aaron came as directed to Dr. John's office. "Hello, Dr. John."

Dr. John rose as he spoke, "Aaron, I'm so glad to see you! I've been worried about you all week." He placed his hand on Aaron's shoulder and squeezed.

Aaron's face looked empty. "I'm sorry. I just decided to stick around home for a while. Fortunately, I only have finals in two classes next week. One professor has agreed to exempt me because I have a 98 average, and I was hoping I could talk to you about your final as well. I'm afraid I'm just not in a good place right now after all that has happened," he explained.

Dr. John interrupted. "I completely understand, Aaron. I don't expect you to come to the final exam. That's not a worry you should have at this time. You're good. Please, have a seat."

"Thank you. I appreciate it."

"Of course," Dr. John assured him.

Aaron struggled to speak. He handed Dr. John a card that had been opened. "It's from Amanda's parents," he managed to whisper.

Dr. John opened the note. . .

Dear Aaron,

It is with great sorrow that Mrs. Watkins and I write to you today. We mourn our loss and know you do too. Amanda knew of your plan to propose on her birthday. She found out through a friend. She was so excited. She had saved her honor, love, and devotion for you. You were the man of her dreams. We would be so proud to call you our son as well. And so, we want you to have the enclosed card. She may have been the

Queen of Hearts—but you were her knight in shining armor.

> *May God bless you always,*
> *Jay & Rhonda Watkins*

"It's inside." Aaron choked.

Dr. John shook the small envelope, and the Queen of Hearts fell out.

"I don't know how I will go on. She was the love of my life. I was going to be on the front seat of her bike!" Aaron broke down.

Dr. John looked at the young man falling apart on the other side of his desk. He hadn't just lost his girlfriend. He had lost the entire life he had planned to live with her. "I understand, Aaron. I really do."

Aaron shook his head as if to say, *No you don't!* "Why would this happen? It's not fair!" Aaron raised his voice, forgetting where he was.

Dr. John remained silent as Aaron cried.

After a minute, Dr. John tried to offer comfort. "There's little that I can say that will make things much better right now, Aaron. But I know from experience that grief is a process. A slow process that all who love must eventually go through. When we love others, we accept the risk that one way or another, the relationship will end with pain."

Aaron looked at the floor with an empty stare. Dr. John stopped. While all that was true, it wouldn't help Aaron right now. He knew what Aaron needed. He sighed. "Let me tell you a story."

Aaron looked up and tried to collect himself.

"More than thirty-five years ago, I married my college sweetheart. Her name was Susan. I met her right here at State U. Although I was not exactly full of promise, I somehow talked her into spending her life with me. She was a beautiful woman—both inside and out. She would go on to become a physician. Very accomplished.

"When we started our family, we agreed that she would forego her lucrative career for a time in order to be with our children. She was a phenomenal mother to our two boys. We had a house in the suburbs. My business flourished. We took family vacations often. We had a wonderful community through our church family. We were living the American dream. And then, one day, a simple phone call shook our foundations. On a routine doctor visit for indigestion, my wife received a devastating diagnosis."

Dr. John felt the old grief, dulled with time to something almost bittersweet, an inextricable part of himself, aching in his chest once more. "We prayed and sought signs of hope. Every two weeks, we traveled five hours each way for the best treatment available. We were diligent in our efforts to fight. Susan was brave and determined to win. But it was only a matter of time. She spent her last days at home. And on her final day, I stayed up and watched her all night. You don't sleep when you know the end is near.

"At about 7:15 a.m., I couldn't explain why, but I decided to go upstairs and wake our boys. It was as though my feet were moving themselves. In looking back, I now believe it was providential. Perhaps even a miracle of sorts. I don't pretend to know how all that works. But when I got upstairs, I simply said to the boys, 'Come down and spend some time with Mom.' They came quietly and quickly.

"We all climbed on the bed. The boys petted her head softly and told her they loved her. I encouraged them to talk to her. I believe she heard and understood all they said. They offered sweet words of affection.

"After several minutes, she opened her eyes ever so slightly . . . as if to say, *OK . . . I can go now. I just wanted to say goodbye and that I love you.* And then at 7:37 a.m., on January 31, she slipped away, surrounded by those she loved most. We wept together.

"I explained to our sons that Mom was now with the angels. After a year and four days of fierce battle, she had succumbed. My wife and their mom was gone. Just like that. It was a moment that will last forever."

Aaron could tell Dr. John was retelling a story that had not been unwrapped for many years. He suddenly remembered Dr. John's words: *I know what it's like to be worrying about the health of those close to you.*

Aaron found himself the consoler now. "I'm sorry, Dr. John. I had no idea."

Dr. John blotted a tear from the corner of his eye and continued as though he had not heard Aaron. As though he had been transported again to that time and place.

"I rose to open the tall curtains in our bedroom. Falling across our wooded backyard were the largest snowflakes I had ever seen. They floated down slowly, covering the ground. Snow is rare in North Texas. I would later say at her funeral that it looked like confetti from Heaven. She was home. The angels were celebrating. But we were still here, to carry on without her.

"Many months went by. I tried to be a good dad, but I was a poor substitute for a mom. The boys coped well for the most part, but it was difficult. Our faith in God had been strong throughout the ordeal of Susan's illness. When cancer invades your world, life gets pretty simple. It boils down to faith, family, and friends. It's all you have. Life is about relationships. And we were so thankful for them. But in the long days that followed, I felt empty, wondering what good could possibly have come from such an untimely death."

Dr. John stared out his office window as he spoke. "The days slowly turned into weeks as we endeavored to reestablish our routines in the midst of our new normal. Then, one afternoon, there was a knock at the door. It was Anicia—a dear friend of Susan's. She had come by to bring us a meal and to give me a book. She knew I was a big reader." Dr. John half laughed.

"What was the book?" Aaron asked.

"I have it in my study at home. But, you know, I don't recall the title right now. Isn't that terrible? But I do remember a profound idea that it contained. 'The greater the love—the greater the sorrow. And the lower the lows are in life—the higher are the highs.' In other words, our lives become more worthwhile as we experience challenges, obstacles, grief—and even danger. We appreciate the good things and the good times more because of our trials and difficulties. It's about growth—and an abiding faith in God no matter what. Perseverance. This book made a profound difference in my thinking. It gave me an avenue to exit the place of depression and sadness I was occupying at the time."

Dr. John half smiled then. "Little did I know that little book would lead to much bigger things!"

"What do you mean by that?" Aaron asked.

"Well, one thing happened, and then another, and . . . I learned to love someone again."

"Who?"

"Her."

"Her who?"

"The lady who gave me the book! Anicia!" Dr. John exclaimed.

Aaron's eyes widened as he suddenly understood Dr. John's closeness to Anicia Kosta and Lisa and Nicole's familiarity with Dr. John's principles in an entirely new light. "Really?"

"That's right. I told you books were good gifts!" Dr. John laughed. "I found the most wonderful woman I could have ever imagined. And while I obviously knew her as a friend of my wife's, she had only been an acquaintance to me, really. But we fell in love. I came to know her in a different way. Well enough, in fact, that we were married fifteen months later. She had two daughters—and now so did I. Anicia lovingly took to my sons as any natural mom would. And through God's grace, we blended a family, and I found happiness again."

Aaron looked at Dr. John. Grief and rage and depression still hung heavily around him, but for the first time since Amanda's death, he could see a glimmer of light in the darkness, a twinkling of hope that there might be something beyond all the pain. "Thank you for sharing that, Dr. John," Aaron said. "You know, Lisa and Nicole have been my study buddies this semester. They're nice girls. It's just incredible how everything came together for you after a tragedy like that. And all your kids seem 'wise beyond their years,' if you know what I mean."

Dr. John smiled. "I think I do know what you mean, Aaron."

"But I still can't believe Ms. Kosta is your wi—"

"Ms. Kosta professionally, yes," Dr. John interrupted. "But at home and with our friends, it's technically *Mrs.* Kosta *Daniels*. We're both old school."

"I get it," Aaron acknowledged. "Thank you for telling me your story, Dr. John. It's amazing."

"I can't disagree. I believe there's no one else Susan would have wanted me to marry. In fact—I can't prove it, of course—but I would not be surprised if Susan had something to do with it, maybe as her first angel assignment. Susan's father even walked Anicia down the aisle at our wedding. There wasn't a dry eye in the place."

"I can only imagine," Aaron said.

Dr. John paused for a moment. Then, gently, he said, "Aaron, I had a year during her illness to adjust to the idea of losing Susan. Getting over Amanda's death is going to be difficult for you. Her young age and the sudden nature of her passing is a huge shock. My hope is that by sharing my story with you, it will be some comfort to you to know you're not alone. You have friends and loved ones that will be here to help you bear this burden."

Aaron braved a smile. It was only skin deep, for now, but it was a start. "Thank you, Dr. John. I appreciate it."

"And Aaron—" Dr. John waited for full eye contact. He placed his hand firmly on Aaron's shoulder.

"Yes, sir?"

"If I could tell you only one more thing to remember, it would be this—*life is for the living*."

Aaron's smile turned into a much smaller, sadder thing. Experience taught wisdom—but Dr. John had never wanted Aaron to learn wisdom like this. He nodded soberly. "Thank you, sir."

Then he turned and walked away.

TWENTY-FIVE

THE FINAL

No bird soars in a calm.

—WILBUR WRIGHT

"Good morning, ladies and gentlemen."

Dr. John's normal enthusiasm was absent. It was one minute before nine o'clock. "Let's go ahead and get started."

The front middle seat was empty. Dr. John stared at it and took a moment to consider the semester and the class that sat before him. He prayed silently. *This may be the most difficult and rewarding semester I've ever had. But thank you, God . . . for the opportunity . . . for these kids.*

He then looked up. "I'm confident you're all ready for today's exam. However—" Dr. John stopped as the classroom door opened and Aaron made his way down quickly to his seat.

"I apologize, Dr. John."

Dr. John stared at the young man. "Uh . . . no worries, Aaron. You're actually right on time. Good to see you." Dr. John looked down to regain his composure, then continued. "As I've quoted to you often, 'Readiness is all.' I know you're all ready for the exam today. But there are times when life events preempt even final exams. I believe this is one of those times. I've never done this before—and I don't know how the dean is going to feel about it—but you'll all get a final exam score that is commensurate with the work you've done in this class all semester. I don't think any of you will be disappointed. If you have any questions about your final posted grade—please contact me."

Either disbelief or relief—in some cases, both—fell over the students' faces. Dr. John continued. "I guess you could say, in a sense, I'm giving you a 'take-home' final. Because everywhere you go and in everything you do for the rest of your life, you will be tested. You'll be tested in ways that you can never anticipate. And this class was always about getting you ready for those challenges.

"Sadly, as Robert Frost famously wrote, 'knowing how way leads on to way,' I will never see or talk to most of you again." Dr. John's voice quivered. "So while I have you as a captive audience one last time—and in light of the difficulties we've experienced as an Eagle family in the last few weeks—I decided last night that, in lieu of an exam, I wanted to offer you a few more thoughts before I let you go."

Dr. John began, "Here are **ten things I hope you will never forget**. Some of these will sound familiar."

He gave the class a moment in case they wanted to take notes and, to his pleasure, saw notebooks coming out of backpacks all over the room. There were no keyboards.

"First things first." He managed a slight smile. "**Life is not fair. Fair is an amusement park with rides.** Thank you again, Mr. Chris Kotten.

"**Beware of fame and fortune**. The only thing more difficult to handle than failure is success. Money has never made anyone rich. Seek *contentment*, for it is the key to happiness.

"**Make each day your masterpiece.** Count your blessings, and then ask yourself, like Ben Franklin: 'What good have I done this day?'

"**Don't lie, cheat, or steal—nor tolerate those who do.**

"**Surround yourself with wise peers and mentors—no matter your age.** They will help you stay focused on things that *never change*. To quote the prophet Joel, 'honor the ancient paths—and walk in them.' I call it old school.

"**Never stop learning. Read today. Lead tomorrow.**

"**It's not just what you do. It's *who you are* that matters most.**

Dr. John looked around the classroom and made eye contact with several students before continuing. "*Everyone* **is important. All are made in God's image. Treat them that way.**"

He thought of Anicia before giving the next piece of advice. "**Seek *truth*—and pass it on.** It's the only way to change the world for good."

"And finally . . ." Dr. John looked up at Aaron. He paused for a moment, then he turned to an adjacent table and sifted through his briefcase. "Yes!" he whispered to himself. Stepping forward, he said, "The last and tenth thing I hope you never forget is this: **every challenge brings with it an equal or *greater* opportunity.**"

He looked to either side and slightly upward, then motioned to his left. "We actually have two witnesses from history today," Dr. John said. "I didn't know if we would have a chance to talk about them, but I'm glad we do. Wilbur and Orville Wright are two of the most impactful citizens in American history. Their famous first flight at Kittyhawk, North Carolina, in 1903 changed the world forever. Two bird-watching, book-loving brothers who owned a bicycle shop in Dayton, Ohio, became perhaps the greatest inventors in history. Failing time after time, they became a symbol of perseverance."

He continued, "During their endless experimentation, Wilbur wrote in his journal this short sentence that describes the essence of a challenge. It has become one of my favorite quotes: 'No bird soars in a calm.' I'm holding in my hand a *challenge coin*. It's common for those who have served in our armed forces, police officers, firefighters, and other public safety personnel to present challenge coins to honor a person—and to challenge them to strive for excellence. I've been privileged to receive many over the years. This one doesn't compare in importance to those given by our heroes—" He held the coin up to show to the class. "But it contains an important concept for its recipients. And for all of you. It's given to members of the Old School, a campus organization for which I'm the faculty advisor. They receive it once they become full members at the end of the school year. From then on, they also have the privilege to present a coin to those they see overcoming any great challenge in their lives," Dr. John explained.

"On one side, it actually says *challenge*—and on the other side, it says *opportunity*." Dr. John turned the coin. "The Latin phrase *verum exquirere* is inscribed on this side as well. It means 'seek truth.'" He flipped the coin into the air and caught it. "When the coin flip of life lands on *opportunity*—what do you do?"

No one answered.

Dr. John smiled and said, "You take it! It wasn't a trick question."

Students nodded.

"But when it lands on challenge—as it does most of the time in life—what do you have?" he asked.

Natalie slowly raised her hand. "An opportunity?"

"That's right!" Dr. John exclaimed. "So no matter what happens in life, it's heads, you win, and tails, they lose. You *can't* lose—unless you quit, and none of you will. You will persevere, because you will learn that the challenges in life are what make it interesting . . . and *overcoming* them is what makes life meaningful.

"Aaron?" Dr. John said.

"Yes, sir?" Aaron replied.

"I want to thank you. First, for even being here today. That took courage. No one here expected you. But we're all glad to see you."

Classmates nodded. Some held back tears.

"It's good to be here. I wanted to ace your final," Aaron said with a small smile.

Nervous laughter filled the room.

"I know you did. But you have aced something more important—a test of life. And for being that example to all of us, I want to present this challenge coin to you."

Aaron stood, and Dr. John extended his hand. They shook firmly, and Dr. John passed the coin to Aaron. The students applauded.

As Aaron took his seat, Dr. John faced the class, took a deep breath, paused, and said, "And now, I bid you all farewell. Most of you are now heading into the workforce. And you will all be . . . *awesome!*" He grinned. "And don't forget to come back and see me—or better yet, drop me a card. Now . . ." Dr. John looked around the room one last time. "*Let's get to work!*"

The class cheered, and there was some scattered applause as students lined up to say goodbye one more time. Aaron, seeing the commotion, stepped forward and gently laid an envelope on Dr. John's desk before slipping out the side door.

There was a lump in his throat and his eyes burned as he stepped out into the brilliance of a warm and beautiful late spring Texas day. Aaron lingered for several minutes in the shade of the building, staring at the ground, pondering.

"Hi, Aaron."

The voice that intruded on his thoughts was kind and gentle. Aaron looked up to see Lisa Kosta standing in front of him. "What are you doing here?" he asked.

"Oh, I just wanted to come by and say so long—and to give you this." Lisa handed him a package. "I'm so sorry for your loss," she offered quietly.

"Oh, thank you. I appreciate it," Aaron said, taking the package.

Both stood awkwardly staring at one another. Lisa looked down at the unopened package. "It's a book," she said. "My mom gave the same book to Dr. John when his first wife passed away. I thought it might be helpful."

"That's very nice of you." Aaron told her. He looked at her then. "Hey, why didn't you ever tell me that Dr. John was your dad?"

Lisa shrugged, smiling a little. "You never asked."

"I guess so," Aaron admitted. "I'm coming back next fall to grad school," he told her. "I'm going to work with Dr. John as a TA and then help in his consulting business."

"I know. He told me. I'm glad you're coming back. Maybe you can come with me and Nicole to an Old School meeting in the fall?"

"Sure, maybe. I've already earned the challenge coin." Aaron took it from his pocket and turned it over in his hand. "How did shirt sales go for your spring fundraiser?" Aaron asked. The small talk felt dull and unimportant, but he remembered what Dr. John had told him—*life is for the living.*

Lisa lit up. "They exceeded expectations! We made over $22,000. We're sending seventy-five kids to Camp Eagle this summer."

"That's great. Congratulations." A thought occurred to Aaron, and he tilted his head at Lisa. "Wait, can grad students come to your meetings?"

Lisa grinned at him. "Of course. Just because you have a degree now doesn't mean you know it all."

Dr. John stepped outside the building and saw Aaron and Lisa as they walked away together. "Will I get an official shirt if I come?" he heard Aaron ask.

"We'll see," Lisa said.

Dr. John smiled. Going into next year, Aaron would need a friend. He was proud he'd helped raise a girl that would reach out to the young man.

He started the trek across campus to his office, examining the card Aaron had left for him on his desk. *Let's see what my new protégé has to say.*

As Dr. John walked into his office, his phone began to buzz. He pulled it out of his pocket. It was Anicia. "Hi, sweetie. What's up?"

"John, I just received a text from Nicole. She said there was a black SUV with two people in it parked in front of our house." Anicia's words came far faster than usual, and an icy hand seized Dr. John's heart.

"Who . . . What people?" Dr. John asked.

"She didn't say. She said a man and a woman came to the door and asked if we were home. When she told them neither of us was, they just said they would wait because they wanted to talk to both of us."

Dr. John hesitated. "A black SUV?" He swallowed. "Were they in uniform?"

Anicia paused.

Dr. John stood up again. "Anicia. Were they in uniform?" he repeated slowly.

Anicia's voice was quiet, full of worry as she answered. "Nicole didn't say. I can ask her real quick."

"No. That's OK. Class is just over. I'm leaving now. I'll meet you at home in five minutes."

"OK. Love you," she said.

"Love you too. And say a prayer . . ."

To be continued . . .

*A teacher affects eternity; he can never tell
where his influence stops.*

—HENRY ADAMS

Dear Dr. John,   *May 14, 20--*

I wish I could explain to you how much this semester has meant to me. I always avoid bringing up my father to you. He left our home when I was two, and so I have no real memory of him. You're the closest thing to a dad I've ever had. Your practical instruction, wisdom, and godly counseling and example have truly been a blessing to me. I can't believe that I will soon be your protégé! I just wanted you to know what a difference you have made in my life. Thank you.

Warmest regards,
Aaron B. Woods

Afterword

First things first: I want to thank you. With over one million books published in the United States each year, the fact that you chose mine is humbling. I know how valuable time is. I can never repay the honor.

The Mentor is my first attempt at fiction and was spawned from my fourth book, *The Old School Advantage*—released in 2016. The original idea for *The Old School* came from a desire to equip my own four children with wisdom from the ages . . . life's foundational principles that don't change.

My goal was to write a companion book with an *aspirational* tenor to motivate readers (and myself) to become better in the future than we are now. Perhaps we can be wise, and good, and kind—like the characters of *The Mentor*. Perhaps our universities can return to the "old school" and follow the ancient paths to restore the focus of higher education to the pursuit of *truth*, no matter where it leads. That is my earnest hope.

I believe *this* generation can be the greatest generation. Those Americans who saved freedom during World War II have rightly held that moniker for three-quarters of a century. They became the greatest because they met the greatest challenge of all time. Unfortunately, I believe the generations of my children and grandchildren will face even bigger challenges—and opportunities. The table is set for their greatness. But it won't happen without help.

While I've spent thirty-five years running my companies, I've always been a teacher and a coach—both at heart and in practice. I believe, at some level, we all are. Therefore, for the benefit of those who come after us, we must be able to understand the culture on one hand and pass down tried-and-true wisdom on the other. Young people want to know how to make sense out of their lives. We can show them.

I am reminded of two young archetypes who were wise beyond their years. They lived over twenty-five hundred years ago. Their names were *Daniel* and *Esther*. Their stories, while not directly related, are found in ancient Biblical texts like these:

> Therefore, they [Daniel and friends] stood before the king. And in every manner of wisdom and understanding . . . he found them ten times better than all that were in the kingdom."
>
> —Daniel 1:19–20

And,

> ". . . Who knows whether you [Esther] have not come to the kingdom for such a time as this?"
>
> —Esther 4:14

In both of their stories, there were elements of economic challenges, eroding cultural values, and at times harsh persecution—and even threats of death. I believe we can easily deduce from these and other historical accounts that Daniel and Esther were true to the wisdom their mentors had instilled in them.

The characters of Aaron, Lisa, Amanda, Nicole, John Jr., Nate, and all the rest represent exceptional young people like those we all know who are equipped with great insights, understanding, and discernment. My hope is that parents, teachers, professors, coaches, business leaders, and mentors of every walk, and in every place in our land, will be in some way inspired by *The Mentor* to pour into the next generation and shepherd them with a renewed commitment and determination. May we all train up as many Daniels and Esthers as we possibly can before our own life's vapor vanishes.

With this in mind, *regardless of your age*, I would ask that you start by making two small commitments—*in writing* (of course). The first is to write below the name of one mentor whom you will endeavor to contact—either to simply say thank you or to reengage. Beside the first blank is another line for a GMAD—the deadline you are giving yourself to accomplish this task.

Mentor _____

GMAD _____

The second is for a protégé whom you shall seek to mentor.

Protégé _____

GMAD _____

May I humbly suggest that perhaps you can start the process by simply giving them a copy of this book, then having a conversation about its lessons?

I believe the battle for the hearts and minds of this generation is not over. It's just getting started . . . again. May your mailbox be filled with cards and letters from protégés like Aaron. If you are younger, thank those who are pouring truth into your lives now, and pray for more mentors like Dr. John, Anicia, Michael, or Coach Joe to whom you might be compelled to express your gratitude.

I hope to return with more about these characters and their lives pursuing wisdom. I'm sure you're all eager to learn whether something has happened to Nathan Daniels and about Aaron Woods's first year of grad school and his growing friendship with the Kosta girls. Maybe around the corner there is one more big court case awaiting Anicia Kosta Daniels or twists and turns for Michael Reedy and John Jr. Maria is just getting a start on changing the world with her family. And surely Eli Driver, Kit Potter, and teammates have more moves to make. Stay tuned, and remember: life is not about *affluence*; it's about *influence*. It's not about giving our children what we've *earned*; it's about giving them what we've *learned*. Because in the end, *the things that matter won't be things*. They will be the wisdom we've gained and the people we've shared it with.

May God Bless You,
J. N. Whiddon

ACKNOWLEDGMENTS

Tell me, and I forget. Teach me, and I remember.
Involve me, and I learn.

—CHINESE PROVERB

First things first, I offer my profound appreciation to my life's mentors: my father, to whom this book is dedicated; coaches Tom Leezer, Barry Arnwine, John Thornton, and Shelby Metcalf; Bob Panky; Frank Thomas; Dr. Don Wass; Charlie Classe; David Vierling; Bob Shank; and Gary Simpson. I will be forever grateful for your guidance and influence over the years.

I also offer my heartfelt appreciation to those who gave extravagantly of their time—and allowed me to draw from the stories of their lives. Maria Elena and Salvador Gonzales, Dr. Nathan Harness, JD Sullivan, Micky Reeves, and Chris Cobb—thank you.

To my manuscript readers and advisors—you all came together to provide the "wisdom of crowds." A sincere thank-you to Chris Atkinson, Dave Berry, Alex Booras, Steve Calvert, Joy Christiansen, Oran Cogdill, Stan Cole, Frances Cordell, Analiese Crane, Blake Crowell, Dr. Charles Ellerich, Russell Garrett, Dawna Guzak, Mark Hendricks, Norris Hodgin, Wesley Holmes, Dr. Joel Holyoak, Dr. Lee Jagers, Charles

Jones, Daniel Jones, Caroline Kirchen, Pat Laubacher, Chuck Lee, Jake Little, Linda Marone, Bill Martin, Dave Martin, Doug McCulley, Jim Musil, Madelaine Pfau, Dr. Tom Pledger, Kate Rimer, Dr. David Shiring, Gary Simpson, Ed Wales, Dr. Sid Walker, Daniel Whiddon, Johnathan Whiddon, and Michael Wykrant. No one can do this alone.

A hearty thank-you is again due to Milli Brown, Tom Reale, and all the exceptional professionals at Brown Books Publishing Group—with special thanks to my project coordinator, Earl Mickens, and my editor extraordinaire, Hallie Raymond.

Finally, to my wife, Nizie Whiddon—we've raised four young adults together—and to our children; you are all wise beyond your years. Thank you for your continual interest and the excellent suggestions you've provided for this project along the way. I love you all very much.

May our sons in their youth
be like plants full grown,
our daughters like the corner pillars
cut for the structure of a palace.

PSALMS 144:12 (ESV)

About the Author

J. N. "Jim" Whiddon is founder and CEO of "The Old School," a professional development and consulting firm specializing in exceptional personal skills and mentoring systems for college programs, young professionals, and corporate executives. After a short stint in college coaching while in graduate school, Jim spent more than thirty years in the financial industry as an accomplished business owner and national thought leader, where he authored three books in the investing genre.

Impassioned with the mission of pouring wisdom into the next generation, Whiddon sold his highly successful financial firm in 2013 and wrote *The Old School Advantage: Timeless Tools for Every Generation*. As a father of four millennials, he felt compelled to write a book containing the how-tos of life. *The Mentor* is an attempt to put the principles he teaches into story form.

Whiddon has been quoted by national media outlets including the *Wall Street Journal*, CNBC, and *Fortune* magazine. He has hosted a daily radio show on CNN Headline News in Dallas and been a Fox News Radio contributor. His work has been published in more than 350 newspapers and publications across the country.

Whiddon is a voracious reader and avid sports enthusiast. He earned his bachelor's degree while a member of the Corps of Cadets at Texas A&M University. He also holds a master of science degree from the American College in Philadelphia.

THE 12 KEYS TO PROFESSIONAL SUCCESS

1. BUILD INSTANT RAPPORT (LAVA)

2. TIME LEADERSHIP

3. WORDS THAT WOW!

4. INFLUENCE AND PERSUASION

5. STORYTELLING

6. READY RECALL

7. YOU'RE ALWAYS INTERVIEWING

8. INDEFATIGABLE CONNECTEDNESS

9. DRESS FOR SUCCESS

10. DECISION MATRIX

11. ASK GREAT QUESTIONS

12. LIFELONG LEARNING

Also by J.N. Whiddon

The Old School Advantage:
Timeless Tools for Every Generation